THE BODYMIND EXPERIENCE IN
JAPANESE BUDDHISM

SUNY Series in Buddhist Studies
Kenneth Inada, Editor

The Bodymind Experience in Japanese Buddhism

A Phenomenological Perspective of Kūkai and Dōgen

DAVID EDWARD SHANER

State University of New York Press

Published by
State University of New York Press, Albany

© 1985 State University of New York

For information, address State University of New York
Press, State University Plaza, Albany, N. Y., 12246

Library of Congress Cataloging in Publication Data

Shaner, David Edward, 1954 –
    The bodymind experience in Japanese Buddhism.

    (SUNY series in Buddhist studies)
        1. Kūkai, 774–835. 2. Dōgen, 1200–1253.
3. Experience (Religion) 4. Buddhism – Japan.
I. Title. II. Series.
BQ8999.K857S5 1985   294.3'422   84-26747
ISBN 0-88706-061-7
ISBN 0-88706-062-5 (pbk.)

For my mother and father

*Special thanks to Koichi Tokei Sensei
and William H. Chalker*

Contents

Preface

1. A Precautionary Note

Wordsworth would caution, "We murder to dissect." There is however much to be gained by an analytical reconstruction of our lives and experience. Individuals benefit from reflection and analysis in their efforts to answer questions and demystify their world. I would suggest that it is possible to at once appreciate Wordsworth's advice and carry out scholarly analyses of our experience. Mystics East and West would underscore that an encounter with Truth can not be adequately described within the limited confines of the spoken word. Nevertheless, we do analyze and share our interpretations of experience because most of us have not cultivated a sufficiently holistic worldview. Hence, we are forced to piece together our many experiences (logical, moral, aesthetic, metaphysical, etc.) into a coherent whole. The systematic reconstruction of our diverse experiences reflects our personal "philosophy."

This is the first of many paradoxes contained within this study. The study itself is paradoxical because I am attempting to describe the indescribable. Such a theoretical obstacle did not stop Lao Tzu from describing the Tao and it has not deterred me from my efforts to describe the relationship between the mind and body in the philosophy of Dōgen and Kūkai. Lao Tzu, Wordsworth and many others share the view that the spoken/written word can not reconstruct accurately the beauty of simple yet whole experiences. This is an important disclaimer to this study. Since the relationship

1

between the mind and body is said to be one, according to the forementioned traditions, then in an important sense I am foolish for attempting to say so much about the nature of their identity. The analyses contained in this work transcend positing this simple thesis about the mind and body. Important issues relating to the discipline of comparative philosophy, phenomenology, and Japanese Buddhist philosophy are also at center stage.

2. An Overview of the Study

The purpose of this book is to help develop an interpretation of "bodymind"[1] experience that will be helpful in understanding some central themes in Japanese Buddhism. The relationship between the mind and body espoused in Japanese religious and philosophical texts, and cultivated in various forms of Japanese Buddhist disciplines (*shugyō*),[2] has not yet been explained in Western philosophical categories. Even though people of different cultures may share the same fundamental experiential structures, the way in which these experiences are articulated and valued may vary appreciably. Therefore, a central experiential concern for one culture may be so peripheral to another that it is ignored philosophically and uncultivated as an ideal in everyday life. Throughout this study the phenomenological method will be employed to describe the eidetic structure of the mode of experience to which bodymind awareness refers in the philosophies of Kūkai and Dōgen. Accordingly, the thesis of this book is not only that the Western phenomenological method is a useful instrument for laying bare the structure of bodymind experience, but also that bodymind experience is a central theme through which the complex philosophies of Kūkai and Dōgen may be penetrated.

The body of the project and final conclusions will be limited to articulating the eidetic structure of bodymind awareness via phenomenological categories. From the beginning, it must be explicitly recognized that these categories merely serve to describe identifiable characteristics of bodymind experience. The categories described within this study do not represent an exhaustive study of the universal categories of experience. Only those categories that help describe the eidetic structure of bodymind experience have been analyzed. The attainment of a comprehensive list describing the eidetic structure or transcendental categories of the myriad forms of human experience would require a complete map articulating the processes by which our *Weltanschauung* is formulated. Since the focus of the study is concentrated within the phenomenological epoché, I will not attempt to justify any ontological status associated with the methodological categories. In addition, my concentration upon bodymind experience is not intended to suggest that the Occident ought to duplicate this emphasis. On the contrary, the phenomenological approach restricts one from making such value judgments. The structure of experience as represented in this project is intended to reflect the value given to bodymind experience by the principle figures, namely Kūkai and Dōgen.

At this early stage, it should also be clarified that my phenomenological analysis of the eidetic structure of bodymind experience focuses upon articulating a viable vehicle through which Kūkai's and Dōgen's philosophical theories may be understood. Since my thesis states that Kūkai and Dōgen are strikingly similar in their understanding of bodymind experience, the reader may appropriately ask why Dōgen ever departed from the teachings of his predecessor, Kūkai. To this question I must reply that this analysis merely serves as two illustrations of the value given to bodymind experience in two schools of Japanese Mahayana Buddhism. Social, historical and perhaps psychological points which explain different emphases between Kūkai and Dōgen have not been articulated within this project. These issues remain beyond the boundaries of phenomenological exegesis. Even though Kūkai and Dōgen were sectarians promoting their own schools, their *implicit* emphasis upon bodymind experience serves as a thread by which one may interpret their similar Buddhist doctrines. Accordingly, this project will be limited to making *explicit* the bodymind thread through which one may lay bare the underlying philosophical compatibility of Kūkai and Dōgen.

Although an analysis of the historical antecedents of the primary significance of bodymind experience exceeds the boundaries of this project, there is textual evidence that suggests that the emphasis upon body and mind inseparability was an inherited tradition. For example, when Kūkai describes an ancient mandala he refers to the Sanskrit and says, "Unite your *dhyāna* with *prajñā* in an adamantine binding."[3] We may explain the significance of this statement as follows. In philosophical traditions East and West there are schools of thought in which the body and mind are defined as being ontologically distinct and there are schools upholding the antithesis that body and mind are one — bodymind. In the West these traditions range from the Platonic and Cartesian schools to the Christian mystics and French Existentialists. In South Asia, East Asia and Northeast Asia the diversity of views with respect to the ontological status of mind and body is equally diverse. By simply acknowledging the plethora of belief systems represented by the six orthodox Indian schools, the myriad divisions of Buddhist philosophy throughout Asia and so on, it becomes clear that it would be irresponsible to stereotype Eastern or Western attitudes concerning the logic of mind and body interactions.

It is noteworthy to suggest that the various philosophical and theological problems associated with defining either the logic of body and mind, or bodymind, reflect antithetical axiomatic attitudes about body and mind. In general, for those who consider body and mind to be ontologically one, *the problem* is to empirically verify this primordial unity. Frequently this is achieved through some form of spiritual practice or meditation in both the East and West. The opposing perspective is reminiscent of the Platonic, Cartesian and Sāmkhyan philosophy in which mind and body are by definition ontologically distinct. *The problem* in this case is to discover the manner in which they interrelate. In short, the problem for some is one of understanding the interconnection between body and mind. For others, the problem is to realize experientially their original oneness. In an effort to interpret adequately only the latter position, this study will utilize phenomenology as a bridge to understand this emphasis within Kūkai's and Dōgen's conceptual framework. I would also like to suggest the possibility of further phenomenological analyses of bodymind experience as described not only by the early predecessors of Japanese Buddhism, but also by those whose philosophical posture is in favor of mind and body dualism.

The significance of my phenomenological interpretation is two-fold. First, by laying bare the bodymind component in our everyday experience (Chapter 2), we will be able to experientially identify with certain salient features of Kūkai's and Dōgen's philosophy. This important step will enable the reader to understand a way of thinking which gives value and significance to modes of awareness uncultivated by the influential Platonic and Cartesian traditions. Once the phenomenological categories clarify the cultivated bodymind experience characteristic of the two Japanese Buddhist schools considered, we will be able to interpret many Buddhist doctrines in relation to this central theme. In this way, our analysis may reveal an atypical conceptual framework by first identifying aspects of the framework that occur in our own everyday experience, and second, articulating the formal structure of the framework itself. This procedure will enable us to understand better the experiential basis of Kūkai's and Dōgen's philosophy.

The second significant point of the study is that it serves as an example of how phenomenological methods may be utilized to interpret philosophical systems that are based upon modes of thinking different from our own. By explicating the structure of the paradigmatic mode of experience cultivated by Kūkai and Dōgen, the culturally dependent emphases within that structure will become apparent. In this way, the reader will be able to intellectually appreciate a new conceptual framework in terms of a structure which describes at least a few identifiable components of his or her own experience.

Acknowledgments

I have been blessed with a supportive family, extended family, friends and earnest teachers. The errors, if any,and inadequacies of this study are a result of my own failures to fully heed their model.

There are many who have been generous with their time and expertise. All of you mentioned below, and more, are my teachers; each of you an inspiration. Thomas Patrick Kasulis helped guide me through many obstacles that early drafts of this work occasioned. Sincere and dedicated, Professor Kasulis is a model teacher-scholar. The first draft of this work was written in Cambridge, Massachusetts in 1980. Memorial Hall, the rooftops on Highland Avenue, the Yenching Library, the red line MTBA and late night short cuts through Harvard Yard are something of a blur compared to the detailed memories of my study located in the attic of a Cambridge three-decker style house.

My interest in topics pursued in this study began well over a decade ago in Val Thorens, France, Bariloche, Argentina and Olympic Valley, California. My downhill ski racing coaches Phillip Mollard, Jean-Pierre Pascal and Michael Rudigoz unknowingly inspired more serious investigations into the psychic and somatic interrelationship during the peak performances of high speed competition. William "Wild Bill" Dyer, Tom Crum, Christen Cooper, Owen Kawakami, Liz and Donny Birnkrant, Kathy and Jeffrey O'Neil, and now Clayton Naluai would, I think, attest to the importance of such considerations on and off the snow. (The sky diving expeditions over Lake Tahoe were really just for fun. Family and loved ones have vetoed a reunion jump for Clayton Sharkey, Chris Belknap, Clayton Naluai and myself).

7

Senseis Robert Taylor and Smokey Beaman introduced me to *Shin Shin Toitsu Aikido* fifteen years ago—thank you. Following a move to Honolulu, thank you Sensei Calvin Tabata, I became indebted to the Senseis at Waipa Lane—Yukiso Yamamoto, Harry Eto and Seichi Tabata. Sensei Clayton Naluai, thank you for the Lokahi Ki Society (East and West) and providing many opportunities to grow. Thank you for continuing to embody the meaning of friendship and (the literal meaning of) aloha. Sensei Shinichi Suzuki, thank you for the continuous inspiration and for believing in and preparing "future generations." Sensei Takashi Nonaka, thank you for giving me the opportunity of a lifetime and risking so much on my behalf. Masue Wakumoto, thank you for warmth and confidence. Master Koichi Tohei (President and Founder, *Ki no Kenkyukai International* [Ki Society International]) deserves special acknowledgement for taking me under his wing as an *otomo* and *uchi deshi* in Japan. Monastic life and *shugyō* require a twenty-four hour a day commitment. Accordingly, Master Tohei's influence is found between the lines of the entire manuscript. To this gentleman, for so many things, I can only say, "*domo arigato gozaimashita*." There is much to be learned and unlearned living in the monastic setting of an *uchi deshi's* existence. Sensei Koretoshi Maruyama (Chief Instructor of *Shin Shin Toitsu Aikido* International and Chief Lecturer *Ki no Kenkyukai*), thank you for enriching that experience, and many recent ones with compassion, generosity and love. Sensei Minoru Oshima, thank you for *all* the *taigis*.

I would like to acknowledge my deep appreciation for the insights and encouragement offered by Professor Yasuo Yuasa and Professor Hajime Nakamura. Their contributions gave important early direction to this project. I wish to thank Ralph Honda and the Crown Prince Akihito Scholarship Committee, Nihachiro Hanamura and the Japanese *Keidanren* and Professor Nakamura's *Tōhō Kenkyukai* for enabling me to conduct research in Japan. For research support related to other aspects of this project I thank the University of Hawaii at Manoa (Department of Philosophy), Harvard University (Department of East Asian Languages and Civilizations), John H. Crabtree Jr. and the Furman University Research and Development Committees, the University of Chicago Center for Far Eastern Studies, the National Endowment for the Humanities, the Fulbright Foundation and

Richard M. Hunt and the Andrew W. Mellon Faculty Fellowship in the Humanities Committee, Harvard University.

There are many who have read various portions of the manuscript at various stages of development. For offering many beneficial suggestions I would like to thank Professors Roger Ames, Alfred Bloom, Eliot Deutsch, David L. Hall, Kenneth Inada, David Kalupahana, Shigenori Nagatomo, Winfield Nagley, Kakuko Shoji, Beatrice Yamasaki and the State University of New York Press copy editors and staff. For supportive colleagues, who make me feel at home at Furman University, I thank Professors Thomas Buford, Lin Chen, James Edwards, Edward Jones, James Leavell, Douglas MacDonald and Mark Stone . . . Special gratitude to David Turner who has helped me to approach some of the tangential epistemological questions I find fascinating. In this context I owe much to Janis Maude, Charles Henry, William Chalker, Nanette and Ira Gordon, Joseph Dadabay, Donna Lynn Guthrie, Richard Kienast, Phyllis and Arch Lhormer, Miriam and Bert Sud and Ralph Sayre who, through their own examples, have helped me to appreciate the significance of formulating questions in the first place.

Thank you, Phyllis Watts, for putting up with many revisions; you have the patience of a saint. There is great joy in being able to stimulate interest in philosophy and comparative studies. For returning the favor, I express my gratitude to the students at Furman University. Specific thanks go to Timothy Bergstrom, Christen Hagebak, David Hills, Brian May, Fred McKay, Greg Gardner, Denise Ann Rosmaita and Cheryl Wicker. Also for returning the favor, thank you, Kathy Matsueda, for an appreciation of words, language and the unspoken.

My acknowledgments for this project would not be complete without thanking Yuriko, Sueka and Robert Masatoshi Nakano for unceasing encouragement, patience and support. Jon Lopez and Carol Wlock thank you for offering assistance whenever and wherever. Jillian Mary Gordon has seen many changes of time and place and endured them all. Jillian, like a magician, uses mirrors, I think, to give me instruction.

Chapter 1

Phenomenology and
Comparative Philosophy

In this study I will argue that the phenomenological method, as defined by Edmund Husserl (1859-1938) in his *Ideas I* (1913), offers an exciting vehicle by which the worldview of one philosophical tradition may be meaningfully described to another by articulating the formal structure of experience at the root of both traditions. This assumes that people, irregardless of cultural influence, share the same transcendental categories through which their experience is ordered.[1] Without the explicit recognition of these structural common denominators, it seems unlikely that any meaningful cross-cultural communication can ever be achieved. That which accounts for unique philosophical orientations East and West entails a quantitative, not qualitative, difference. One tradition may place paradigmatic significance upon a particular mode of experience in order to apprehend Truth. A second tradition may seek the Truth by placing greater emphasis upon a mode of experience that may be completely ignored and uncultivated by the former. The point is that the philosophical positions of both traditions may be understood by one another if those who study them explore reflexively the common denominators of the structure of experience itself in order to reconstruct first their shared axioms and second the value and significance they attach to those axioms. (The word *reflexive* indicates *the act of turning one's inquiring glance back toward the presuppositions of the discipline under investigation, or the presuppositions of the inquiring subject, for the purposes of understanding the powerful determining influence of themes, ideas, or [Kantian] transcendental categories,*

11

operating at the axiomatic level of experience). The reflexive philosophical posture required to lay bare the *structure* of our experiential encounter with the world is best accomplished by using the phenomenological method.

1. What is phenomenology?

Philosophy itself is a reflexive enterprise. Early philosophers East and West were filled with a sense of awe and wonder. They began to question the nature and purpose of their very existence in an effort to demystify the world around them. The apparently orderly processes of nature, life cycles and the cosmos itself inspired a sense of speculation and questioning that continues today. Socrates encouraged us to question, to thoroughly examine ourselves in an effort to clarify our beliefs, opinions and knowledge. In time, when the questioning process became more specialized, it became clear that our different modes of experience required parallel methodologies by which a more detailed investigation could be accomplished.

The specialized study of different sorts of experience became associated with different philosophical disciplines. For example, our experiences enabling us to recognize formal relationships between like and unlike expressions or entitites may be said to be investigated under the rubric of logic. Understanding our sense of conscience or experiences associated with that which is good or bad might be investigated according to different methods in the field of ethics. Experiences related to our learning processes might be explored in epistemology while religious experiences might be interpreted according to entirely different criteria. In short, the disciplines of logic, ethics, epistemology, ontology, metaphysics, philosophy of religion, philosophy of science and so on, all bare a distinctive philosophical trademark — the constant critical questioning process that is directed reflexively back toward the basic presuppositions of each discipline. Without this challenging spirit we could become victims of our own conceit, intellectual prejudice, covetous and dogmatic opinion. Like Euthyphro, we may build a philosophical ivory tower that rests upon false ideas and unexamined opinion.[2] Such a situation would be unfortunate because it implies being a prisoner of one's own ideas rather than being free to utilize and change one's ideas autonomously. For many this never ending questioning process appears at first glance as unproductive idle speculation; a dog chasing its tail. Upon closer examination it becomes clear that the discipline of reflexive questioning itself is of great value. The chasing/questioning is more important than reaching a definite answer because the so called "definite" or certain answer may not be true for all time in all places. Only the critical questioning and constant re-examination of our beliefs allows us to temporarily posit new answers which more satisfactorily explain a wider range of phenomena. This process is of course crucial for any inductively based discipline. The great scientific discoveries of our culture are marked by the vision of the genius who critically challenges and questions the basic premises of his or her discipline. One can describe this procedure as a *reflexive* process because the analysis is turned back toward an investigation of the legitimacy of the discipline's axioms upon which all subsequently derived theorems are based. If new data are collected that are not in accord with the predicted data, then it is the genius who, following the Socratic maxim ("The unexamined life is not worth living"), re-examines the discipline's basic presuppositions upon which the hypotheses are based. Without accurate premises or axioms, the derived theorems and hypotheses are sure to faulter in their ability to predict our experience.

Edmund Husserl, the founder of the phenomenological movement, sought to underscore this reflexive, radical questioning orientation in science and philosophy. In so doing he sought, somewhat anachronistically, to direct philosophy toward a scientific ideal. Husserl believed that the phenomenological method would assist him in articulating the a priori structure of human experience. By proceeding in the manner of a "rigorous science," Husserl sought to reveal the most fundamental axioms of experience thus paving the way for a "first philosophy" grounded upon apodictic evidence. Taking experience as his starting point, Husserl wanted to articulate that the essential (the qualities without which something could not any longer be itself) or eidetic (from the Greek *eidos* meaning form) structure of experience was the ground through which the content of human experience is ordered. It is through the employment of the phenomenological method as a rigorous science that the eidetic essences are shown to be primordially given even before existential thetic positings, i.e., before our experiences are colored by our attitudes, desires, feelings, and judgments. Husserl therefore believed phenomenology to be both reflexive, rigorous and a first philosophy because of its radical orientation towards what he called "things themselves" (*zu den Sachen selbst*).

Since this philosophical orientation reflects Husserl's life and times, it should be noted that Husserl recognized that there were perhaps even loftier ways of doing philosophy. This is an often overlooked but important point. Husserl was searching reflexively to ground philosophy upon apodictic certainty, via phenomenological methods, in order to lay bare the fundamental axioms of experience. Husserl's claim that this approach is the most objective, proceeding scientifically, is one that he openly acknowledges and is indicative of the scientific culture in which he lived. (Later within this chapter the sense in which phenomenology is scientific will be critically examined.)

Husserl's ambition then was to establish a method to be employed by phenomenologists for generations to come in an effort to ground philosophical studies upon unshakeable rational truths. The phenomenological method was to be the vehicle through which the arbitrary and contingent became selectively cast off until only the absolute and necessary objects of knowledge were allowed to remain. For Husserl, however, absolute certainty could only be attached to essences. Here Husserl is reflexively drawn into a science of essential being, purposefully disregarding the posited existential world which bares each individual's ontological judgment. Knowledge of the existential world could only be considered knowledge of particulars, hence only contingent knowledge and thus could never be a candidate for absolute knowledge based upon apodictic certainty. Husserl believed philosophical inquiry ought to be concerned with only the highest truths (essences) wherein each step of the rational progression of ideas is verified thus contributing to the development of a rigorous, scientific, first philosophy.

Recognizing that Husserl's quest for certainty led him away from the posited existential world and toward the realm of essences is crucial for understanding the most important feature of the phenomenological method — the phenomenological *epoché* or reduction of the natural standpoint. Husserl begins to explain this aspect of his method by suggesting that people have an undoubtable *attitude* that there is a world which exists independent of their consciousness (*Ideas I*, section 31).[3] This attitude is universal to human consciousness and serves as a backdrop or "horizon" for all experience. That is, the lived world is ontologically posited by one's consciousness upon which other worlds, e.g., arithmetic, may be intended (section 28). Husserl begins with this ordinary experience of the world because this is how "the man in the street" believes his world to exist "out there" for him (section 39, c.f., 66). This general thesis about the world is actually thetically posited. Husserl calls this the view of the "natural standpoint" whereby we *assume* the "spatio-temporal fact world" to be out there as a separate ontologically existing "it" independent of our apprehension of our shared world (section 30).

Husserl cautions his readers by emphasizing that this general thesis is only an assumption and should not therefore lead us into making absolute distinctions between subject and object as if there were two separate worlds — one "out there" (objective) and one "in here" (subjective). This observation helps to explain an important element of Husserl's method. This is his employment of the concept "intentionality" (section 34). Experience is said to be intentional because it is directed from subject to object. Consciousness is always directed (section 35 and 36). In an effort to avoid the ontological and metaphysical assumptions attached to the words "subject" and "object," Husserl referred back to the Greek and spoke of our intentional experience in terms of the point of origin or "meaning-bestowing aspect" (noesis) and the intended object or "object-as-experienced" (noema). In this way, Husserl maintained the spirit of phenomenological investigation (*zu den Sachen selbst* and *Wendung zum Objekt*) where one is led to an analysis of the intentional structure of experience.

This approach enabled Husserl to be able to distinguish two *modes* of experience, subjective (noetic) and objective (noematic). Husserl suggests that subjective experience is private and unconfirmed by others and objective experience is public, about which we receive more feedback from others, leading us to believe that the content of this part of our experience is shared. The manner by which the phenomenological method reveals this often overlooked aspect of experience is by "suspending" or "bracketing" those aspects of our belief which tend to cloud or distract one's attention from the actual eidetic structure of experience, e.g., ontological or ethical thetic positings are removed from consideration. Accordingly, the purpose of bracketing the natural standpoint is to allow the phenomenologist to become more aware of the primordial a priori structure of consciousness (section 31 and 32).

Suspending the natural standpoint does not imply detachment from the world. On the contrary the phenomenologist becomes closer to the world as it is directly or pre-reflectively experienced. The world is neither affirmed nor denied. The world is seen as it is given, via "pure experience" (*Erlebnis*), for consciousness. The phenomenologist is interested in becoming aware of the world devoid of ontological judgments.

Once the so-called natural standpoint is suspended, Husserl utilizes an imaginative technique called "free fancy" (section 70) in order to distinguish the arbitrary, or accidental, from the necessary ways in which our experience is connected. This procedure allows one to become familiar with the universal eidetic essences which govern our experiential apprehension of the world (Section 69). Free fancy simply means that one conceives what an entity or event would be like without certain characteristics. If the definition of the entity is significantly altered by the absence of a defining characteristic, then the characteristic is said to be necessary, e.g., a necessary characteristic of a right triangle is that one angle be ninety degrees while the remaining two angles may vary; they are arbitrary. Hence, free fancy enables one to concentrate upon the essential relations of experience rather than the noematic content. Ideally, the a priori structure of experience becomes juxtaposed with the ordered sense datum.

The forementioned phenomenological techniques, outlined in *Ideas I*, were utilized by Husserl in order to (1) lay bare the eidetic essences at the base of our experiential encounter with the world; and (2) clarify the implications of intentionality. The contemporary interest in hermeneutics and deconstructionism reflect a continued effort to understand the intentional character of experience. If the meaning of an expression is conditioned by an author's noetic or meaning-bestowing act, then hermeneutic problems develop when we consider that the same expression may be read or translated with a different sort of noetic interpretation. Although Husserl recognized the importance of acknowledging discrepancies of meaning, it was not a novel discovery. This observation alone did not fuel his philosophical investigations. What did interest him however was that if the *intention* of an expression constituted its meaning, then a thorough investigation into the eidetic structure of intentional acts would reveal the essence of meaning. In order to penetrate reflexively into an understanding of the essence of meaning, Husserl sought to bracket his own intentional positings and confront the immanence of essential being via a priori intuition. Explicating the intentional structure of experience is the thread linking everything from Husserl's first published work, *Die Philosophie der Arithmetik* to his last *Die Krisis der europaischen Wissenschaften und die transzendentale Phänomenologie.*

Most of Husserl's philosophical writings focused upon method in order to reveal the immanent, and therefore self-justifying, essences of conscious activity. Husserl's preoccupation with method reveals the strong influence of Descartes and Kant. Descartes' emphasis upon method was important in order to eliminate all contingent, and therefore doubtable, objects of knowledge. Husserl, following Descartes' lead, sought to ground his rationalistic philosophy upon only those truths which are both necessary and immanent. And, like Kant, Husserl systematically resisted metaphysical speculation in favor of returning to an investigation of subjectivity itself. A reasoned (*logos*) study of transcendental categories and eidetic essences, which define the parameters of our finite experiential encounter with the world, requires a strict methodology to ensure that the focus of the investigation always be fixed deeper and deeper into the heart of human subjectivity.

Husserl's criticism of his predecessors does not therefore focus on their strict use of method. Rather, Husserl suggests that their reflexive investigations were not radical enough thus stopping short of entering into the gateways of immanent, apodictically given, experience. The phenomenological reduction of the natural standpoint can therefore be seen as that feature of Husserl's methodology that allowed him to bracket the metaphysico-onto-logical presuppositions that hindered his predecessors' reflexive inquiries into human subjectivity. From Husserl's perspective, Descartes' *cogito* was too steeped in ontological and causal assumptions regarding subject and object. Similarly, Hume threw out the baby with the bath water. His rejection of necessary causal relations between subject and object led him to be skeptical about the possibility of adequately explaining their interaction. Although the direction of Hume's study towards the things themselves is in the same spirit as phenomenological studies, Hume was unable to escape the naturalistic assumptions of Berkeley and Locke. These empiricists argued from the perspective of the natural standpoint and thus could not escape basic ontological attitudes concerning phenomenal objects. The revolutionary ideas of Kant demonstrated that Humean skepticism could be overcome by probing even deeper into transcendental subjectivity. Here the formal categories of our experiential encounter with the world could be exposed. To use a contemporary metaphor, this approach likens our mental processes to a grand computer. The description of Kantian transcendental categories at once illuminates the computer's program, but simultaneously sets the limits of reason. While Kant found it necessary to deny reason in order to make room for faith, he opened the door to all sorts of metaphysical speculations about "things-in-themselves," God, etc. Husserl's position was to resist all such temptations in order to extend further, not limit, the scope of his first philosophy grounded upon apodictic evidence.

2. Is phenomenology truly presuppositionless?

Thus far the themes of reflexivity, "to the things themselves" (*zu den Sachen selbst*), and "constant returning" have been underscored in order to set the context of Husserl's phenomenology. A critical analysis of Hussel's position however requires an explicit recognition that Husserl *presupposes* that the proper direction of philosophical studies is reflexive. That the source of a clear immanent, self-justifying, apprehension of our world is best achieved by transcendental methods is itself assumed. Husserl assumes that the source of objectivity, and therefore universality, is in man's direct, primordial encounter with the world. This is to focus upon the common denominators of all human subjectivity devoid of the particular and contingent positings of individuals. The unique character of individuals can be understood when one can reveal the source of their posited (noetic) configurations that account for discrepancies of intended meaning. To superimpose a Buddhist metaphor, Husserl assumes that humans possess an innate mirror (experiential apparatus) through which the world is perceived. A polished mirror uncluttered by metaphysico-ontological positings is *assumed* to be the best source of understanding our experiences as they are primordially given (reflected). Here the radically empirical suppositions of Husserl become clear. There is an explicit assumption that since experience is our window to the world, a rigorous phenomenological description of eidetic essences will allow one to see the world not necessarily as it really is, but as it is in the only way which one can know it – as it is presented to consciousness.

Husserl believed it is not necessary to posit things-in-themselves since things are immanently, and therefore objectively, given in primordial experience, i.e., chronologically prior to intentional thetic positings. Unlike Kant and Hume, Husserl supposes that a thoroughly reflexive (phenomenological) investigation of experience reveals that the *form and content* of experience appear as one. In this primordial apprehension essences are apodictically intuited, not discursively derived. In fact, Husserl's method prohibits him from moving beyond immanent experiential data given necessarily. Contingent knowledge must be discarded (free fancy) if his philosophical investigations are to be grounded upon immanent self-justifying knowledge. The fact that Husserl superimposes these criteria for the development of a so-called presuppositionless philosophy itself constitutes a violation of presuppositionlessness. Since it is difficult for Husserl to escape this problem of circularity, his radical empiricism must itself be regarded as his philosophical preference.

The circularity problem seems unavoidable if we accept Husserl's first argument that consciousness is always of something. Intentionality is contrary to the Lockean *tabula rosa* for the mind is not understood to be a passive receptor but rather as a projector, i.e., as a vector (noesis) moving towards noematic objects and situations. Consciousness is considered personal since each individual is responsible for his/her particular perspective (not excluding Husserl). Husserl seems to imply that the phenomenologist might overcome this problem by a strict recourse to method. Phenomenologists strive to make their attitudes as unbiased as possible while striving for a true objectivity that is primordially given. Husserl assumes it is possible to experience the world in a direct, immediate and immanent way (Section 38). Here he relies upon Franz Brentano's notion of an inner perception. Since inner perception is a reflexive *activity* and not a thing, Husserl is able to make the connection between activity and intentionality by which consciousness is understood as an *attitude* of the observer. Nevertheless the phenomenologist must be aware that the *act* of analysis itself may suggest a certain perspective. Objects (noemata) are not *apprehended* but are *intended* such that the object is not given in a vacuum of feelings. The noema might be appreciated, believed, ignored and so on (section 37).

As long as one's experiences are intended, they are also finite as they are limited to the particular perspective characterized by the noetic/noematic relation. Husserl seeks to open a new region of "Being" (sections 33 and 50) by bracketing the perspectival, and therefore limited, dimension of experience. Once this has been accomplished, Husserl says one is left with a "phenomenological residuum" (section 60). The reflexive approach is then said to have reached the domain of the totally immanent and is thus non-perspectival. When consciousness is directed, perspectives are limited since there appears to be an infinite variety of spatio-temporal ways to apprehend noemata. However, when consciousness is immanently intuiting essential Being, Husserl suggests the possibility of complete and necessary knowledge that is non-perspectival (sections 43, 49, and 50).

A brief mention of the Socratic tradition, will help to underscore that Husserl's whole project, as summarized above, is a matter of philosophical preference. If philosophy is the "love of wisdom" or "pursuit of Truth," it is important to acknowledge the philosopher's assumptions regarding *where* Truth is to be found. Socrates and Plato, in response to the Sophists, upheld a philosophical realism in which they sought to clarify that there were standard objective truths (Gk. *physis* lit. "nature," in this case indicating a source of authority corresponding to the law-like regularity of the physical world, e.g., the law-like regularity of the seasons, which function independently of human intention) that applied for *all* mankind. Man is *not* the measure of all things and the laws (Gk. *nomos*) of society ought to approximate these standards in every possible way. According to Plato, Truth exists in the eternal, non-spatial, metaphysical world of the forms. These forms were thought to be purely objects of knowledge known via a process of recollection. Husserl, one might say, similarly pursued Truth but in a radically different place. The objective world or abode of universals was sought not in the metaphysical world of forms but in the immance of primordially given experience. Both "places" (Gk. *topos*) were believed to be the domain that serves to unify all mankind under a single, non-discriminatory, lawlike Truth (*physis*). The forms exist eternally and unify mankind insofar as man has the ability to remember those objects of knowledge which are innate.

For Husserl, man's experiential apparatus, or mirror if you will, is that which serves as the common denominator and therefore standard of objectivity. The phenomenologist pursues Truth (*physis*) in regions confirmed by immanent intuitions. Experience is the window on to the world which Husserl prefers. His is a sort of empirical pursuit of *physis* in the essential core of our Being. Revealing this new region of Being would allow *all* the various disciplines (ethics, political science etc.) to ground their law-like (*nomos*) first principles (*archai*) in accord with the methodologically revealed *physis* at the base of experience. The phenomenological method is limited to the domain of a technique (*techné*) assisting phenomenologists to intuit eidetic essences. The method is therefore directed toward *physis* reflexively, Husserl's preference, and is designed to expose only our *experience* of objectivity or universality and does not guarantee the *existence* of *physis*. Such latter judgments lay outside the domain of the phenomenological reduction.

Now, it should be clear that phenomenology is best understood in the context of method. Husserlian phenomenology, requiring a reduction of the natural standpoint, can not succumb to metaphysical or ontological urges while making claims about "reality" itself. Rather the method is designed to help the phenomenologist understand and describe the structure of experience. Phenomenological studies are limited to analyses of the empirical world as experienced within the phenomenological *epoché*. These studies are further limited by language. Since phenomenology is a descriptive affair, the method is plagued by all the limitations which accompany the use of language. The different configurations of grammar and syntax necessarily reflect culturally dependent conceptual frameworks which dictate a parallel form of psychological ordering. To recognize the significance of this point is to further challenge the possibility of Husserl's method as the ground of a truly presuppositionless first philosophy. The method may assist the phenomenologist to set aside culturally dependent intentional positings but then the practitioner must return to the natural standpoint in the process of describing the structure of pre-reflective experience. Here Wordsworth might legitimately claim, "we murder to dissect" yet we dissect whenever we accept the conventions of language for the purposes of communication.

While phenomenological description will never replace the clarity and originality of immediate experience, the method is extremely valuable as it may point to new regions of experience that may be systematically or unconsciously covered by unique individual configurations. To return to the mirror metaphor once again, one might suggest that a clear, well-polished mirror (consciousness) reflects the world as it is primordially given. As individuals develop specific attitudes, prejudices and skills, dust begins to collect upon the mirror forming a particular configuration. Those with whom one associates are likely to have configurations of similar proportion. In this sense friends might be inclined to "see" their world similarly. Yet a reinforcement of such specific or parochial views only serves to dust over, suppress and do violence to other possible perspectives on the world. Soon even cultural archetypes might be generalized to the point of serious misunderstandings between cultures. Just as an individual might say of a friend "I've always liked David but I could never understand some particular dimension of him," one might generalize about a culture and say, "I've always loved Hawaiian culture but I could never understand the Hawaiian attitude toward X." The artificial block lay in the fact that individuals and cultures may differ with respect to the paradigmatic value noetically superimposed upon certain types of experiences. In these instances the assumption of the phenomenologist, that human beings are endowed with the same mirror (experiential apparatus), work positively and optimistically to enhance intersubjective and intercultural understanding. The method works to distinguish (free fancy) between subjective positings (dust), which limit one's awareness, and objective essences indicative of the polished mirror itself. In this way, the phenomenological method assists comparative studies by opening, or at least pointing in the direction of, regions of being and awareness that may have been previously covered over.

An analogy may be helpful. Those who live comfortably in two distinct cultures and are bilingual report that their image of themselves and others change with respect to their environmental setting. When the configurations change so does one's sense of identity. To dream in one's non-native language for the first time often conjures up a whole new set of axioms by which the self is identified. Similarly, one might like one culture for one set of reasons and another for different reasons. Neither setting is entirely satisfactory. When in one place X is good but one misses Y. Yet, in another place, the converse is true. It is possible to account for such changes by thoroughly examining the value and significance noetically attached to different sorts of experience. In this way, phenomenology may be a useful instrument for laying bare the structure of experience and thereby exposing patterns of culturally dependent behavior.

The project of this study may be likened to that of Watsuji Tetsurō who, in 1926, wrote the following passage in his essay *"Shamon Dōgen (Dōgen, the Monk)*:

> I am not here insisting that my own interpretation is the only one on the truth of Dōgen itself, in the understanding of which I am least confident. I can safely say, however, that a new path of interpretation has been opened up here, to say the least. Thereby Dōgen is no longer the Dōgen the founder of the sect but *our* Dōgen.[4]
> (Italics mine)

Like Watsuji, I do not insist my interpretation of Dōgen and Kūkai is the only viable one. I am hardly in a position to make such a claim. Yet, phenomenological exegesis may help to make many of the following doctrines of two schools of Japanese Buddhism *ours*. Often, in the past, the doctrines of East Asian Buddhist thinkers have been labeled alogical, mystical and secretive. These labels may more accurately reflect the limited configuration of the foreign analyst who may be unable to appreciate or understand the *rationale* of others. This new rationale or way of thinking may attach paradigmatic value to modes of experience uncultivated by the outsider as an ideal in his or her everyday life. The temptation is to label that which does not fit into one's configuration as alogical or illogical. Human beings per se are rational but their differing modes of reasoning or rationale may be based upon entirely different sorts of experience. The use of phenomological methods in this study are intended to make these doctrines *ours* within the limits of language and our shared experience.

Although phenomenological methods of interpretation help identify, and therefore better understand, uncultivated modes of awareness, we must once again recognize the limitations of the method and not overextend our philosophical conclusions. Once our interpretation informs us that an experiential mode of awareness is cultivated with greater frequency in one culture than another, we may be tempted to develop all kinds of explanations for such phenomena while assuming that the explanations were justified by phenomenology. Once the method has informed us about the modes of awareness given the greatest value and significance, we must search for additional methods to help explain *why* a specific type of experience emerges as paradigmatic. Explaining why different emphases occur would entail additional criteria other than experience. For example, one may wish to investigate the anthropological, historical, social, or religious background of a given culture in an effort to become more familiar with the intellectual history preceding the era in question. Phenomenology, on the other hand, is a method of description exclusively oriented towards introspection upon the axioms of the experiential process. Therefore, one must recognize that answering "why" questions may transcend the areas of discourse within which the phenomenological method operates. In short, the method may allow us to see Kūkai and Dōgen in a new light (and make them ours) but we must limit our conclusions to underscoring this new insight and not exceed our phenomenological boundaries by attempting to make claims regarding the ultimate reality of Japanese Buddhism or solutions to mind-body dualism.

The philosophical orientation of Husserl is a major reason why the phenomenological method is particularly appropriate to an investigation of Dōgen and Kūkai. The forementioned themes of reflexivity, returning to things themselves and so on reflect the orientation of Dōgen and Kūkai as well. The "place" wherein Truth is to be found is centered in man's direct, immediate experience of the phenomenal world. These two Japanese thinkers share with Husserl a spirit of radical empiricism. In terms of philosophical preference, Husserl, Dōgen and Kūkai share assumptions that Socrates and Plato would have explicitly rejected. Although the compatibility of the phenomenological method and these two Buddhist thinkers will be progressively clarified throughout chapters three, four, five and six, it should be noted that the close alliance between these traditions has already been noted in a recent work on Japanese phenomenology. The relationship is explained as follows:

The other important observable feature of the Japanese philosophical thinking may be found in its ontological apprehension of man's existence and the world. . . . Japanese philosophy, in fact, never accepted the ultimate reality or its principle as "existing" apart from and independent of the concrete, lived world of experience, although they are separable in our theoretical thinking.[5]

The "lived world of experience" is the source of authority for most schools of Japanese Buddhist philosophy. One thesis of this study will be to demonstrate that thetically neutral experience is given value and significance by the Shingon and Sōtō Buddhist schools. This thesis and its implications will be developed by describing this unique philosophical structure, via phenomenological interpretation, thus making it "ours" as it were. I believe similar phenomenological methods of investigation may be utilized to make other aspects of Japanese culture ours as well. The fact that phenomenology shares a commitment to experiential verification with Japanese philosophy makes the success of such studies most likely.

3. The Relation between Philosophy and Culture

Two main points regarding the relation between philosophy and culture need to be clarified early in this study. These points not only serve to accentuate insights ascertained throughout this investigation, but they also serve to guide future cross-cultural studies utilizing phenomenological tools. First, different cultures attach different values to particular modes of experience and produce distinctive philosophical structures. We have already discussed this issue with respect to the suspect labeling of the Japanese Buddhist philosophical structure as alogical, mystical and secretive. The fact that different people cultivate different paradigmatic modes of experience does not imply that both cannot be equally rational in their methods of cultivating or sedimenting these experiences.

Since the method relies upon description in order to expose culturally dependent philosophical structures, one must recognize that even the best desciption can never serve as an accurate replacement for the original experience. This problem is compounded when one attempts to articulate experiences indigenous to environments with which one is most unfamiliar. For this reason a phenomenological interpretation has been employed to bridge this cultural gap by concentrating upon a description of the a priori structures of all experience.

The second point regarding the relation between philosophy and culture is that distinctive philosophical structures significantly color subsequent philosophical endeavors. That is, given a specified structure, certain philosophical and practical (in the sense of *praxis*) problems are more or less predetermined. By examining the axioms or presuppositions of a particular philosophical orientation, basic assumptions may be clarified. If these assumptions include specifiable rules of logic, definitions, and preferential attitudes regarding "where" Truth is to be found, then many philosophical problems may be anticipated. In this way, not only are problems anticipated but it may be possible to see that solutions to the issues are fundamentally impossible without recourse to devising a *new* rationale, rules of logic, definitions, etc. The mind-body antinomy may be irresolvable unless the Platonic or Cartesian assumptions about "what is mind" and "what is body" are reconsidered. Exploring new paradigms and atypical modes of thinking often inspire new and creative ways to examine age-old problems. Creativity is difficult when one's thoughts are encrusted with stale habits. Here phenomenological methods might serve as a vehicle to tap new perspectives that may have been heretofore dusted over. At the same time, the phenomenologist recognizes that the relationship between philosophy and culture is so intertwined that one must consider the distinctive structures of experience before passing judgment upon one culture's paradigmatic modes of thinking while using the criteria of another.

The important role of comparative philosophy today is thus underscored. Comparative studies, East and West, can play an important role in global understanding and cooperation through education. Philosophical studies can not afford to remain steeped in narrow disciplines wherein fixed configurations limit the vision of those who, more than any other, bare the responsibility of pursuing Truth wherever it may be. It is, of course, impossible to stay abreast of all the developments within one's field yet it seems that the contemporary philosopher may possess a unique perspective and skill (*techné*) for seeing the forest as well as the trees. The need for contemporary philosophy to expand its vision drawing upon "the width of civilized experience" is succinctly described by David

L. Hall in his recent work *Eros and Irony: A Prelude to Philosophical Anarchism.* He writes:

> The positivistic character of contemporary culture as a realm of posited, yet essentially unexamined, values expresses the failure of philosophy in its speculative mode. Philosophy is the critic of posited value, or it is nothing worthwhile. In his role as articulator of importances, the speculative philosopher confronts the condition of contemporary cultural existence and finds that some of the unexamined consequences of the dominance of the moral and scientific interests are deleterious in the extreme since they have led to the suppression of burgeoning interest in alternative modes of activity aimed at the realization of aesthetic and religious value.
>
> Despite all of the single achievements this specialization has permitted, the dominance of moral and scientific interests has occasioned a significantly narrowed and dulled complex of cultural experiences. The endeavor to release the aesthetic and religious sensibilities from the constraints of the scientific and moral impulses is an important cultural imperative. By performing this task contemporary philosophy can lay claim to its distinctive importance. Thus it is primarily the responsibility of the contemporary philosopher of culture to articulate the importance of aesthetic and religious interests, thus enriching our cultural expressions by enabling us to draw upon the width of civilized experience.[6]

Husserl believed that the employment of the phenomenological method, as a "rigorous science," would assist philosophers to better understand the width of human experience. To an extent, this is the thesis of this study as well. The relationship between phenomenological and scientific methodologies requires, however, a critical evaluation. In order to clarify my own use of Husserl's method to this end it is necessary to enumerate major differences between our epistemological presuppositions.

4. The Relation between Phenomenological and Scientific Methods: A Critical Appraisal

For Husserl the goal of philosophy is to ground normative studies, e.g., ethics, upon apodictic evidence. In fact he believed any discipline required a sturdy foundation in which its axioms were known to be universal, objective and apodictically certain. Husserl also recognizes the limitations of any inductively based science. Knowledge of facts will not guarantee the validity of ideal norms that transcend the contingency of the physical world. Accordingly, Husserl's critique of empirical psychology and the natural sciences centered around their inability to grasp *essences*. The essences of experience reflect the formal structure, the universals and the objectivity of our experiential encounter with the world. Without presupposing that humans share the same basic experiential apparatus through which one perceives the world, then there is no basis for supposing the possibility of genuine intersubjective understanding. Phenomenological methods are unique and scientifically rigorous in that they are employed reflexively. Through introspective analysis, the eidetic structure of the acts of consciousness are themselves laid bare. In this sense, Husserl sees phenomenology as being the most rigorous, the most reflexive and the only "science" capable of transcending the contingent fact world in order to intuit the necessity and objectivity of eidetic essences.

It would seem appropriate to ask, if this is Husserl's vision, in what sense is phenomenology at all a science? To call phenomenology a "science" of essential being might seem consistent with Husserl's intent, however one must question the accuracy of calling immediate intuition of essences an inductive enterprise. Here Husserl transcends the method of the sciences in order to ground them. Through direct, immediate and immanent intuition, Husserl seeks to confront essential being, reflect upon that primordial experience and then describe, as best as possible within the limits of language, the universal aspects of experience that bind us together.

The democratic[7] presuppositon that people encounter the world through the same transcendental categories would seem to be required if one believed in the possibility of true interpersonal understanding. The source of commonality and objectivity would rest in the supposition that one person's window to the world is at least structurally like another's. This supposition is one to be acknowledged if one is optimistic about the possibility of genuine or accurate intersubjective understanding. I would disagree with Husserl, however, that this grounds "objective" knowledge with apodictic certainty. While phenomenology is unique as a vehicle to discover sources of commonality between individuals, it does not, as Husserl believed, ground objective and necessary Truth. Knowledge of the structure of the acts of consciousness tells one something about how human beings encounter the world but it does not break the barrier of human finitude. This point of departure might best be underscored by examining Husserl's conception of science.

Husserl's high hopes for scientific endeavors appears to be rooted in a sort of seventeenth century optimism. His training in and love for mathematics reflects a Newtonian conception of the world. In the *Crisis* Husserl writes:

> Mathematics showed for the first time that an infinity of objects that are subjectively relative and are thought only in a vague, general representation is, through an a priori all-encompassing method, objectively determinable and can actually be thought as determined in itself or, more exactly, as an infinity which is determined, decided in advance, in itself, in respect to all its objects and all their properties and relations.[8]

The use of mathematics coupled with the scientific method inspired Husserlian optimism. His belief in man's ability to come to understand the "rational systematic unity" of the universe is underscored in the *Crisis* as follows:

> Philosophy in its ancient origins wanted to be "science," universal knowledge of the universe of what is; it wanted to be not vague and relative everyday knowledge—*doxa*—but rational knowledge—*episteme*. But the true idea of rationality, and in connection with that the true idea of universal science, was not yet attained in ancient philosophy—such was the conviction of the founders of the modern age. The new ideal was possible only according to the model of the newly formed mathematics and natural science. It proved its possibility in the inspiring pace of its realization. What is the universal science of this new idea but—thought of as ideally completed—omniscience? This, then, is for philosophy truly a realizable, though infinitely distant, goal—not for the individual or a given community of researchers but certainly for the infinite progression of the generations and their systematic researches. The world is in itself a rational systematic unity—this is thought to be a matter of apodictic insight—in which each and every singular detail must be rationally determined. Its systematic

form (the universal structure of its essence) can be attained, is indeed known and ready for us in advance, at least insofar as it is purely mathematical. Only its particularity remains to be determined; and unfortunately this is possible only through induction. This is the path — infinite, to be sure — to omniscience. Thus one lives in the happy certainty of a path leading forth from the near to the distant, from the more or less known into the unknown, as an infallible method of broadening knowledge, through which truly all of the totality of what is will be known as it is "in-itself" — in an infinite progression.[9]

Here Husserl is cognizant of the limitations of the sciences yet he retains the Newtonian view that the clockwork of the world is fixed, following mathematically predictable laws, and is therefore eventually theoretically knowable. This presupposition lies behind all epistemic acts. Eidetic intuition is an epistemic act yet, unlike inductively derived knowledge, it is assumed that intuition is a more accurate vehicle to come to know the concrete universe both acts describe. That there is such an objectively valid world to know seems to violate the spirit of the phenomenological *epoché*. The view of the world *via* eidetic intuition may guarantee an epistemic act that is direct, immediate, and immanent but it can not claim both necessity and objectivity. Eidetic intuition only underscores the structure of the experiential window throught which we gather information about the posited world. The common denominators binding human experience may be revealed but can these denominators also guarantee apodictic certainty, as Husserl would suggest, or are they merely the most accurate description of man's epistemic apparatus?

Again, in the *Crisis*, Husserl gives the impression that there is a fixed construction of our universe that is ultimately knowable. He writes:

We have not two but only *one* universal form of the world: not two but only *one geometry*. . . . The bodies of the empirical-intuitable world are such, in accord with the world-structure belonging to this world a priori, that each body has — abstractly speaking — an extension of its own and that all these extensions are yet shapes of the one total infinite extension of the world. As world, as the universal configuration of all bodies, it thus has a total form encompassing all forms and *this* form is idealizable in the way analyzed and can be mastered through construction.[10]

Husserl's optimism seems to permeate his quest for undoubtable Cartesian truths. Where inductive methods fall short, the reflexive phenomenological method is said to unveil eidetic truths, i.e., the axioms describing the truths of our "universal configuration" (structure of the acts of consciousness). Just as twentieth century physics asked whether or not the Newtonian configuration of the universe was satisfactory, I would argue that a similar re-examination is required of Husserl's version of phenomenology as a rigorous science. Can the objectivity, necessity and universality of eidetic intuition be retained in the wake of the discoveries of twentieth century physics? Some of these themes are introduced below to question whether or not the apodetic certainty associated with phenomenological techniques describes true objectivity as it were, or merely—yet significantly—the common denominators and universal structure of our experiential encounter with the lived world.

The figure illustrates that our common sense everyday world is lived within the domain of the relatively large (sizes greater than 10^{-10m}) and relatively slow (speeds less than 10% the speed of light). Classical Newtonian physics explains phenomena within specifiable ranges of speed and size. When our lived world becomes enlarged, due to technological developments allowing us to "see" and measure phenomena which are increasingly small (sizes less than 10^{-15m}) and fast (speeds approaching the speed of light), early theories and laws that appear inadequate must be complemented by more comprehensive laws capable of describing a wider range of speeds and sizes.[11] For this reason the classical terms of momentum, energy, position and time may be extended to describe relatively large objects approaching the speed of light (relativity physics), small objects at slower speeds (quantum physics) and small objects approaching the speed of light (relativistic quantum physics). An accurate description of phenomena smaller than the atomic nucleus 10^{-15m} and larger than say 10^{25m}[12], remain unresolved (at least for now). As our lived world becomes enlarged, as it were, our experiential/sensory apparatus becomes inexorably linked with our technological apparatus allowing for increased awareness. This observation underscores the finitude, frailty, and ultimately, fallibility of the view of our world as it is eidetically constructed via conscious acts. Kant's transcendental categories denied reason to make room for faith. Husserl however has vowed to resist metaphysical urges based

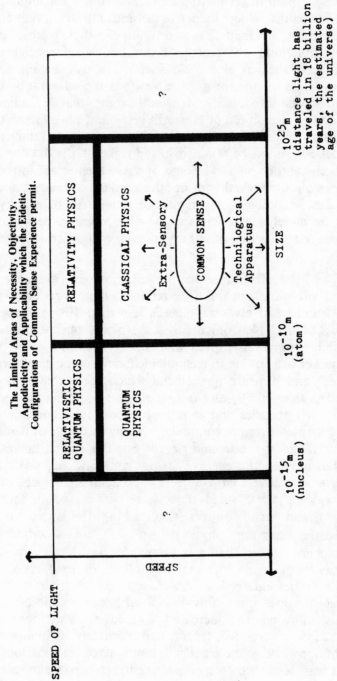

Paradigms for Explaining Physical Phenomena:

The Limited Areas of Necessity, Objectivity,
Apodicticity and Applicability which the Eidetic
Configurations of Common Sense Experience permit.

Adapted from Richard T. Weidner and Robert L. Sells, *Elementary Modern Physics*, ed. 3 (New York: Allyn and Bacon, Inc.)

upon faith. If one follows Husserl's radical empiricism, then it seems necessary to also acknowledge explicitly the epistemic limits imposed upon man as a result of the eidetic configuration of human experience. Such limits define our finitide. Our unaided perception such as auditory and visual sensation are limited to a specifiable range of octives and light wavelengths respectively. It is becoming more clear that our aided senses are also subjected to various limitations. This forces a person to tolerate a degree of uncertainty that may be specifiable within statistical limits, e.g., Planck's constant,[13] and reexamine dreams of necessary and certain knowledge.

In the aftermath of the Heisenberg Uncertainty Principle, the Newtonian deterministic model of nineteenth century physics has largely been discarded in this century.[14] The scientist, like the phenomenologist, begins to understand something by describing it and measuring it. The act of measurement and description turns out to be a problematic vicious circle when one recognizes that the physical world and its measurement are so entangled that it becomes impossible to separate the object from the influence of its measurement or description. The phenomenologist loses the primordial giveness of an experience during reflective description and the nuclear physicist may be unable to measure the primordial "path" of an electron thus being forced to accept only a statistical description of its location and velocity. As Heisenberg himself cautioned — we have to remember that what we observe is not nature herself, but nature exposed to our method of questioning.[15] Similarly, the phenomenological method of questioning is defined by, and limited to, the configuration of the eidetic structure of consciousness itself. The phenomenologist can claim no authority cerning universal objectivity and necessity beyond the a priori manifold of conscious acts. Husserl's method can direct one to the realm of the direct, immanent intuition of eidetic essences. However, the cautious epistemological position that twentieth century physics inspires, reminds phenomenologists to restrict their investigations within the phenomenological *epoché*. The eidetic structure of the acts of consciousness reflect the common denominators of human experience. Accordingly, claims regarding the necessity, objectivity and universality of truths based upon apodictic evidence must reflect the structure of the finite and fallible epistemic windows which, it is presumed, all people share.

In spite of this epistemological limitation, the phenomenological method assists one in understanding the eidetic character of
experience itself—the only window to the world available. The
possibility of mapping the common denominators of our shared
experiential apparatus underscores the a priori objectivity that
binds human experience everywhere. In this way, phenomenological techniques may help to describe perspectives and values
that may otherwise be dusted over (adopting a Buddhist metaphor)
by individualized noetic positings. Here phenomenology may illuminate new insights by helping us to appreciate and understand
the myriad forms of intentionality. The value and significance attached to paradigmatic modes of experience by one philosophical
orientation may become at least theoretically understood by
another and thus enable the interpreter to tap a wider range of the
plethora of culturally dependent experiential, and consequently
philosophical, preferences. Just as twentieth century physics tells
us our assumptions, tools of measurement and methods are tied
into a knot, phenomenology helps us realize that experience itself
is bound to specifiable configurations based upon the encrusted
habits of intentional acts. And, just as twentieth century physicists
bring to their investigations particular presuppositions, so the
phenomenologist operates according to preferences that are not
entirely "presuppositionless" as Husserl claimed. The reflexive
direction of phenomenological inquiry and preference for radical
empiricism reflect just two of Husserl's suppositions.

In this light phenomenologists, like physicists, must work collectively within a degree of epistemological tolerance somewhat
less than absolute certainty and necessity. The axioms of the acts of
consciousness may describe the parameters of our shared experiential encounter with the lived world. Yet, as long as man's window
on the world is incomplete, finite and continually evolving over
millions of years, then even the eidetic structures of human consciousness can not be known with *complete* apodictic certainty nor
can one expect to achieve an exhaustive typology of eidetic structures. A further implication underscores that the so-called "real"
world can not, as Kant cautioned, be known independently of our
finite transcendental categories which ultimately shape our
method(s) of questioning. Nevertheless, the phenomenologist's
work, within the phenomenological reduction of the natural standpoint, allows for meaningful investigations uncovering the framework of our shared and evolving conscious configurations.

The implications of working exclusively within the limits of the phenomenological *epoché* are numerous. In the following chapter the most important implication, the phenomenological preoccupation with essences, will be explained. Once this distinguishing feature of phenomenological studies is clarified, the stage will be set to employ the phenomenological method as one possible pedagogical vehicle by which the philosophical views of Kūkai and Dōgen may be articulated.

Chapter 2

A Phenomenological Description
of Bodymind

The main purpose of this chapter is to conduct a phenomenological analysis of body and mind. The analysis will lay bare the essential, in the sense of phenomenological essences (Gk. *eidos*, form), characteristics of the experiential correlates to which the terms body and mind refer. It will be clear from the onset that the noematic body and mind, as directly experienced, are unlike the abstracted concepts body and mind. The direct experience of bodymind will be unpacked, by means of an analysis based on eidetic structures, and demonstrated to be a phenomenologically viable interpretation. Before this interpretation, it is necessary to discuss some of the implications of conducting this analysis exclusively within the phenomenological reduction of the natural standpoint.

1. Phenomenology as the Study of Essences

The reduction of the natural standpoint in which the ontological positings of the "man in the street" (see Chapter 1) are suspended, prepares the way for an analysis of the essential (the qualities without which something could no longer be itself) a priori structure of the acts of consciousness. Husserl's preference for a study of essences can best be understood by recalling his early training as a mathematician. The constitutive function of mathematical relations allowed Husserl to appreciate the way in which consciousness might order an infinite variety of sense data in accord with far fewer axiomatic or constitutive processes. These processes reflect the eidetic structure of experience. The essences are given primordially and are not adduced, deduced or induced from one's experience of the fact world or world of "things" (the view of the natural standpoint). Essences are directly and immanently intuited as ideal ordering a priori rules and are not themselves dependent upon experience or intentional acts to uncover them. Essences are therefore known as immediately in intuition as physical objects are in perception. Like Plato, Husserl seeks to uphold the objectivity of consciousness by discovering the universal ideals that link human experience. (Note however, in Chapter 1, that Husserl is searching for objective universal standards in a different "place.") The essential ideals are grounded in the constitutive acts of consciousness. The immediacy, self-givenness, objectivity, necessity, and ideality of essences are one for Husserl. The phenomenological reduction of the natural standpoint strips the intentional positings bare, thus allowing a phenomenological residue to be given in a sort of "pure experience" (*Erlebnis*). Contingent knowledge, which interferes with primordially experiencing necessary essences, is discarded, thus revealing the epistemological acts to which Husserl attaches the greatest value and significance.

Husserl's belief that the ideality of eidetic essences could be infallibly known with apodictic certainty led him to suggest that phenomenology was a "science" of essential Being. (Note once again Husserl's dated optimism regarding scientific investigation.) Essences are not law-like ideals *inferred* from sense data, but are given directly in intuition. In the study of pure phenomena (phenomenology), no causal metaphysics is assumed. Rather, essences are said to be primordially given in experience. Knowledge that is based upon conjecture is, for Husserl, meaningless. The proper realm of philosophizing, then, is to collectively work to complete a total picture of the essential structure of cognition. Understanding the form and content of our apprehension of the lived world would give us the most complete and accurate knowledge about ourselves. In fact, Husserl suggested that the intuitive grasp of essences is the only act revealing immediate knowledge and is therefore the most important byproduct of a methodology that brackets the natural standpoint thus grounding phenomenology as the science of sciences.

At this point, a cursory overview of the implications of attempting phenomenological descriptions of eidetic essences is in order. The phenomenologist must always be alert to the methodological ramifications associated with the suspension of the natural standpoint. The interpreter must be cognizant of the important difference between; (1) descriptions of eidetic essences; (2) abstract explanations of ontologically posited entities; and (3) ontologically defended explanations of mere abstractions (concepts without direct experiential correlates).

To begin, the phenomenological description of eidetic essences ("1" above) exposes the a priori structures of human experience by revealing, with apodictic certainty, the most fundamental axioms of experience. This is accomplished by the fact that phenomenological description never strays from the act of experience. (In the context of this particular study, the distinction between concepts about body and mind gained through abstract speculation versus knowledge of body and mind gained through pre-reflective experience, is at the heart of the issue). By bracketing common intentional assumptions—those aspects of belief which tend to cloud or distract one's attention from the essential structure of experience, e.g., ontological or ethical attitudes—thetic positings are removed from consideration. In this way experience is described as it is given to consciousness. A ramification of this method is the recognition that the "what" aspect precedes the "that" aspect in experience, i.e., the essence precedes existence. Through phenomenological description, eidetic essences are shown to be primordially[1] given to our consciousness before ontological thetic positings; hence Husserl's preference for the noesis/noema terminology. The phenomenological reduction does not detach one from the world but focuses upon the world as it is primordially experienced before the ontological status of the world, as exemplified by subject/object phraseology, is affirmed or denied. There is an explicit Husserlian assumption that since experience is our window to the world, a rigorous phenomenological description of eidetic essences will allow us to see the world not necessarily as it really is, but as it is in the only way which we can know it—as it is presented to consciousness.[2]

When following this approach, all abstract explanations of ontologically posited entities ("2" above) and ontological explanations of mere abstractions ("3" above) must be examined because both violate the spirit of the phenomenological reduction of the natural standpoint. To give an abstract explanation of an already ontologically posited entity is to have assumed a perspective, with respect to that entity, before the investigation has begun. For example, if I assume that body or mind exist and then attempt to explain their existence via abstract doctrines (causality or temporality), then I have assumed from the start that which I am attempting to prove. Or, if I were to argue for the ontological necessity of an abstraction, I would be attempting to give ontological status to something which has no exact experiential correlate. There is nothing inherently wrong with attempting to argue for the ontological status of an entity nor defending the ontological necessity of an abstraction. However this does set both apart from phenomenological descriptions of eidetic essences. The latter concerns itself solely with the relations and process of experience. *Ideally*, during phenomenological description nothing is presupposed (the difficulty if not impossibility of this has been critically evaluated in Chapter 1), no perspective is assumed nor is any theory substantiated. The motive behind descriptions of essences is to become aware of the eidetic structure of experience. The motive behind explanations of ontologically posited entities is to demonstrate their relation with other entities in accord with an abstract system or theory. In short, phenomenological description attempts to be true to experience as it is given to consciousness, whereas abstract explanations of ontologically posited entities and ontological explanations of abstractions attempt to be consistent with some criterion other than the act of experience itself.

The value of phenomenological description is to lay bare the first principles of various fields of study. The phenomenologist is concerned with the necessary relations of experience and does not argue for the ontological necessity of noemata or abstractions. The danger of assuming from the beginning that noemata or abstractions ontologically exist is that such an assumption may allow an entire system of thought to be built upon false foundations. For example, abstractions like the axioms and theorems of Euclidian geometry became so commonplace that there was a time when most everyone assumed that the universe *really was* Euclidian. Since Euclidian geometry was successfully used to construct buildings and bridges etc., people began to assume that this system of constitutive abstractions was something which actually had an existential counterpart operative in the universe. The arrival of the new geometries, which more satisfactorily explained the behavior of small entities (such as those studied in atomic physics, nuclear physics, and quantum physics), large entities (studied in astro physics), and entities approaching the speed of light (in relativity physics), shocked the scientific community only because they broke the encrusted habits of geometric thought based upon a Euclidean model. The universe may appear to be Euclidian, Riemannean or Lobachevskiean depending upon the speed and size of matter in the part of the universe under analysis and the relative position of the observer. The point is that the constitutive geometries are not themselves absolute; they are abstractions and possess a pedagogic value, not an ontic one. As Einstein once remarked, our common sense is a layer of prejudice we gain prior to the age of eighteen. Analysts who utilize phenomenological description are concerned with understanding the experiential ground of a particular area of study in order to clarify the modes of experience through which the world is presented to consciousness. This methodology forces the phenomenologist to break through Einstein's "common sense" world or Husserl's world of the "man on the street" (natural standpoint). For example, Euclidian axioms can be recognized as abstractions when we remember that they are based upon the consistent relative relationships among noemata. The relationships are seen as constitutive eidetic essences and are not confused with the content (noemata) of experience. Accordingly, there is no temptation to posit ontological or causal metaphysical status to, for example, Euclidian axioms and theorems.

In this chapter we will make use of phenomenological descriptions of eidetic essences when examining body and mind. This procedure will guide the entire investigation in order to understand the body and mind as they are primordially presented to our consciousness.

2. A Phenomenological Description of Bodymind Experience

How is it possible to discover the first principles, eidetic essences, and fundamental axioms of an experience of body and mind? To begin, the phenomenological reduction of the natural standpoint must be employed. One must suspend, as much as possible, the ontological beliefs and judgmental presuppositions which might be brought to an investigation of body and mind. Physiological, psychological, theological, anthropological and philosophical suppositions must be suspended so that one may remain open to include all perspectives of body and mind that may be given as a direct ramification of a phenomenological analysis.

The phenomenological methodology directs one's attention to the primordial giveness of the act of experiencing body and mind. In accord with a phenomenological reduction we will attempt to understand the body and mind as they are experienced directly. And, in accord with a phenomenological description of eidetic essences, we will investigate the eidetic structure of the act of experiencing body and mind. We will not search for an abstraction of body and mind that will be consistent with some presupposed criterion other than the act of experience itself. Again, since experience is our only window onto the world, a rigorous phenomenological analysis will allow us to describe the primordially experienced character of body and mind presented to consciousness. The concern for primordial giveness will lead the inquiry to the activity of experiencing body and mind. Since this is achieved within the phenomenological reduction of the natural standpoint, it should be understood that the activity of experiencing body and mind is the same as describing the primordially experienced body and mind. Following this procedure we will search for the first principles of body and mind as they are known through experience. Once we have described body and mind in a phenomenologically viable manner, we must accept the additional responsibility of describing the eidetic structure of body and mind as experienced.

How then does one experience mind and body? Phenomenologically speaking, one can never experience an independent mind or body. That is, neither mind nor body can become the noematic focus of a noetic glance. This is not meant to imply that body and mind are meaningless terms, for they may have a meaning that is *abstracted from experience*. There may be a mental dimension or "mind-aspect" of some complex experience, but a "mind"[3] may never be experienced as a noema completely independent from the "body-aspect" giving meaning to the experiential background or "periphery"[4] within which the noema is circumscribed. "Mind-aspects" and "body-aspects" have been abstracted so frequently that there is a tendency to believe that these terms have exact independent experiential correlates. The history of this dualism can be traced back to Plato where the mind (*psyché*) was interpreted as having an independent metaphysical status capable of participating, as it were, in the knowledge of the world of forms. The body on the other hand, was interpreted as an aspect of the physical world and was therefore a deterrence or hindrance to a person's epistemic and spiritual development. Phenomenological inquiry, however, demonstrates that it is difficult to isolate either mind or body as perceivable noemata. Although there may be mind-aspects and body-aspects within all lived experience, the presence of either one includes experientially the presence of the other.[5] This relationship may be described as being "polar" rather than "dual" because mind and body "require each other as a necessary condition for being what they are."[6] The relationship is symbiotic. The abstractions mind and body share the same misunderstanding that affected ontological interpretations of Euclidian axioms and theorems. There are no exact one-to-one experiential correlates for the terms body and mind.

Think, if you will, of some experience that may focus upon body or mind. In this experience where does the mind stop and the body begin? What is mind totally disconnected (abstracted) from body? Through what medium would mind gain knowledge of the world? Using the technique of free fancy, would our definition of the lived-body be significantly altered by the absence of the mind-aspect and vice versa? Is the relationship between mind and body experienced in such a manner that the presence of one is a necessary condition for the presence of the other? It can be said that there are mind-aspects and body-aspects within all lived experience. In many respects the remainder of this chapter will serve as a description of these "aspects" in all experience.

To begin to unpack this thesis let us imagine the following situation. A young boy and his first girlfriend are at the movies and have been sitting together quietly for some time. The boy has spent the last half hour trying to get enough courage to hold the young lady's hand. Finally he reaches over and clumsily touches her hand. The girl, unaware of his intention and action, had been engrossed in the movie. The noematic object of her experience was her favorite actor. The periphery of her experience was no greater than the mountainous terrain surrounding the actor. Suddenly she felt something strike her hand and her first pre-reflective reaction was a slight jump back into her seat as the cold feeling was quite unexpected. At that moment the noematic core of her experience shifted from the actor to the physical object still clutching her hand. The boy's hand is, at this initial moment, experienced by the girl as body-as-object (*der Körper*), i.e. to the girl the cold feeling could have been any number of foreign objects. Upon reflection, however, as she became more aware of the "horizon"[7] of the new noematic focus, the meaning of the experience gradually unfolded. As her noematic focus shifted from body-as-object to body-as-subject (*der Leib*), i.e., from an object on her hand to his hand holding her hand, she recognized that the cold feeling was her boyfriend's hand. At this time all the implications of his hand holding her's begins to unfold as the horizon and meaning of the experience becomes clear.

The first implication of this situation was one of embarrassment. She was embarrassed for having been frightened unexpectedly. She knew too that he must feel somewhat embarrassed by her sudden reaction. Feeling self-conscious, the direction of her noetic glance turns more and more reflexively upon her own plight. What should she do now with her palm on her own knee, and his hand on top of hers? The meaning of the situation becomes even more clear as she discovers his hand is clammy. She realizes that he must be very nervous if his palm is moist. She is flattered he overcame his nervousness and reached to hold her hand. Again, her attention shifts to his hand and she decides she will turn her palm over to reciprocally hold his hand. At this point the meaning of the situation is clear: from a simple experience of sudden contact on her hand the meaning of the experience unfolded as the horizon became more accurately understood.

This description reveals a number of points at which we must look more carefully. First, the situation is very complex since the girl changes her noetic glance to focus upon different noema many times. Each shift of the meaning-bestowing noesis changes the meaning of the noematic focus. The recognition of a cold object upon her hand broke the flow of her attention which had been directed toward the movie screen. Since this cold object startled her, she spontaneously jumped back into her seat. At the next moment the meaning of the cold object (body-as-object) changed as she discovered it was *his* hand (body-as-subject). Gradually the meaning of the situation began to unfold becoming more complex as she concerned herself with the implications of *his* feelings, *his* nervousness, *her* embarrassment and *her* next reaction and so on. Accordingly her noetic glance could have been directed toward mind-aspects or body-aspects yet, in either case, the *meaning of the experience includes, in the horizon, body-aspects and mind-aspects respectively.* The meaning and significance of an experience is due to our awareness that in the lived world each experience contains both mind-aspects and body-aspects. For example, his hand holding her hand is understood as a sign of affection from one person to another. The moist hand signifies that the boy is nervous. The fact that he continues to stare at the movie is a sign that he is too scared to look in her direction. And when both hands join in this mutual context, it is a sign of mutual affection. In daily life we act as though the visible body-aspect is a reflection of the invisible mind-aspect. We act as though one is necessarily connected to the other.

Phenomenologically, we know that the relation between noesis and noema is one of inseparability. As the meaning of a situation unfolds, the noesis and therefore noema, change meaning. And, since understanding an experience, for example a cold object upon one's hand, is enriched when the periphery and horizon of an experience is understood, we can say that to fully understand the meaning of a specific noematic focus, we must understand it in relation to the entire situation. In this way we may begin to appreciate the complexity of experience which always includes mind-aspects and body-aspects in either the noematic focus or horizon. Mind-aspects and body-aspects may be separated from the context of lived experience only through abstraction. It is only through abstraction that mind-aspects or body-aspects may become noematic foci, for example, in reflection, imagination, or reverie. In daily life we act as though the meaning of our experience simultaneously includes both mind-aspects and body-aspects. Accordingly, henceforth we will refer to the presence of both aspects in all experience as "bodymind." This is necessary since our experience, as it is given to our consciousness, is not broken up into "mind-aspects and body-aspects." Rather we are conscious, aware and act in a bodymind way. Given the radically empirical predelections of Husserlean phenomenological analysis, the mind and body seem to share an organismic process in which they are mutually dependent.

This may be further explained by looking at a few everyday

experiences. Our memory is often triggered by one of our five senses. The sight of a house in which we were reared, the sound of a favorite song, the smell of a special dish cooking on the stove, etc. may all trigger long since forgotten memories. Similarly, emotions often trigger bodily reactions. We jump for joy, fidget in boredom or impatience, blush when embarrassed, quiver when scared, shake when nervous, slouch when tired, wrinkle our brow in anger, and so on. A close examination of the relation between mind and body in our lived prereflective experience reveals that there is no mediate relationship. We experience and live body and mind as one.

It is possible, however, to abstract the mental and physical aspects from an experience. There is indeed a "psychic" and "corporeal" aspect of consciousness. Nevertheless, if we are to describe experience as it is given to our consciousness, we must pay particular attention to the presence of both the corporeal and psychic aspects which accompany all experience. Although in abstraction we may speak of a mind-aspect which wills or intends and a body-aspect which is said to carry out the will or intention, this bifurcation is not experienced directly in daily life. There is no experiential correlate that substantiates this common separation of the respective roles of mind and body. In fact in our pre-reflective lived experience one might suggest that we think with our body and act with our mind and vice versa. Our actions are a direct reflection of how we feel. Again we jump for joy, fidget in boredom, etc. Moreover, our action toward others is determined by the mode of the other's physical presence, i.e., we cannot see another's mind but we act as though his/her body is a reflection of his/her mind. We say things like she "looks tired," "seems nervous," "appears unhappy," "acted unusual," "revealed emotion," "was visibly upset," "seems to carry a problem on her shoulders," "held back the tears," "let her inhibitions go," etc. Our language is full of many idioms that presuppose a direct, immediate relationship between a person's physical appearance and mental condition. In daily experience people act as though the lived relation of mind and body were not dual but polar. We act in a manner accurately represented by the term "bodymind."

However, we must further explore the forementioned notion that if the body and mind share an immediate relationship (bodymind), then we may say that "we think with our body and act with our mind and vice versa." Bodymind depicts the way in which we act, think, and experience. We do not experience mind as the sole decision-maker or active intender. We feel the "weight" of our decisions before we formally act upon them. We arrive at some decisions by contemplating whether or not some forthcoming action will "feel right." We may even imagine some grotesque situation and become nauseous. In each case, body and mind are experienced as one — bodymind. Using experience as our criterion for judgment, we may say that the idea that the mind intends or wills and the body follows these orders is a popularly perceived but phenomenologically unsound concept. There are of course many alternative or competing philosophical perspectives that give rise to different interpretations of mind and body. The myriad forms of these other interpretations are grounded, however, upon methodologies that do not share the existential signification of phenomenological studies.

To demonstrate how bodymind is operative and expels the forementioned misconception, look in the direction in front of you. Tell yourself "now I will turn and look behind me." Of course, we may then turn and look. It appears as though "in our mind" we decide to turn *and then* our body follows the command. But now imagine that you are in a body brace and are physically constrained from turning around. You must truly imagine that you are unable to move. Now tell yourself once again to look behind. If you find it impossible to turn, it is because the mind and body are one. The body-aspect is as equally involved in the intention required to initiate an action as the mind-aspect is involved in the physical tension required to perform that action. In each of the above cases there was no (1) intended mental stimulus and (2) physical response. That is, there was no "time 1" when the mind intends and "time 2" when the body acts. It is not the case that in the first situation we try to turn (t1) and then do (t2) and in the second situation we try to turn (t1) and then are unable (t2). Rather in both situations at (t1) and (t2) there is the awareness of will (mind-aspect) and physical constraint (body-aspect) simultaneously. At (t2) one may *will* to turn but, at the same time, there is within the horizon of the experience an awareness that one is not *able* to turn. Intention is not merely saying to oneself "now I will turn around" and then later discovering that one cannot. Intention or will is merely one aspect of a complex experience. Intention or will may be a predominate aspect of experience at a given time. However, if all aspects of the experience are laid bare, then the complement (mind-aspect/body-aspect) of the predominate aspect may also be recognized to be within the horizon of the complex experience. Insofar as there are mind-aspects and body-aspects influencing our experience and behavior at all times, then we may suggest that "we think with our body and act with our mind and *vice versa.*"

In order to further clarify the notion of bodymind and the phenomenological means of laying bare further characteristics of experience, we will proceed to the next section.

3. The Essential Bodymind Quality in All Experience

It is possible to classify all experience based upon the degree of bodymind awareness as follows:

First Order Bodymind Awareness — only in this mode of experiencing is there a direct awareness of bodymind within the horizon. All thetic positings are neutralized. There is no specifiable noetic vector towards a privileged[8] noematic focus. There is only an awareness of the horizon *in toto*. Example: pre-reflective neutral[9] consciousness in which there is no intentionality.

Second Order Bodymind Awareness — in this mode of experiencing there is only one specific noetic vector directed towards a single privileged noematic focus. This is, however, the most primordial form of intentionality. The awareness of bodymind is secondary to the awareness of the intended noematic focus. Example: pre-reflective, assiduous consciousness as exemplified by an athlete during intense competition or a musical artist during a performance.

Third Order Bodymind Awareness — in this mode of experiencing there may be many overlapping noetic vectors towards a multiplicity of noematic foci. This is the most complex form of intentionality. The awareness of bodymind is filtered by a myriad of noematic foci. Example: reflective discursive consciousness.[10]

Thus far the study has underscored the importance of the phenomenological search for first principles, eidetic essences, and fundamental axioms that are discovered as a result of a rigorous analytic description of experience as it is given to consciousness. Since first order awareness is the only mode of experiencing wherein there is a direct awareness of bodymind within the horizon, a phenomenological description of this order will serve to ground this investigation. An analysis of first order bodymind awareness follows.

a. *First Order Bodymind Awareness*

A phenomenological approach demands that we attempt to remain presuppositionless[11], that we assume nothing and that we begin our analysis by describing what appears (noema) and the way we look at it (noesis). However, since our definition of first order bodymind awareness states that "there is no specifiable noetic vector towards a privileged noematic focus," an analysis which requires a description of "what appears (noema) and how it appears (noesis)" would seem problematic, if not impossible. This problem is, however, dissolved when we search for the primordial giveness of bodymind. That is, if we maintain the spirit of phenomenology (*zu den Sachen selbst* and *Wendung zum Objekt*), then we are led to a mode of experience *prior* to intentional experience. This is due to the discovery that bodymind awareness occurs only when all thetic positings are neutralized. In first order awareness, bodymind may never occupy the intended noematic position in experience. Bodymind is only presenced amidst the intentionally neutral experiential horizon.

In order to understand how one might arrive at such a conclusion, we need to unpack our methodological approach even further. Since our phenomenological reduction suspends the natural standpoint, we are led to a description of the noetic and noematic aspects of experience. The reduction, therefore, leads us from a description of ontologically posited objects to a description of the eidetic components of thetic experience. However, if the noetic/noematic intentional relationship is retained, then our reflexive analysis will not go beyond second order bodymind awareness in which there remains "a specific noetic vector directed towards a single privileged noematic focus." Therefore, *an additional reduction which leads us to the primordial giveness of bodymind within the horizon is necessary*. This additional reduction is the means to lay bare the level of *Ur-doxa* or *proto-doxa*[12] upon which all doxic modifications are posited. This even more radically reflexive reduction serves to neutralize all thetic positings and leads us from a description of the noetic and noematic aspects of experience to the primordially given, non-privileged horizon. Husserl only hints at such a maneuver in his *Ideas I*. I would like to underscore the importance of a second reduction in order to move beyond even the noetic/noematic distinction.

Ur-doxa is characterized as the ground of consciousness upon which positive and negative judgments are constituted. It is a neutral ground exposed by the second reduction of the noetic/noematic distinction. Although a few twentieth century philosophers have pointed to this backdrop of consciousness as the ground or precondition of imagination, and therefore constitutive of our consciousness of the world itself,[13] it is important to underscore that this ground *not* be interpreted as a *negative* backdrop for affirmative thetic enterprises. On the contrary, the horizon is given directly as *neutral*; a source of pure potentiality reminiscent of the Taoist uncarved block. This first order experiential ground becomes the non-privileged arena and source of second order noetic vectors (affirming or negating) bestowing intend meaning upon specifiable noemata.

The emphasis on the second reduction in this study is one consistent with Husserl's overall philosophical *Weltanschauung*. Like the original reduction of the natural standpoint, which constantly forces the phenomenologist's analysis towards apodictic giveness and away from the mind's natural tendency toward objectivism, the second reduction deliberately puts aside the noesis/noema distinction in order to sediment or habituate an awareness of the *ground* of the constitutive intentional structure of consciousness itself. One must acknowledge that this reflexive move pushes Husserl's orientation even further in one direction at the expense of other possible methodological avenues. However, since it is argued in this study that Husserl's philosophical orientation is not entirely dissimilar from the perspectives of Kūkai and Dōgen, it will become apparent that this often overlooked second reduction is crucial for demonstrating the unique character of phenomenology as a potentially viable hermeneutic for this and other comparative studies. The second and more radical reduction exposes the immanence of consciousness and the backdrop upon which the constitutive eidetic structures become manifest. The methodological rigor required to habitually "see" the world from this neutral perspective may be as difficult as sedimenting paradigmatic modes of awareness encouraged by the techniques of Kūkai and Dōgen.

Husserl's analyses throughout his life were typified by constantly starting over—returning to the things themselves (*zu den Sachen selbst*). He was never quite satisfied that his methods were ever complete. This preoccupation with the process itself, versus the goal, is one also shared by Kūkai and Dōgen. It is the way one carries oneself, the way one lives and the way one perceives the world that is important. As soon as one thinks the process has been completed, stagnation and rigidity begin to force one's consciousness into a fixed and therefore limited awareness. Just as the Zen master's teachings are like a "finger pointing to the moon," allowing students to perceive truths for themselves, the phenomenological techniques merely prepare the way for personal intuitional experiences of the direct, immanent ground of conscious acts.

Although one might immediately criticize Husserl's transcendental philosophy as having solipistic tendencies, one must keep in mind the "place" (see Chapter 1) where Husserl seeks universal objectivity. Consistent with his radical empiricism, Husserl argues that the ground of individuals' shared understanding, experiences of intersubjectivity and experiences of universal objective standards (our common denominators) lay in the shared structure of human consciousness. The second reduction therefore assists one to at least theoretically confront the structural base of intentional acts (the noesis to noema vector) shared by all human beings. Given his orientation one can understand why Husserl was adamant in repelling complaints about psychologism or relativistic solipisism in favor of a sort of realism rooted in a reflexive analysis of the eidetic structure of human consciousness. This methodology, for Husserl, allowed one to cut through the contingent elements of the facticity of our unique situations and cultures. This procedure eliminates all non-rational contingent elements so that only those necessary, apodictic truths of reason may be emminently given. The evidence for universal objective truths is therefore directly given and not intended, based upon some criterion other than present experience itself. Contingent facts are said to be suspended in order to lay bare the essential truths which provide for the possible conditions and sustaining power of a collective human consciousness. In this way, the second reduction exposes the ground for intersubjective experience and all its ramifications; for example, any ethical doctrine requiring recognition of the autonomy of another with the same rights as oneself.

The importance of the second reduction of the noesis/noema distinction has now been underscored. The second reduction constitutes the main difference between first order bodymind awareness and second order bodymind awareness defined above. In the neutral, non-vectoral mode of first order bodymind awareness the experience of bodymind within the horizon is immediate and direct. Bodymind can never be experienced as the noematic focus of experience because this first order awareness occurs prior to the noetic/noematic distinction. Accordingly, bodymind holds no privileged position amidst the entire experiential horizon. At this *Ur-doxic* or primordially given ground level, bodymind is experienced as part of the horizon prior to thetic judgmental positings.

An example of the second order mode of experience, as opposed to the first order, may be presented as follows. I put down my pen, sit back in my chair and look up from my desk. If I were to look around and direct my attention (noetic vector) to different objects (noematic foci) within the room, I might think to myself "there's that old door that needs to be fixed . . . or should I replace it entirely . . . it looks like the flowers need some water . . . I've always liked that picture . . . oh well I better get back to writing and stop wasting time." This mode of experiencing is not first order experience. By speaking to myself my thoughts were given the syntactical and grammatical structure of my language. I shifted my attention to four different noematic foci (door, flower, picture, self), I assumed a specific noetic attitude with respect to each noema, and I made a judgment about each noema. In short, my intentions were numerous and somewhat disconnected.

Let us consider the same situation from the perspective of first order awareness. I put down my pen, sit back in my chair and look up from my desk. This time I am merely aware of the situation; I "presence"[14] the situation as it is given to consciousness. There is no judgement and no silent speaking. I superimpose no structure, linguistic or otherwise, upon the situation. Since all intentions are neutral, no specific vector points toward anything which might otherwise have a privileged noematic position within the horizon. In this way, all of my senses are keen. The size of the experiential periphery expands since my awareness is not concentrated in any specific direction. There is no reflection, abstraction, recollection, wish, hope, desire, etc. There is only the activity of "presencing"[15] the horizon as it is given to consciousness. This does not imply that I am merely registering Humean patches of grayness and redness, etc. Insofar as I am familiar with my surroundings, I presence the horizon in a gestalt. That is, the horizon includes within it, as distinguished from the periphery, the meaning and historicity of familiar objects. The horizon, therefore, is given a structure in accord with the experiential history of its contents. For example, as I sit at my desk I need not be concerned about a train running through the wall since the structure of my present situation is given to consciousness already sifted of such a possibility. Accordingly, I may feel relaxed and comfortable presencing the horizon.

The awareness of bodymind occurs during the forementioned situation. When our intentions are neutralized, it is as though the vectors work to broaden and add greater sensitivity to the awareness of the ground of experience. The greater the conflux of overlapping intentions the more narrow the periphery becomes. For example, while deciding whether or not to fix or replace "the old door" I was aware of little other than that towards which my intentions were directed. However, when I merely presenced the situation in the manner of first order experience, I was aware of not only the door, flowers, picture and self but also temperature, street noise, stuffiness within the room, and so on.

Another brief example of the relationship between the neutralization of intentions and an expanded periphery is as follows. Body-aspect tensions, like mind-aspect intentions, cloud one's sensitivity. Tensions and intentions are like mud put into a clear stream of first order experiencing. They dam the flow of presencing and muddy one's awareness of the non-privileged horizon.[16] When tensions and intentions are neutralized, one's responsiveness to the situation may be immediate. To demonstrate this, play your favorite piece of music. Tense your muscles and listen. Can you hear all the instruments clearly? Can you respond and tap your foot in time to the music? Or, close your eyes and imagine you are blind. Now tense your muscles once again or create some intentions by reflecting or imagining. Can you feel the objects around you clearly? Can you hear the sounds around you? It seems as though our awareness is increased during neutral first order experience unlike any other mode of experience. Once mind-aspect intentions and body-aspect tensions are neutralized, presencing with an expanded periphery seems to arise as a natural consequent.

In an effort to more clearly describe first order experience, three qualities of bodymind awareness within the horizon will be examined.

(1) BODYMIND AWARENESS AS THE CONDITION FOR NOETIC AND NOEMATIC RELATIONS.

The relationship between noesis and noema is one in which a change in the meaning bestowing noesis creates a change in the meaning of the noema. One may ask how is it that the above changes can be so sensitively experienced? Such determinations are ascertainable only against a background of first order bodymind awareness. The presence of noesis and noema already entail a second or third order experience. If there is one initial second order experience, it is difficult to utilize additional second order experiences in order to ascertain subtle shifts between the noesis and noema within the initial experience. Such additional intentional vectors only serve to cover the single assiduous perspectives characteristic of second order experience. Additional thetic analyses only serve to focus attention toward specific aspects of the initial (chronologically prior) experience, thus abstracting some unique features of experience from their original context. This process does not serve to describe the subtle relations within the original pre-reflective experience. A description of the subtle changes between noesis and noema within a second order experience requires a description of the entire context within which the changes occur. The changes themselves are experienced against a background of neutral bodymind awareness wherein the horizon is clearly presenced. Being neutral, the horizon surrounding the privileged intentional vector reflects all the changes clearly. In this way, first order bodymind awareness of the non-privileged horizon serves as a backdrop against which noetic/noematic changes, characteristic of second and third order intentional experience, may be understood.

An analogy, although overly simplistic, may serve to clarify this point. Bodymind awareness acts as the original, neutral canvas upon which the subtle intentional changes of color, texture, and brushwork are recorded. The artist's intentions are fulfilled and recognizable against this background. In a similar way, the bodymind background is a necessary epistemic condition for ascertaining changes in the noetic/noematic relations. An artist's intentions are not recognized by creating additional intentions (color, texture, brushwork) for this would only serve to color over the initial painting, i.e., the initial experience. Similarly, each meaning bestowing noetic vector is possible and recognizable due to the neutral bodymind awareness that acts as a ground. Furthermore, just as the artists's intended object is usually not the same as the blank canvas upon which it is painted, unless of course one intends a blank canvas to represent space or emptiness and so on, an intended noematic focus is not the same as the neutral nonprivileged horizon against which it is recognizable. Similarly, the awareness of bodymind within the non-privileged horizon can not occur as a noematic focus. The awareness of bodymind permeates the horizon of pre-reflective experience but can not, during that experience, be specified as a privileged noema. For example, a simple brush stroke is visible because of the blank canvas upon which it is drawn. In contrast, a purely blank canvas is something which is experienced in toto for one's attention is not drawn to any privileged noema. The blank canvas, like first order bodymind awareness, is experienced as a whole prior to any intentional noetic vectors which may be drawn upon it. In this way bodymind, like the blank canvas, can never be experienced as an independent noema. In reflection, bodymind can become the noematic focus of a reflexive glance; however, such an intention would abstract bodymind from its unassuming position within the horizon of prereflective experience. In short, one is aware of bodymind in its primordially given form, not as a noematic focus, but as one aspect within the non-privileged horizon.

The relation between noesis and noema is, therefore, understood by describing the subtle shifts of meaning bestowing (noesis) and meaning (noema) that are directly experienced against a neutral background. It has been suggested that the neutralization of the mind-aspect intentions and body-aspect tensions increase one's awareness of the entire horizon of our experience. In fact, neutralizing intensions and tensions appears to be the means of becoming most aware of bodymind and its role as the ground upon which intentional vectors are possible and recognizable. Now we are prepared to examine the *second* essential quality of bodymind awareness within the horizon.

(2) BODYMIND AWARENESS AS THE DYNAMIC QUALITY OF ALL EXPERIENCE.

During the first order mode of experiencing when all thetic positings are neutralized, bodymind does not "declare" or "reveal"[17] itself. Rather, one is aware of bodymind as one aspect within the experiential periphery; it does not draw attention to itself as a privileged noematic focus. Accordingly, bodymind cannot be thoroughly grasped. That is, it can never be experienced in toto because of its dynamic nature within the horizon. It is this dynamic feature that restricts bodymind from becoming authentically captured as the static noematic focus of a noetic glance. Since the dynamic quality of bodymind awareness explains why it can never be thoroughly grasped and why it can never be authentically posited as a noematic object, this notion needs to be clarified further.

There are many ways in which one can experience an object. In each case the degree to which one can know the object depends on the intrinsic nature of the object. For example, if a tree is a noematic object then it is possible that an infinite number of perspectives could be directed upon it. The tree could be viewed from perspectives 360 degrees around it and could also be viewed from a variety of attitudinal noetic stances. It could be viewed from a "Cartesian" perspective ("with an accurate description of the tree's color, the shape of its leaves, the texture of its bark" as it is seen on a bright sunny day) or it could be viewed from a "druidic" perspective (when the "tree emerges from an overwhelming nearness of presence and is eery, bespeaking its druid or spirit within" as it is seen "on mistry nights and windy mornings in the half-light of dawn").[18] If, on the other hand, $1+2=2+1$ is the noematic core instead of a tree, then there would be only one immediate apprehension of its meaning. The awareness of bodymind however must be distinguished from each of these ways in which one can know an object.

To begin, bodymind can never be primordially presenced as a noematic focus. Bodymind is experienced within the horizon of the first order experience. Since the entire horizon in which bodymind is included is thetically neutral, it is not static. The horizon is given no rigid structure during the act of presencing. The meaning of the horizon is given to consciousness as it is. There are no superimposed categories or definitions into which the contents of the experience must be compartmentalized. In the first order mode of experience bodymind is primordially given and is experienced as the dynamic ground for all experience. During an experience, for example of looking up from the desk, I am aware of the myriads of possible ways in which I may focus my intention. At this time one is aware of bodymind as the ever-changing dynamic reservoir from which an infinite number of vectors may be posited. Moreover, during our awareness of bodymind, there is a recognition of a dynamic fluidity which allows our sensations to be keen throughout the expanded periphery.

This dynamic characteristic of bodymind is also experienced during a variety of experiences of the same static object. The variety of attitudes and perspectives that could be taken towards a tree have already been mentioned. This variety is possible because the changes of perspective issue from the dynamic bodymind ground. This dynamic nature of bodymind is experienced in an obvious and overt manner. When one has neutralized all thetic positings this does not mean that one "does not do anything" (a negative thetic positing) or "strips away every meaningful thing" (a nihilistic attitude) etc. Rather one could liken neutralizing all intentions with positing only one intention, viz., nothing. This approach has the advantage of carrying with it the notion that there is an activity even within the first order mode of experiencing. There is no denial of the world but an active positing of nothing. One is literally *doing* nothing. From this perspective it is perhaps easier to recognize the dynamism which pervades the horizon. The fact that perceptual objects given to our consciousness are never completely known is due to the fact that (1) experience is perspectival and therefore limited, and (2) it is an on-going process with a seemingly infinite reservoir of possibility. Accordingly, not only is it impossible to be totally knowledgeable of bodymind as it is directly presenced amidst the horizon, but it is also impossible to know bodymind in reflection as the noematic focus of a noetic glance. Nevertheless, we have seen that the dynamic quality of bodymind may be directly experienced within first order experience as the ground of subsequent thetic positings. Finally we are prepared to describe "the third essential quality of bodymind awareness within the horizon."

(3) BODYMIND AWARENESS AS THE CONDITION FOR THE SPATIO-TEMPORAL CHARACTER OF EXPERIENCE

Another dimension of experience is that it is a process known to be our own. Bodymind is experienced as that aspect of experience which enables us to know that it is our own. During the first order mode of experience, the ground is recognizable as the center of the periphery. That is, the periphery is always given to consciousness located in some "place."[19] If some noetic attitude were to arise as an intentional vector, then this vector's point of origin would be this same place. This place is bodymind. Bodymind is the phenomenological ground for all experience since all experience is both located and directed.

Our communication and interaction with the world is through visual, tactile, and auditory experiences. Each of our sensations has a range within which information is gathered and analyzed. The vertex of these sensory experiences is bodymind. For example, as I sit and look up from my desk in a first order manner, all thetic positings are neutralized and the periphery of my awareness expands. I am aware of the entire visual field before me, the auditory sound around me, and the climate within my surroundings. In each case experience is known to be mine since I am, phenomenologically, nothing more than the place through which dynamic experience flows. If I choose to focus my attention upon "door," "flower," "picture," or "self" while at my desk, then the intentional vector will be directed from "here" to "there." The common belief is that this spatial locale affects both body-aspects and mind-aspects. However bodymind, as the ground of experience is the condition for the spatial character of experience. For experience to occur it must occur in some place — bodymind.

In addition, bodymind is experienced as the temporal ground of experience. Again, our temporal locale seems to affect both body-aspects and mind-aspects because bodymind is the condition for the temporal character of experience. For experience to occur, it must occur with respect to some temporal ground — bodymind. In first order experience bodymind is recognized as a dynamic function that binds experience together in time. Within a completely neutral horizon, the primordial continuous stream of experience is presenced without interruption. As this time, the past and future have no meaning apart from the now in which they are presenced. One becomes aware that just as the mind and body have no exact one-to-one experiential correlate, the past and future have no correlate other than their meaning as abstracted from the stream of present experience. The past and future can only be *experienced* as present memories or anticipations respectively. I am not concerned with discrediting the very pragmatic utility of such abstractions; however, by focusing upon primordially given time-as-experienced, one is able to describe the experiential ground of temporality itself — bodymind.

During first order experience, past, present and future occur simultaneously. Since the horizon is experienced in toto, there is no succession of moments. There is no t1, t2, t3 in which a series of before and after may be constructed. Moreover, there is no noematic object which is given a status unique to the rest of the horizon. Once intended, a noematic object may be seen as something which stands apart; it is something capable of undergoing relative change in space and time. Spatial change is possible for a noematic object may be observed to move across the periphery relative to the rest of the horizon. This, in turn, is possible because one is aware of a specific moment (t1) in which the noema became the specific object of our attention. Once focused upon, it may acquire a history relative to the rest of the horizon, i.e., it may do X at t1, Y at t2, and Z at t3. However, in first order experience wherein the horizon is presenced in toto, there is no recognition of anything specific. Therefore, there is no recognition of something changing in space or time relative to everything else. The horizon is presenced as it is in a *simultaneous* manner. Since nothing stands apart from the horizon, there is no experience of relative space or time. Only the dynamic simultaneity of the horizon is experienced as the reservoir of possible relative spatio-temporal distinctions.

The awareness of bodymind within this simultaneity may now be clarified. Above I described how the horizon is experienced in toto simultaneously. We noticed that when a noetic vector aims at an intended noema, this noematic focus stands apart (privileged) relative to the remainder of the horizon. If we were to become totally involved with the noematic focus, then we would find ourselves mentally and physically separated from the horizon, i.e., our awareness of bodymind as the ground necessary for spatio-temporal distinctions would be greatly diminished. For example, suppose I am in a new city shopping for a gift. I discover to my delight an incredible children's toy. As I walk out of the store, I marvel at my new purchase. I take it out of the box and proceed to play with all of its gadgetry. Unknowingly, I walk for blocks and blocks. Finally, as I look up to check my whereabouts, I discover myself in completely unfamiliar surroundings. As I check my watch I learn, to my amazement, that half an hour has passed since my purchase.

In this case total involvement with the noematic object resulted in a complete lack of awareness of my surroundings. In other words, the noematic object was observed with a limited periphery (tunnel vision). In such a situation the noematic object, and my complete involvement with it, became abstracted from what we might call a "normal periphery"[20] under the circumstances. In short, I was aware of only the object relative to nothing else. Cut off from the normal periphery, I lost my awareness of space and time. This is because space and time are experientially grasped by relative changes between the periphery and noemata. When I finished walking I did not know my location nor how long I had walked. I had made the periphery of my experience the same as the noema. Accordingly, the relative contrast between noema and normal periphery necessary for awareness of space and time was absent. The only awareness of space and time occurred within the very narrow periphery surrounding the toy, i.e, the toy itself has a spatio-temporal character; its lights blinked on and off in succession and its odd shape stood out against a background consisting only of the tops of my shoes and the sidewalk.

From this description one can see that spatial and temporal characteristics accompany all experiences in which a noematic object is posited. The noema may be experienced relative to the periphery of the experience no matter how large or small. It has also been suggested that when no noematic object is posited, there is no thing against which relative spatio-temporal distinctions may be determined. In this way, one recognizes that space and time are conditions which accompany only thetic experience. In contrast, primordial neutral experience is characterized by bodymind awareness which serves as the condition and ground (simultaneity) for the spatio-temporal dimension of thetic (second and third order) experience. One might also recognize that space and time are solely components of our experience. When fixed upon a specific noema, spatial and temporal dimensions are experienced in relation to the size of the periphery and horizon.[21] For example, if the periphery is only as large as the above mentioned toy, then the spatio-temporal considerations regarding my position within the city and time of day go completely unnoticed.[22] Accordingly, space and time are experienced as qualities which allow for the possibility of intentional experience. As such they provide the structure by which the noemata may be distinguished from the rest of the horizon. Without such a structure all experience would be first order experience and one would only be aware of the dynamic bodymind pervading a simultaneously given horizon.

Having described the three essential qualities of bodymind in first order experience, we are prepared to add some observations regarding second and third order experience. The discussion of the latter two modes of experience will be limited to characteristics pertinent to a phenomenological description of bodymind.

b. *Second Order Bodymind Awareness*

We may recall that in this mode of experiencing there is only one specific noetic vector directed towards a single privileged noematic focus. This is, therefore, the most primordial form of intentionality. The awareness of bodymind is secondary to the awareness of the intended noematic focus. Example: pre-reflective, assiduous consciousness as exemplified by an athlete during intense competition or a musical artist during a performance. The description of second order experience will be restricted to the degree to which it offers insight into the nature of bodymind. The awareness of bodymind in second order experience is not direct; instead it is recognized by the degree of awareness and clarity of the horizon. Since bodymind can only be directly experienced as part of the horizon in toto, it will be helpful to examine the manner and degree to which one can be aware of bodymind in second order experience.

To begin, let us examine a "pre-reflective, assiduous" experience. For an experience to be assiduous, it must be "marked by careful, unremitting attention or persistent application."[23] Driving a nail into a board calls for "unremitting attention" on a single noematic object — the head of a nail. And, *via* "persistent application," one can become so talented at driving a nail into a board, that his or her attention may actually be allowed to wander. Consider that I am an unskilled carpenter. Whenever I attempt to drive a nail into a piece of wood, my attention is sporadic. I am *worried* about driving the nail straight, *concerned* about bending the nail, *afraid* of accidentally striking my thumb or forefinger holding the nail, and basically have so many noetic concerns operative that inevitably my unremitting attention to driving in this nail is less than adequately achieved. It would appear that "unremitting attention" is the product of "persistent application," i.e., practice makes perfect. An assiduous experience is, therefore, one which requires "cultivation."[24] The skilled carpenter drives in 99% of his nails straight and true in two or three swings of a hammer. His unremitting attention is present yet, through his training and confidence, it looks and feels easy. In fact these skills have become so internalized that the carpenter is free to actually daydream while performing a difficult task. The term "internalized" signifies that a certain skill has become incorporated into one's subconscious. However, since "subconscious" usually denotes a mind-aspect phenomena, I would like to suggest *"sedimentaion"*[25] as a term meaning the process of internalizing skills with the mind-aspect and body-aspect, i.e., to perform skills with an awareness of bodymind. Accordingly one might say that an artist, sportsman or carpenter, for example, possess sedimented skills when they can pre-reflectively perform the skills operative in musical or athletic improvisation, or even in striking a nail through a board.

In daily life there are many such assiduous experiences. There was a time in our lives when even walking created "worry," "concern," and "anxiety." Once we learned how to walk it became a sedimented skill. Once able to walk pre-reflectively, we acquired such skills as running, jumping, and skipping. Similarly, we learned to speak and recite multiplication tables pre-reflectively. All of these skills eventually become sedimented. Many of us who have learned to drive a car with a manual clutch remember having to concentrate on the clutch, brake, accelerator, steering wheel, and shifting column independently. Once the skill is internalized the mind-aspect and body-aspects (bodymind) can pre-reflectively perform the skill by relying upon sedimented patterns of behavior. While driving, for example, some of us have experienced a type of reverie in which one continues to drive down a familiar road while concentrating upon something totally divorced from our driving situation. One continues to perform the skill of driving by apparently relying upon sedimented patterns of behavior acquired by persistent application.

During pre-reflective assiduous experience, our attention may continue to focus upon the single noematic object or, if the activity has been sedimented, we may direct our attention elsewhere. Our attention may be directed away from the immediate situation, as in reverie, or it may focus upon the noema with even greater concentration, therefore perfecting the sedimented skill even further, or it may become neutral. In the latter case, the experience changes from second order experience into first order awareness of the horizon in toto. Once the skill has been sedimented, the practitioner is capable of continuing to perform the activity while presencing the horizon as it is primordially given to consciousness. It is from this special type of first order experience that one hears accounts, particularly from artists and sportsmen, of rather euphoric experiences during exceptional performances. First, the performance is exceptional because all the extraneous intentions, e.g., worry, anxiety, have been neutralized. Second, the sedimented skills are performed pre-reflectively. And third, since even the primary noetic intention is neutralized, the artist or sportsman becomes unhampered by a desire to concentrate and try too hard. Accordingly, the skill is performed with greater spontaneity and naturalness.

The artist or sportsman often considers the experience euphoric or even mystical because the skill was performed well without thinking or trying. Moreover, that which the individual does experience is a completely neutral horizon in which the entire situation may be experienced simultaneously. The expanded periphery and increased awareness enables the performer to experience and feel the skill as never before. Oftentimes, in reflection, one is capable of remembering and feeling every detail of the skill as if it were performed in slow motion. This type of first order experience is usually the most striking insofar as the performance of a familiar skill constitutes the horizon.

The awareness of bodymind may be the most dramatic during this special "transitional"[26] first order mode of experience. This experience is unique because the antithesis of the commonly accepted abstraction that the mind intends first, and then the body responsively moves, is experienced. For example, during a pianist's or dancer's improvisation, in which all noetic intentions are neutralized and the performance is inspired by the habits of sedimented skills, the body-aspect is as much an instigator of movement as the mind-aspect. The origin of this performance is directly experienced as arising from the historicity of the horizon in which bodymind is included. Since the meaning and context of the situation may be familiar, the horizon is filled with past habits, performances and skills. The kinesthetic impressions are pre-reflectively meaningful due to the wealth of their history and sedimentation, and thus their meaning need not originate via a meaning-bestowing noesis. Since the patterns of movement are sedimented they may be projected, without a noetic vector, at once as a gestalt. In short, since the horizon of an experiential situation with which we are most familiar is rich with sedimentation, it is in this situation that the awareness of bodymind can be most pronounced. If we are very familiar with the horizon of performing a skill, and if we neutralize the single noetic intention, the direct awareness of bodymind strikes our attention as it is the most unfamiliar aspect pervading the horizon. Bodymind is thus recognized immediately within a familiar horizon. We are now prepared to describe the pertinent characteristics of third order bodymind awareness.

c. *Third Order Bodymind Awareness*

In third order bodymind awareness there may be overlapping noetic vectors towards a multiplicity of noematic foci. This is the most complex form of intentionality. The awareness of bodymind is filtered by a myriad of noematic foci. Example: reflective discursive consciousness. The phenomenological description of second order bodymind awareness demonstrates that the awareness of bodymind is heightened when one can continue to perform an activity even though the single noetic and noematic relationship has been neutralized. This, we remember, is achieved through persistent application and the eventual sedimentation of skills. When the sedimented habits "take over" as it were, the performance of the skill is maximized since all intentional attempts to concentrate or try *too* hard are neutralized. Just as this neutralization of extraneous intentions maximizes the performance, the addition of unneeded noetic intentions tends to detract from the performance. For example, if an artist or sportsman feels pressure to perform well, additional noetic positings (worry, concern, fear, and so on) may distract the individual from the specific activity that must be done. These additional noetic concerns may cause an individual to focus only upon privileged noemata, thus narrowing the size of the periphery (tunnel vision). In the case of an orchestra conductor or quarterback, this may severely affect their performance.

Even in daily life too many foci entering the periphery of our attention may result in, for example: (1) driving through a red light; (2) forgetting to turn off the stove; (3) saying things in an argument we really do not mean; or (4) finding ourselves working at a project all day and never getting anything accomplished. A lack of concentration may occur as a result of either an inability to neutralize extraneous intentions or a tendency to be distracted by movements or noises within the periphery. The additional maze of intentional vectors not only hampers one's ability to perform a skill but also creates a filter making it difficult to be directly aware of bodymind at the ground of experience.

The fact that the third order mode of experience is not optimal for performing a specific skill must be seen in its proper context. To perform the skills of an artist or sportsman etc., the second order mode of experience is most successful. Anything which involves concentration upon a single activity is best achieved *via* second order experience since "you can only do *one* thing at a time." However, sometimes it is more pragmatic to consider many things at once. On these occasions, as in complex decision making, many factors may have to be considered simultaneously. Accordingly, the third order mode of experience allows for the possibility of many noetic intentions to be weighed simultaneously.

Within this category one finds the experiences of complex reflection, abstraction, imagination, and speculation. Mind-aspects and body-aspects can always be detected within these experiences as well. Bodymind is the condition for the noetic/noematic relation, the spatio-temporal character and the dynamic quality of third order experiences as much as first and second order experiences. The only difference one may discover is that a phenomenological description of these aspects requires one to neutralize a greater variety of intentional positings. Imagination, abstraction, and reflection, all refer back to bodymind ultimately. For example, while imagining one is dancing, the kinetic form is experienced spatially. One does not see oneself as object (although this is possible from yet another spatial perspective). Instead, one's spatial presence pervades the horizon in which one is included. We seem to be aware of our space and movement in a way that describes a blind person's ability to "see" with the tip of his cane. In this way, it is possible to choreograph a dance in our imagination and still know if it "feels right."

In conclusion, we have seen that while third order experiencing may be beneficial under certain circumstances, it is the least effective mode for bodymind awareness. The third order mode is the most removed from pre-reflective awareness of the primordially given horizon. The second order mode of experience moves closer to an awareness of the primordially given horizon. In fact, in transitional cases when the primary noetic intention may be neutralized and the activity is able to persist through sedimentation, the individual may become directly aware of the horizon including bodymind. The first order mode of experience requires all thetic positings to become neutralized. In this way, bodymind may be experienced as the condition for noetic/noematic relations, the spatio-temporal quality of thetic experience, and as the dynamic quality characteristic of all experience.

Chapter 3

Kūkai: A Descriptive Philosophy

The purpose of Chapters 3, 4, 5 and 6 is to investigate phenomenologically some philosophical themes and religious practices related to bodymind awareness in two schools of Japanese Buddhism. It will be maintained throughout that the type of experiences emphasized as the goal of various religious practices reflect, implicitly or explicitly, the eidetic structure of first order bodymind awareness. Accordingly, first order bodymind awareness will emerge as a common thread in the two Japanese Buddhist schools discussed — Kūkai's (774–835) Shingon-shū, and Dōgen's (1200–1253) Sōtō-shū. In addition, the analysis of each school will further illuminate not only first order bodymind awareness, but also an entire philosophical structure that has for its ideal this mode of experience. The unique set of problems accompanying this philosophical structure will also be emphasized. Specifically, the problem of the relation between practice and enlightenment in Japanese Buddhism will be phenomenologically analyzed in light of first order bodymind awareness.

In Chapters 3 and 4 the experiential basis for Kūkai's Esoteric Buddhist theory will be investigated. By elucidating the relation between tantric religious practice, Esoteric Buddhist theory (Chapter 3) and first order bodymind awareness (Chapter 4), it will be possible to de-mystify, and therefore clarify, Kūkai's complex philosophical system. This interpretive technique will begin to unveil important themes for understanding first order bodymind awareness and its role in the subsequent development of classical Japanese Buddhism.

1. Introductory Background

Kōbō Daishi Kūkai (774–835) was the founder of the Shingon school of Esoteric Buddhism. He was born in the Sanuki province on the island of Shikoku. A precocious child and a member of a scholar-aristocratic family, Kūkai received instruction in poetry and Confucian classics. He was on his way to a career as a government bureaucrat, under the guidance of his maternal uncle Atō Ōtari, the tutor to the Crown Prince Iyo, when he abruptly forsook the wishes of his family and turned to Buddhism. The exact reasons for such a drastic change are difficult to determine, but it has been suggested that Kūkai's attraction to Buddhism was related to a predilection for religious practice rather than theology or a career in public service.[1]

When Kūkai left the university at Nagaoka, he went to the mountains to devote himself to the practice of meditation. It is believed that he spent some time with the *Jinen chishū* (Sect of Natural Wisdom) and was influenced by *Shugendō* (Way of Mystical Practice). Each of these mountain religious activities appealed to what has been referred to as the "archaic"[2] aspect of Kūkai's personality. That is, part of Kūkai seemed to identify with an earlier era of Japanese history in which natural phenomena, such as the light, wind, and heavens were glorified as objects of worship. Believing that gods (*kami*) permeated nature, Kūkai was exposed to various religious practices at sea and in the mountains. Yet, at the same time, Kūkai was one of the most progressive intellectuals of his age. Even though theory and study were less important than practice, his gifted intellectual analytic abilities enabled him to systematize Shingon doctrine and to excel in his studies of Chinese, Sanskrit, calligraphy, and numerous other artistic endeavors. In addition to this archaic and intellectual blend, Kūkai was extremely energetic. His achievements as the founder of the monastic center on Mt. Kōya led to such impressive accomplishments that, today, it is difficult to distinguish his actual contributions from the myriads of legends spread by his wandering priests (*Kōya-hijiri*).

While in the mountains as a youth, Kūkai internalized the notion that *kami* were embodied within the forests, streams, rocks, wind, and mountains. According to this Shinto tradition, these natural phenomena were said to be the offspring of *Izana-gi* and *Izana-mi*—the mythical creators of the universe. Of specific interest to us is the child *Amaterasu* (Sun Goddess) who gives light to the entire universe. This point is worth noting for the following reason. It is said that in a dream Kūkai was told to consult the *Mahāvairocana Sutra* (*Daibirushana jōbutsu jimben kajikyō*, popularly known as *Dainichikyō*).[3] It has been suggested that the "ultimate Buddha" (Sk. *Tathagāta Mahāvairocana*, Jp. *Dainichi Nyorai* lit., 'great' + 'sun' + 'Thus-come[gone]-one') was understood by the Japanese as "Buddha-nature that shines like a great light within all things."[4] In other words, the pervasive infinite character of *Mahāvairocana* (Dharmakāya) was likened to the *Dainichi* (Great Sun) which not only shined over the entire universe, but also, in the sense of *Amaterasu*, shared the same heritage with all other natural phenomena, i.e., as offspring of *Izana-gi* and *Izana-mi*. Just as *Amaterasu* participates in and shares the same reality as that upon which she shines, Dainichi Nyorai, as the anthropomorphization of the Dharmakāya, permeates all things. However, possessing only this parallel from which to work, the esoteric doctrines and many symbolic explanations describing interrelationships within the *Dainichikyō*, were probably too complex for Kūkai to understand alone.

Convinced that understanding this sutra would enable him to grasp the highest truths of Buddhism, Kūkai went to China (804) in search of a Tantric master to instruct him. Kūkai met the esoteric master Hui-Kuo (746–805) and was received by him as his long awaited successor. In thirty months Kūkai studied Sanskrit, poetry, calligraphy, other minor arts and became the eighth patriarch of Esoteric Buddhism. In addition, having spent a twenty year government stipend, he returned to Japan (806) loaded with valuable sutras and paraphernalia necessary for esoteric practice. Kūkai was thus able to return to Japan thoroughly instructed in Esoteric Buddhist theory and practice. His early understanding of the *Dainichikyō*, relying upon parallels to the Shinto tradition and a limited knowledge of Esoteric Buddhism, gave way to thorough knowledge of oral instructions passed on to him as the *dharma* successor to Hui-kuo.

2. The Prescriptive and Speculative Aspects of Kūkai's Metaphysics; the Secret and Mystic Aspect of Enlightenment

Kūkai's metaphysics is often portrayed as prescriptive or speculative since Kūkai *assumed* the supremacy of the *Dainichikyō* as a result of (1) a mystic dream experience and (2) the *Dainichikyō's* long established credibility throughout the history of the Esoteric Buddhist tradition. Kūkai's tenets are said to be speculative since esoteric wisdom is not demonstrable. Based upon the assumed authority of only one specific sutra, Kūkai's doctrines would appear to be intellectual speculations without a concrete experiential base. Furthermore, the complex mystic symbolism of ritual practice and the need to learn both Chinese and Sanskrit alienated the masses from Esoteric Buddhism. Accordingly, Kūkai's philosophy developed a reputation for being secret, mystical and impenetrable beyond the capabilities of layman and esoteric scholar-monks alike.

Kūkai's contention that Esoteric Buddhism represents the highest stage of Buddhist understanding similarly connotes a notion of supremacy. He claims that an individual can attain enlightenment in his present body through esoteric practice. He continues to say that this same enlightenment would take aeons through exoteric practice. For these reasons Kūkai's philosophy is often considered prescriptive, speculative, and mystical, beyond the experience and understanding of average human beings. Once an account of the major tenets of Kūkai's philosophy has been given, it will be possible to begin a phenomenological analysis (Chapter 4) of the experiential basis of the apparent prescriptive, speculative, and mystic elements of his philosophy.

a. *Exoteric and Esoteric Buddhist Philosophy*

In the *Benkenmitsu nikyō ron* (Treatise on the Difference Between Exoteric and Esoteric Buddhism), Kūkai distinguishes four salient features of each.[5] First, the exoteric doctrine is preached by the *nirmānakāya* (historical Buddha-body) and is geared for his audience's level of understanding. In contrast, the esoteric doctrine is preached by the Dharmakāya Buddha (Dainichi Nyorai) for his own enjoyment without the use of instructional techniques, i.e., it typifies his innermost enlightened experience. Second, the exoteric doctrine states that this experience of enlightenment is mystical and transcends linguistic description. However, esoteric doctrine states that such a linguistic description is possible *via* "true words" or *mantras* (Jp. *shingon*). Third, in the exoteric tradition it is believed that enlightenment is a gradual process taking aeons of life-times to achieve. In the esoteric tradition, proper practice enables a person to "instantly unite with the Dharmakāya Buddha and attain enlightenment."[6] And finally, in the exoteric tradition sentient beings are classified according to their spiritual capability. In the esoteric tradition, *all* sentient beings are able to realize enlightenment. Such a realization may be aided not only by "true words" but also by works of art and various mental and physical practices. Each of these differences will be discussed in greater detail in the context of our explanations of some representative doctrines.

b. *Hosshin seppō*

Hosshin seppō means "the Dharmakāya expounds the dharma." This term refers to an experience wherein "each and every thing we experience (*hosshin*) is teaching, expounding or explaining (*setsu*) the *dharma* (*hō*)."[7] Hence, the third Buddha-body (Dharmakāya) expounds the truth (*dharma*) by manifesting itself immanently within each and every thing. For Kūkai, this term had far reaching implications and occupied a central position in his system. Originally, the term "*dharmadhātu*" (literally the Realm of the Dharma) referred to the "subjective essence of enlightenment, Absolute Truth and the all-embracing totality of the infinite universes (realms of experience) revealed within Enlightenment."[8] In Kegon thought, *dharmadhātu* was equivalent to Dharmakāya, the third Buddha-body of which Mahāvairocana, immanent within each and every thing, was believed to be a manifestation. The Tendai view of the Dharmakāya was equivalent to "Buddha-nature," and the theory of "Original Enlightenment" (*hongaku*).[9] For Kūkai, these became subsumed together under the heading of *hosshin seppō*. In his *Benkenmitsu nikyō ron*, Kūkai used *hosshin seppō* "as a criterion by which to distinguish Esoteric and Exoteric

Buddhism."[10] Kūkai insisted that the esoteric truth (*dharma*) was preached by the Dharmakāya by manifesting itself within each and every thing. Kōshirō Tamaki suggests that

the main line of Japanese Buddhism itself can be seen from the fact that one of the fundamental characteristics of Esoteric Buddhism which Kūkai has further developed on the ground of the Kegon Sect is this sermon by the Dharmakāya [*hosshin seppō*].

In the same discussion Tamaki cites Kūkai's own explanation contained in the *Shōji jissō gi* (The Meanings of Sound, Word and Reality):

The five elements all have sound. The ten realms are endowed with speech. The six kinds of defilements all are letters. The Dharmakāya is verily the real state.[11]

In numerous passages of this type, Kūkai accentuates the esoteric notion that the Dharmakāya's sermon speaks to us through every thing. At this point, we are prepared to discuss Kūkai's personification of the Dharmakāya in terms of Dainichi Nyorai (*Tathāgata Mahāvairocana*).

In the *Dainichikyō* is it said that the realization of the presence of the Dharmakāya in all things is *immediate*. Since Kūkai believed that Dainichi Nyorai was "the cosmos itself, limitless, without beginning or end," there was no place for mediate interrelationships with respect to Dainichi Nyorai, i.e., distinctions could be made with respect to some other criterion but all things were equally endowed with the spirit of Dainichi Nyorai.[12] In this way, earth, water, fire, air, space, mind and matter were all considered inseparable and equal. Accordingly, Kūkai believed that there could be no mediate or indirect awareness of Dainichi Nyorai. The Nyorai was considered to be directly knowable as it manifested itself in all things.

The explanation given for Dainichi Nyorai's participation in the world is that his grace (*kaji*) works to aid the practitioner to participate here and now in Dainichi Nyorai himself.[13]. Using "expressive symbols" (*monji*), Dainichi Nyorai can make his presence felt in the objects of sight, hearing, smell, touch, taste and thought.[14] Accordingly, included in the implications of *kaji* are the notions of "communication" and "penetration." That is, since

Dainichi Nyorai permeates all reality without exception, his presence is "communicated" to all individuals by "penetrating" the very existence of all things. These aspects of *kaji* have been characterized by the expressions *Nyūga Ganyū* "[the Buddha] entering into me and I entering into [the Buddha]"), and *ga soku butsu* ("I am the Buddha and the Buddha is myself").[15] Kūkai also often describes this character of Dainichi Nyorai by the term *hōben* (Sk. *upāya*). *Hōben* literally means "expedient," "means," or "instrument" and originally meant "the way of evangelization to lead people, or the means of saving them." Yuasa Yasuo calls it "sacred expedient" and refers to it as that which leads the practitioner to the common universal truth—Dainichi Nyorai.[16] Together *kaji* and *hōben* represent the all-pervasive, penetrating and benevolent character of the personified Dharmakāya included in the meaning of *hosshin seppō*.

Given the forementioned background information it is possible to piece together the meaning of *satori* (enlightenment) for Kūkai. *Satori* is immediate and describes the condition of seeing the *dharma* nature of all things (*hosshin seppō*). *Satori* is made possible through the grace (*kaji*) and permeation of Dainichi Nyorai in all things. A discussion of the "three mysteries" (*Sanmitsu*) will further claify Kūkai's conception of enlightenment.

c. *Sanmitsu*

The three mysteries (body, speech, and mind) are qualities of every human being. Together these are said to possess all secrets through which people may realize their Buddha-nature. Collectively, the three answer the question, "How is man to realize Dainichi Nyorai?" Dainichi Nyorai, as the personified Dharmakāya, is the body of action (*karmakāya*) through which the dharma is perpetually taught. Thus, it is through the actions of body, speech, and mind that one comes to be aware of Dainichi Nyorai expounding the dharma (*hosshin seppō*). The mysteries of the body include *mudras*, postures of meditation, and the handling of ritual instruments. The mysteries of speech include *mantras* while the mysteries of mind include *mandalas* and various meditative techniques. These are all considered "mysteries" (*mitsu*, literally, "close, intimate") since, for Kūkai, they are transmitted orally from master to disciple. Since they are never transcribed in book form, they remain inaccessible to both the lay community and exoteric priesthood. Nevertheless, the mysteries are the vehicles through which man becomes aware of Dainichi Nyorai's omnipresence. By understanding the manner in which the three mysteries are related within oneself, the practitioner learns the manner in which the three mysteries relate to all reality. It must be underscored that since Dainichi Nyorai pervades the universe, all things are interrelated insofar as they equally reflect the spirit of Dainichi Nyorai. Accordingly, if one understands the three mysteries' microcosmic interrelationship, one also understands the macrocosmic interrelationship of all reality.

By synthesizing these concepts we may begin to piece together Kūkai's system. The three mysteries are related to the three actions of man — bodily action, verbal action and mental action. The mysteries forever remain mysteries unless there are means of communication by which man may become aware of their mutual interrelationship and participation with Dainichi Nyorai. These modes of communication (deeds, words, and thought) are the "three mysteries of primordial being" (honnu sanmitsu)[17] granted everyone by the grace (kaji) of the personified Dharmakāya — Dainichi Nyorai. In Kūkai's own words the relationship among sentient beings, the three mysteries and Dainichi Nyorai is as follows:

> Sentient beings are infatuated and blind and know no way of attaining enlightenment on their own. Through grace (kaji), therefore, the Nyorai shows them the way to return [to realize their originally enlightened state]. The basis of the way to return cannot be established in the absence of superior teachings. The superior teachings cannot arise in the absence of sound and word. When sound and word are distinct, reality (the symbolized) will be revealed clearly. So-called Sound-Word-Reality is, indeed, the universal Three Mysteries of the Dharmakāya Buddha, the innate maṇḍa (essence) of all sentient beings. Dainichi Nyorai, therefore, by revealing the impact of Sound-Word-Reality, arouses sentient beings from their long slumber.[18]

Kūkai suggests that if we understand the inseparable interrelationship among the mystery of speech (sound), the mystery of mind (word) and the mystery of body (reality), then the same interrelationship characteristic of all reality will become clear. In addition,

Kūkai instructs that such understanding is possible because the personified Dharmakāya bestows "grace" (*kaji*) upon the universe by offering a teaching vehicle or method (*hōben*), i.e., the actions of the three mysteries. Kūkai's methods of practice allow one to cultivate these actions (*karmakāya*) via deeds (body), words (speech) and thought (mind).

Having described the basic function of the three mysteries, we are prepared to investigate phenomenologically each mystery in terms of the corresponding activity to be cultivated. The following analysis will clarify the "mystic" elements of various forms of practice illustrative of each mystery, specifically, *mantra* (speech), *mandala* (mind), and *mudra* (body). To begin, it is necessary to examine one of Kūkai's most important presuppositions. This Shingon axiom explains how enlightenment, the awareness of the mysteries' interrelationship, can occur in this lifetime thus eliminating the need for aeons of exoteric study and practice.

d. *Sokushin jōbutsu*

Sokushin jōbutsu ('this very' + 'body' + 'attain' + 'Buddha, enlightenment'; hence lit. "This very body attaining Buddha"). In part a. above, it was stated that Kūkai believed esoteric practice enabled one to be enlightened here and now. For Kūkai this is a natural consequence of the theory of original enlightenment (*hongaku*- part e. below). That is, since Dainichi Nyorai pervades all things, the Dharmakāya is always present. If a practitioner is able to cultivate the proper actions in accord with the three mysteries and join in communion with the Nyorai, then he has attained enlightenment in this very body — *sokushin jōbutsu*. The crucial point is that enlightenment is not some other-wordly truth to be grasped *via* a mystical experience. Rather, it involves a keen awareness of that which is already present.

A closer etymological examination of the term *sokushin jōbutsu* will reveal the breadth of its meaning. The full significance of the following paraphrase of Kūkai's etymological discussion will remain uncertain until we have the opportunity to apply our phenomenological categories in the latter half of this chapter and Chapter 4. Kūkai exclaims that the "four characters [of *sokushin jōbutsu*] contain boundless meaning." He adds "none of the Buddha's teaching goes beyond this one phrase."[19] In a work entitled *Sokushin Jōbutsu gi* (*The Significance of Sokushin Jōbutsu*) Kūkai explains four aspects of *sokushin* and four aspects of *jōbutsu*. First, the essence of *sokushin* is that it is "mutually unhindered, everlasting, and in harmony (with Reality)." Since all things are to be eternally in harmony, Kūkai says that there must be "mutual agreement and penetration which are the meaning of the '*soku*'. Second, the form of *sokushin* is "not separate." For example, the "four kinds of *Mandalas*"[20] are like "space and light" in that they are "mutually unhindered and unobstructed." In this way, "not separate" is the form of *soku* or *sokushin*. Third, Kūkai explains that the *function* of *sokushin* is recognized through the "Three Mystic Practices" (Body, Speech, Mind). Fourth, the *shin* of *sokushin* is "unhindered." For example, just as the jewels of Indra's net are "perfectly fused and unhindered," *shin* refers to the perfectly fused and unhindered relationship between "one's own body, Buddha's body, and sentient beings' bodies. . . . These bodies are in manifold relationships and are like a lamp and its images in the mirrors, penetrating each other."[21]

The four aspects of *jōbutsu* (attaining Buddhahood or enlightenment) will be familiar to us as we have already outlined a few characteristics of enlightenment. Kūkai states that *jōbutsu* includes in its meaning (1) "attainment to the Buddhahood of Dharmakāya Buddha," (2) "innumerablesness," and (3) "perfection." "Attaintainment" refers to the fact that all sentient beings are already endowed with Buddha-nature (*hongaku*). "Innumerableness" refers to the infinite abode of the Dharmakāya. Since the Dharmakāya pervades all things, it is boundless in every way including wisdom. Hence, it is "perfect." Finally, *jōbutsu* includes in its meaning (4) "reason" because, in Kūkai's words, "it functions like a clean mirror; it is called Reality-Enlightenment Wisdom."[22]

In short, these eight aspects of *sokushin jōbutsu* are summarized by the Shingon school in the following manner:

(1) "'*Sunawachi mi nareru*,' (in itself one's body is an actualized [Buddha])."
(2) "'*mi ni sokushite butsu to naru*,' (with the present body one becomes a Buddha)."
(3) "'*sumiyakani mi butsu to naru*,' (quickly one's body becomes a Buddha).[23]

At this stage we are familiar with Kūkai's contrast of Esoteric versus Exoteric Buddhism, *hosshin seppō*, *sanmitsu*, and *sokushin jōbutsu*. However, before we can begin to analyze phenomenologically any experiential basis for these notions, we must examine one more important doctrine which contributes to the prescriptive/speculative aspects of Kūkai's metaphysics and secret/mystical aspects of his philosophy of enlightenment, namely *hongaku shisō* (The Theory of Original Enlightenment).

e. *Hongaku*

This doctrine was derived from the *Awakening of Faith* (Ch. *Ta-ch'eng ch'i-hsin lun*), "which maintains the intrinsic nature of Enlightenment, contending that if man was not originally Enlightened, he would have no hope of ever attaining Enlightenment." This work maintains that "all that is necessary is for the individual to realize or actualize his 'Original Enlightenment.'"[24] Yoshita Hakeda says:

> Kūkai was [one of] the first in Japan to hold that man is originally enlightened (*hongaku*). His insistence that one can attain enlightenment here and now was grounded on this belief, a belief derived from the simple insight that unless a man is enlightened from the very beginning he has no way to reach enlightenment.[25] (brackets mine)

For Kūkai, everything from the lowest to the highest level of mind possesses an original, spiritually enlightened, character. It follows, from our discussions above, that all sentient beings are originally enlightened because the Dharmakāya expounds the dharma (*hosshin seppō*) in *all* things. Since sentient beings live within a world that is permeated by the presence of the Dharmakāya, their own enlightened character can be authenticated through any interaction with the phenomenal world. To realize this through the three mysteries is one avenue to realize one's originally enlightened condition. Kūkai explains this relationship in his *Introduction to the Mahāvairocana Sutra* (*Dainichi-kyō kaidai*) as follows: Dainichi Nyorai "is the One whose own nature is the Dharmakāya, that is, the Body of Principle, which is intrinsic and original enlightenment (*honnu hongaku*). Accordingly Dainichi Nyorai, as the Body of Principle, "is the element of original enlightenment in all sentient beings."[26] Kūkai explains the problem of realizing man's original condition in his *Precious Key to the Secret Treasury* (*Hizō hōyaku*) as follows:

> He [the practitioner] should know that by virtue of the Dharma he is to abide in the all-pervading great enlightened Mind. All sentient beings are innate bodhisattvas; but they have been bound by defilements of greed, hatred, and delusion.[27] (brackets mine)

He continues to state that all the devotee need do is cultivate the Esoteric Buddhist practices and he "will perceive his original Mind, which is serene and pure like the moon whose rays pervade space without any discrimination."[28]

Kūkai's emphasis upon esoteric practice is constant. The secret and mystical interpretation of his philosophy of enlightenment is furthered by his emphasis on practice. Since the practical understanding of the teaching is to embrace the theoretical system, and since the theoretical system is, in part, based upon the three mysteries and the secret oral transmissions from patriarch to patriarch, a practical understanding seems contingent upon mysteries and secrets. Nevertheless, Kūkai's own example and teaching suggest that one must pursue enlightenment and observe all precepts in spite of all obstacles. The goal of religious practice is nothing short of achieving the mind of Dainichi Nyorai. This state of esoteric meditation is called *himitsu sammaji* (secret samadhi) or *himitsu zen* (mystic meditation). And, insofar as the three mysteries are innate (*honnu sammitsu*) and provide the vehicle for meditation, Kūkai's practice of Esoteric Buddhist meditation may be interpreted as a systematic effort to experience what the doctrines (*hosshin seppō, sanmitsu, sokushin jōbutsu* and *hongaku*) mean.

For Kūkai, even proper study and interpretation of the Buddhist sutras depends upon proper practice. The only way to understand the passages and sutras is to meditate upon them. Kūkai was extremely critical of blind acceptance and recitation of the sutras. In fact, he considered one of the distinguishing features of Esoteric Buddhism to be its rejection of mere scriptual or textual justification for doctrines that could be empirically verified. In the words of Yasuo Yuasa, "Kūkai insisted that the substance of religion should be understood not through letter and doctrine intellectually, but through religious experiences . . . in man's soul."[29] Kūkai's insistence in this regard is due to the fact that

Dainichi Nyorai "is free from aspects," "beyond speech" and thus cannot be thetically/intellectually taught. Rather the Nyorai must be "intuitively realized" for he "does not correspond to the teachings but [to the experience of] enlightenment alone."[30] Briefly summarizing this point, one of Kūkai's unequivocal statements concerning the importance of practice may be cited: "if we establish our faith and devote ourselves to religious practice, we will at once realize enlightenment."[31]

At this juncture, we are familiar with the central role of the three mystic practices (*sanmitsu*), the secret oral transmissions, as well as the prescriptive or speculative nature of *hosshin seppō*, *sokushin jōbutsu*, and *hongaku*. Apart from a few historical and textual explanations, we have yet to examine the philosophical bases for each of these doctrines.

3. Kūkai's Metaphysics and Philosophy of Enlightenment: A Descriptive Account

In this section the basis for Kūkai's *interpretations* of traditional doctrines and his systematization of Esoteric Buddhism will be shown to arise from his description of a specific type of experience. The thesis presented below suggests that the central doctrines of Kūkai's Shingon-shū are grounded in Kūkai's description of a paradigmatic mode of experience which approximates the structure of first order bodymind awareness.

a. *Phenomenalism and Reflexive Phenomenological Methodology*

Kūkai's emphasis upon meditative practice points to the most central and important aspect of Kūkai's system—the "innermost spiritual experience of the Dharmakāya Buddha."[32] This emphasis upon a direct experiential encounter with the Dharmakāya is a contributing factor to the subsequent radically empirical tenor of many schools of Japanese Mahayana Buddhism. The emphasis upon experience as the ground and proper starting place for philosophy reflects a position consistent with radical empiricism, phenomenalism and even phenomenology. Specifically, for Kūkai, the "innermost spiritual experience" is not an experience of another world but an experience grounded in *this* world. For example, the formless Dharmakāya "is transformed into perceptible bodies through his wonderful power [*kaji*], so that every sentient being is able to see the bodies, hear the voices, and know the mind of Dainichi Nyorai."[33] In the *Precious Key*, Kūkai criticizes doctrines espousing ascetic practices and denial of this world. For Kūkai the direction of cultivating the "innermost spiritual experience" is systematically reflexive, i.e., it begins with techniques for meditative self-examination. Since Kūkai's reflexive approach is akin to the direction of phenomenological inquiry, the analysis will begin by describing the nature of experience according to Kūkai. Specifically, we will want to examine the experiential basis for Kūkai's description of that which is innate in every living being. The doctrines of *hongaku*, *hosshin seppō*, and *sokushin jōbutsu* will be shown to originate from reflexive (turning back) introspection and a corresponding conceptual orientation that examines one's thought processes from experienced effects to experienced causes.[34]

b. *Exoteric and Esoteric Thinking:*
   Modes of Experience and the Pathway to Enlightenment

   Exoteric thinking is characteristic of Exoteric Buddhism and esoteric thinking is characteristic of Esoteric Buddhism. Whereas exoteric thinking represents modes of experiences consistent with second and third order bodymind awareness, esoteric thinking refers to a mode of experience characteristic of first order bodymind awareness. The purpose of this section will be to describe phenomenologically the nature of experience according to Kūkai and defend the above statement.

   Kūkai, as a Buddhist, embraces the doctrine of no-self (Sk. *anātman*, Jp. *muga*). Using phenomenological vocabulary for *hermeneutic purposes only* it may be suggested that the *experience* of no-self is grounded upon a mode of experience that is structurally not unlike first order bodymind awareness. Since second and third order bodymind awareness are characterized by thetic positings from noesis to noema (from subject to object), the self (Sk. *ātman*, Jp. *ga*), with a privileged position within the periphery, is implicitly posited. In first order bodymind awareness, however, neither the self nor any specific noematic focus is posited. Thus, this mode of experience is "without self." Unfortunately, no-self implies a negative thetic positing and therefore carries with it an inaccurate sense of self denial. The term "without self" more accurately describes the actual experiential process and contents of first order bodymind awareness, i.e., "without self" conveys a notion of non-posited self or a self without a privileged position within the horizon. A description of first order bodymind awareness includes a description of the non-privileged horizon in which even the self that is affirmed during thetic experience is neutralized. It is important to reaffirm that Kūkai did not utilize the phenomenological vocabulary with which we have become familiar in Chapter 1 and 2. His written works do however include descriptions of such meditative experiences. The phenomenological exegesis utilized throughout is not intended to anachronistically make Kūkai or Dōgen into phenomenologists. Rather, the contemporary techniques are utilized as hermeneutic devices.

For example, we know that for Kūkai the phenomenal world is not some less than absolute image projected by Dainichi Nyorai. Rather, Dainichi Nyorai, as the Source of all beings, is actually the sustainer of all beings through which the *dharma* is revealed. For Kūkai, "the world of mankind is not a mere image projected from ideation. . . . phenomenal appearances of this world are more important than theoretical idealism of the Reality."[35] Given the analysis in Chapter 2, one might suggest that first order bodymind awareness is the mode of experience most appropriate for experiencing the "phenomenal appearances of this world." Similarly, the third order mode of experience is more appropriate for the "theoretical idealism of the Reality." The reflexive or introspective process of neutralizing thetic positings allows the experiencer to presence the phenomenal world as it is given to consciousness. This process is paradigmatic for Kūkai for it allows one to experience the given world in a *non-discriminatory* manner. The doctrines of Exoteric Buddhism allude to a manner of "seeing" things as one and inseparable. Yet, we will see that Kūkai's systematic approach to Esoteric Buddhism is to provide the vehicle or techniques to aid the practitioner to *experience directly* the oneness of the phenomenal world, i.e., via first order bodymind awareness. In order to clarify Kūkai's explanations of the content of a non-discriminatory experiential understanding of the phenomenal world, we shall interpret the following passage:

1   In the 'revealed' [*kenkyō*; Exoteric] Buddhism, earth
     water, fire, wind, etc., are considered non-sentient
     beings; whereas with the 'secret' [*mikkyō; Esoteric]*
     doctrine, these are indeed deemed the symbol of
5   *Nyorai.* These Great Five (*Go-dai*) exist without being
     separated from the Great Mind (*Shin-dai*). Though
     there are differences recognizable between mind
     and matter, yet their essential nature is that they
     are one and the same. The matter is but mind, and the
10   mind is indeed matter: Between the two there is
     no hindrance nor any barrier to separate one from
     the other. Wisdom which is subjective is the sphere
     for that which is objective, therefore the sphere is
     indeed wisdom. Like wisdom which is cognitive is
15   indeed the essential principle for that which is
     cognizable, and the essential principle is indeed
     wisdom; both interacting with each other unrestrictedly
     and unimpededly. Although from an ordinary standpoint
     one can discriminate between the two as though one were
20   the generating and the other the generated, yet in
     reality they are of but one generation, the former
     only being viewed through the aspect of activity
     while the latter of passivity. How can there be
     any such thing as the generating or the generated
25   with each other confronting the other in the truth
     of Nyorai? Both terms, i.e., the active, namely
     the generating, and the passive, namely the generated,
     are the 'secret' [Esoteric] terms of Nyorai; therefore
     man should not, by clinging to the ordinary way
30   of thinking, debate about these 'secret' terms with
     trifling and fruitless arguments.[36]

As we have mentioned earlier, Kūkai's reputation as a mystic
is in part due to his symbolic and often impenetrable explanations
drawn from his knowledge of Sanskrit, Chinese and secretive tantric religious practice. Yet, by interpreting phenomenologically
Kūkai's instructions in a line by line fashion, we will be able to
penetrate the meaning of the above quotation. We will find that
Kūkai's symbolic language actually constitutes a description of
both the nature of experience and the specific characteristics of the
paradigmatic enlightened mode of experiencing.

To begin, we may note that in lines 1-6 the "Great Five (*Go-dai*, [earth, water, fire, wind, space])" symbolically refer to all phenomenal existents. Together these represent the noemata of the "Great Mind (*Shin-dai*)" which designates the Mind of the personified Dharmakāya — Dainichi Nyorai. Like first order body-mind awareness in which the noetic/noematic distinction is neutralized, Kūkai says the Great Mind (noesis) and Great Five (noema) "exist without being separated." Thus from the all-pervasive and permeating perspective of Dainichi Nyorai (and enlightened individuals), there is no primordial experiential separation of self-other, noesis/noema, or even mind/matter. In this latter regard we may note that in lines 6-12 Kūkai explicitly acknowledges apparent differences "recognizable between mind and matter" (as in second and/or third order bodymind awareness), yet continues to state that "their essential nature is that they are one and the same." In other words, from the perspective of the most "essential" mode of awareness, neither mind nor matter are given a privileged position within the horizon. Both participate in a simultaneous non-privileged manner within the experiential periphery and are thus empirically verified as being "essentially" one.

In lines 12-18 Kūkai approximates our phenomenological language. First, we note that wisdom is described in a manner reminiscent of mind-aspect, the "subjective sphere for that which is objective." Moreover, Kūkai is even sensitive to the relation between the "cognitive" (noesis) and the "cognizable" (noema). When these "interact" (as in first order bodymind awareness when all positings are neutralized), they are said to permeate each other in an "unrestricted" and "unimpeded" way. This is precisely the manner in which the horizon displays its characteristic dynamism (see Chapter 2). The most important theme running between the lines of Kūkai's keen understanding of the primordial mode of awareness is that "wisdom" and various levels of knowledge are a result of different modes of concrete phenomenal experience. Kūkai displays a sensitivity to phenomenological ways of thinking by implying that experience is our window to the world and clear presuppositionless experience is the most authentic means of acquiring widsom.

For example, in lines 18-23 he distinguishes two modes of awareness in which one is said to be a more authentic presencing of the world as it is given to consciousness. We may interpret this section as follows: He says, *although from an ordinary standpoint* (the sedimented second or third order bodymind awareness) *one can discriminate between the two as though one were the generating and the other the generated* (that is, the 'cognitive' and 'cognizable' are discriminated via the 'generating' [noetic intentional vector] and the 'generated' [noematic focus]), *yet in reality they are but one generation* (in first order bodymind awareness when the experiencer presences the ground of all thetic experience, the phenomena within the periphery appear as "one generation"—the horizon in toto), *the former only being viewed through the aspect of activity while the latter of passivity* (the former noetic vector is viewed through the intentional activity whereas the latter noematic foci appears as the passive focus of a noetic glance).

Then, in the next statement (lines 23-26), Kūkai asks how there can be such a (noetic/noematic) bifurcation in the mode of awareness of the Nyorai. Surely, the Nyorai's awareness is the most true, authentic presencing in which there is no "confrontation" whatsoever. Kūkai resolves this apparent inconsistency via a form of phenomenological observation (lines 26-31). First one must recognize that the "active generating" (noesis) and the "passive generated" (noema) are merely "terms" of the Nyorai, i.e., they are abstractions which help to describe the nature of the experiental process by isolating various distinguishable features of primordial awareness. Nevertheless, if "one clings" to these bifurcations as "the ordinary way of thinking" (sedimented second and third order awareness), then one mistakenly attaches a metaphysical or ontological value to these mere abstractions and thus enters into "trifling and fruitless arguments." Hence, the apparent inconsistency above lies in the error of attaching an existential value to mere categories that name various structural components of experience. Consequently, the authentic (first order) mode of awareness of the Nyorai and enlightened individuals may be a direct experience of the horizon and still be described using such abstract distinctions as "cognitive/cognizable," generating/generated," "mind/matter" or our own hermeneutical noesis/noema. Each of these distinctions occur during second or third order bodymind awareness. Yet, from the primordial perspective of first order awareness, they become neutralized in the abode of the non-privileged horizon.

The challenge of Kūkai's descriptive endeavor, and ours as well, is to articulate a thetically neutral mode of awareness. In order to describe this experience, one must thetically isolate its various structural features and this necessarily removes one from the act of neutral experience. Whereas Kūkai often resorted to symbolic metaphorical language to break this thetic barrier, our hermeneutic concerns are directed toward understanding phenomenologically the eidetic structure of experience. While this approach enables us to articulate the phenomenological structure of a thetically neutral mode of awareness, *we must be cognizant of the fact that our categories statically compartmentalize a dynamic primordial mode of awareness.* By explicitly recognizing the hermeneutic problem, we are prepared to at once *sympathize* with Kūkai's question—regarding the unavoidable use of distinctions, viz., "generating" and "generated" (line 24) when referring to the Nyorai's non-discriminating mode of awareness—and *appreciate* the unavoidable paradox that arises when we employ abstractions to describe this non-discriminating first order awareness.

The distinction between exoteric and esoteric thinking should now appear more obvious. Kūkai has emphasized that the non-discriminating mode of experience (first order) is preferable to modes of experience which, in effect, divide or separate the experiential horizon. By giving value and significance to this particular mode of experience, as the authentic manner of viewing the phenomenal world, Kūkai emphasizes the primary importance of meditative practice (first order) and the secondary importance of intellectualizing *via* debate, argumentation and theoretical study (third order). We have seen that he cautions his students not to argue fruitlessly about terms whose meaning can only be known through esoteric thinking. Abstractions like good, bad, mind and matter do not have fixed meanings independent of each other. On the contrary, from the perspective of esoteric thinking (first order awareness) these concepts have no independent experiential correlate. Each must be *directly* experienced as given to consciousness. The practitioner learns that "good" and "bad" are relative terms, without ontic significance, and are the product of reflective judgments that do not have direct experiential correlates in the phenomenal world. In the same way, "mind" and "matter" (body) are experienced as inseparable (bodymind) aspects of the horizon. The meaning of noematic objects is never fixed or permanent. If one clings to exoteric thinking (second or third order), then one may be apt to be attached to the static meanings which have been thetically imposed upon objects divorced from their experiential context. For Kūkai, such an attachment not only signifies that the individual has not experienced the basis for the Buddhist doctrine of impermanence, but also demonstrates that the individual's attachment to exoteric thinking may create more intentions, e.g., desire, craving and lust, which only serve to further cloud the esoteric thinking process (first order bodymind awareness).[37]

Kūkai believed that the esoteric (first order) moder of experience enables one to "see" the objects of our sensation in relation to the experiential horizon. In his own words:

Though raindrops are many, they are of the same water
Though rays of light are not one, they are of the same body.
The form and mind of that One are immeasurable;
The ultimate reality is vast and boundless.[38]

Here he describes his realization that the particulars (noemata) of our experiential life are grounded in the experiential horizon from which they are posited and abstracted. Similarly he says:

The objects of sight — colors, forms or movements — . . . are the products of the unconditioned [horizon]; in other words, they are the manifestations of the Body and Mind [Bodymind] of the Dharmakāya Buddha. . . . Seen from the relative [exoteric] point of view, the bodies of the Buddhas and their lands have distinctions of large or small, coarse or fine, but seen from the absolute point of view they are equally the undifferentiated One.[39] [brackets mine]

Kūkai sums up this distinction by saying that the "marks of distinction" (noemata) are the "expressions" (*monji*) of the unconditioned world, i.e., the horizon primordially given to consciousness. Having distinguished esoteric from exoteric thinking, we are prepared to analyze phenomenologically the paradigmatic modes of experience which serve as "pathways towards esoteric thinking."

(1) THE VEHICLES FOR FIRST ORDER BODYMIND AWARENESS.

The purpose of Kūkai's systematic approach to Esoteric Buddhism is to aid the practitioner to move from exoteric (second and third order) to esoteric (first order) thinking. The practitioner is led to the "secret" truths of Esoteric Buddhism grounded in experience. Kūkai utilized *mantras*, *mandalas*, and *mudras*, in conjunction with the three mysteries (*sanmitsu*), in order to inculcate habits of esoteric thinking. By directing practitioners to esoteric thinking, Kūkai assists them in experiencing the bases for such doctrines as *hosshin seppō*, *hongaku*, and *sokushin jōbutsu*. One must remember that the truths of Esoteric Buddhism have to be experienced directly to be fully understood. Therefore Kūkai, unlike Śākyamuni Buddha and Exoteric Buddhists, would not preach for the benefit of the audience. Instead he would point systematically in the direction of esoteric thinking and thereby encourage the student to verify empirically Buddhist truths for themselves. In this way, the practitioner could realize the truth (*dharma*) as preached by the Dharmakāya himself—Dainichi Nyorai. In the *Dainichikyō* various teaching techniques and the power of symbolism are emphasized for this purpose. The reason for this procedure is that "only the way to enlightenment can be talked about . . . the perfect sea of enlightenment cannot be talked about."[40] For Kūkai, the *hōben* "point the way" in two directions—from man to Buddha (*kōjō*) and from Buddha to man (*kōge*).[41] The actual direction of the aid however is unimportant for such a designation arises from relative exoteric thinking (from here to there). From the perspective of absolute esoteric thinking, there is a thorough permeation of the presence of Dainichi Nyorai within the experiential horizon. From this first order perspective, the practitioner realizes the meaning of the Buddhist expression "*ga soku butsu*" (I am Buddha and Buddha is myself).

Although Kūkai says, "there is no clearly defined method of teaching," he does emphasize three paradigmatic *hōben*, viz., "the gates to enlightenment of the three secrets" (*sanmitsumon*):[42]

When the grace [*kaji*] of the three mysteries is retained, (our inborn three mysteries will) quickly be manifested, the Three Mysteries are the mysteries of body, speech, and mind. . . . If there is a Shingon student who reflects well upon the meaning of the Three Mysteries, makes mudras, recites mantras, and allows his mind to abide in the state of samadhi, then, through his grace, *his three mysteries will be united with the Three Mysteries*; thus the great perfection of his religious discipline will be realized. (brackets mine)[43]

The importance of the three practices is to aid the student to experience the horizon wherein the Three Mysteries are experienced as one, i.e., there are no posited distinctions. This direct experience is possible since body, speech, and mind (which are inseparable during first order bodymind awareness), are the three actions through which the dynamic body of the Dharmakāya is presenced. The practitioner's body of action (*karmakāya*) allows him to become aware of the original *dharma* permeating his body, speech, and mind. The three mysteries are thus experienced as "three secrets of primordial being" (*honnu sanmitsu*).[44] As is the case in first order bodymind awareness, when the "Dharmakāya perpetually teaches dharma [*hosshin seppō*] by these three actions . . . the listener has no body to touch, no ear to hear, and no mind to understand."[45] It is no wonder that the three actions of the Dharmakāya are called mysteries and secrets. During first order bodymind awareness all distinctions such as body, speech and mind are neutralized and are experienced as mutually inseparable and individually unrecognizable. Here even the relative directional pathways (*kōjō* and *kōge*) which help to achieve this experience become neutralized. One becomes aware that the attainment of body, speech, and mind of the Buddha is something which has always been present (as *hongaku*) though covered by thetic positings. Before we can further analyze the relation between the experiential basis for Kūkai's doctrines and first order bodymind awareness, we need to examine phenomenologically exactly *how* the use of *mantras*, *mudras* and *mandalas* leads one to the paradigmatic first order bodymind awareness.

(a) *Mantras*

Traditionally a *mantra* (Jp. *shingon*, "true words") has been defined as "an instrument for evoking or producing something in our mind, specifically a holy formula or magic spell for working or bringing to mind the vision and inner presence of a god."[46] Kūkai used *mantras* to help the practitioner experience the presence of the Dharmakāya. By making sounds, the practitioner uses his own body as a vehicle for enlightenment. By reciting and concentrating upon a *mantra*, one naturally neutralizes all intentions other than the single focus upon the sound. Sounds are most appropriate for this purpose as they are dynamic. Since sounds seem to continue infinitely, a practitioner may focus a stream of unwaivering attention upon them. A static noematic focus is inappropriate since intentionality is dynamic. The dynamic noetic activity is therefore channeled toward the uninterrupted dynamic sound. Kūkai instructs, "Meditate upon it [the sound] until you become united with it. Then you will attain Perfection."[47] This phenomenon is akin to a transfer from second order to first order bodymind awareness (see Chapter 2). When this practice has been cultivated and sedimented the activity of recitation and concentration occurs without effort. Once sedimented, the primary intention focused upon the sound may also be neutralized. It is at this time that "we become united with the sound." The practitioner neutralizes all intentions and suddenly experiences first order bodymind awareness.

The pragmatic meditative effectiveness of a *mantra* is what distinguishes them as "true words" (*shingon*). *Mantra* literally means "'mystic doctrine' that cannot be expressed in ordinary words."[48] The *mantra* may be characterized as "mystic" and "true" because, when properly understood, it is not a sound uttered by the practitioner at all. Rather, Kūkai states that a *mantra* is the "Preaching of the Dharmakāya" and "voice of the Dainichi Nyorai."[49] The sound is therefore understood as the mystery of speech which is a part of the body of action (*karmakāya*) of Dainichi Nyorai. It follows that this sound of Dainichi Nyorai is not a referential device as in ordinary language. Rather the sound evokes the meaning of Reality, i.e., it leads the practitioner to experience the phenomenal world in its primordially given form (in the absence of thetic positings).

The important characteristics of the mystery of speech and sound are as follows: First, all sentient beings are said to be endowed with the gift of speech. They can all make the sounds, through the grace of Dainichi Nyorai, that aid meditative practice. Second, that the mother of all sounds is "A," is symbolically meaningful for our analysis. Kūkai says:

> The very act itself of opening the mouth in order to utter any sound is accompanied by the sound A; therefore, apart from the sound A, no sounds are possible. The sound A is the mother of all sounds.[50]

The "A" sound is important because it is the most primordial; it is the first sound of a baby. Primordiality is the criterion for Kūkai's saying that "the sound A is the mother of all sounds." Moreover, it is toward primordially given experience that the incantation of "A"

leads. That is, we have described above that the continual utterance of the sound provides a noematic object that is dynamic
and can therefore harmonize with the dynamic noetic intention.
This serves to neutralize all intentions other than a single on-going
process of concentration. The practitioner's dynamic noetic process does not waiver from static object to static object because the
dynamism of the noematic sound is complementory to, and even inspires, continued unhindered concentration. Once sedimented,
this single intention may be neutralized, thus introducing the practitioner to first order bodymind awareness. Accordingly, sound
has served to make the practitioner aware of what is *primordially*
given to consciousness (via first order bodymind awareness).
Third, concentration upon sounds helps the practitioner to
become aware that "all sounds, words, speeches, and letters are the
true undifferentiated whole of the *Dharma*."[51] That is, the primordial first order mode of experience unveils the mystery of speech.
In this mode of experience the horizon is experienced *in toto* and
the contents of the experience are presenced equally, i.e., nothing
stands out possessing a privileged position. Thus, one realizes that
all sounds are equally the preaching of the Dharmakāya.[52]

In *The Meanings of Sound, Word, and Reality* (*Shōji jissō gi*),
Kūkai makes the same observation:

> Sounds and letters are differentiated into ten kinds based on ten
> realms. As to their truth and falsity, from a horizontal view, *they
> are all equal*, because all sounds and letters are the true entirety of
> the Dharma, but *vertically, they have differences.*[53] (italics added)

Once again Kūkai's struggle to explain various levels of awareness
is apparent. Interpreting phenomenologically, we may equate the
"horizontal view" with a view of the experiential horizon. All
distinctions, including "truth" and "falsity," are experienced as
"equal" from this first order perspective. In contrast, the "vertical
view" designates a mode in which "sounds and letters" are
specifically intended as noemata and are thereby given a privileged
status amidst the horizon. Intended as such they "have
differences" as in second or third order bodymind awareness.

Another example of Kūkai's description of the actual procedure for *mantra* meditation—and the inculcation of the
"horizontal," or in this case "original," mode of awareness—may
serve as an additional reference:

1   The student of meditation . . . should first
     by means of meditation on the letter A bring forth
     the brightness of his original Mind and then gradually
     make it distinct and brighter and realize his innate
5   wisdom . . . The Buddhas of great compassion,
     therefore, with the wisdom of skillful means, taught
     them [bodhisattvas] this profound Esoteric Buddhist
     yoga . . . By means of this practice each
     devotee will perceive his original Mind, which
10   is serene and pure like the full moon whose rays
     pervade space without any discrimination. . . .
     Just as we hear the sound A when we hear all
     sounds, so we perceive that which is the limit,
     the 'originally uncreated,' when we perceive the
15   arising of all phenomena. He who perceives that
     which is the limit, the 'originally uncreated,'
     will come to know his mind as it really is. . . . Thus this
     single letter [A] is the mantra of Dainichi Nyorai.[54]
     (brackets mine)

By employing our phenomenological hermeneutic once again, we can begin to recognize the consistency of Kūkai's descriptions which share some basic structural common denominators. The sound of the letter A (line 2) serves as a single noematic focus. Kūkai instructs the student to "gradually" (line 3), through sedimentation, bring this sound into a "distinct" focus, for this activity serves to neutralize all extraneous intentions. Accomplishing this, the student is prepared to neutralize this final intention "and realize his innate wisdom" (lines 4-5), i.e., he enters the mode of first order bodymind awareness of things as they are. Next Kūkai metaphorically describes this mode of awareness in terms reminiscent of an expanded periphery. This mode is also referred to as the "limit" or "originally uncreated" (lines 13-14) which may be interpreted as the primordially neutral experiential ground that is presenced prior to thetic "creations." This interpretation seems especially appropriate since one could "perceive the [thetic] arising of all phenomena" (lines 14-15) only by first presencing the original ground of subsequent thetic experience which posits individualized noemata, i.e., "all phenomena." In sum, the practice of *mantra* meditation awakens the student to the "originally uncreated" mode of awareness (lines 15-18).

Properly utilized, a *mantra* can "induce" practitioners "to attain enlightenment." However, if one clings to some abstract meaning which the word or sound represents, then it can "delude" practitioners like a harmful poison.[55] Again, *mantras* have the power to "induce" one into primordial neutral experience because the recitation of sounds share the dynamic quality of first order bodymind awareness. The dynamism of a myriad of possible noetic vectors is channeled into a single focus whose noematic object (sound) shares the dynamism of its horizon. In this way, sedimentation may occur and this final focus is neutralized. Thus, the *mantra* helps to break the encrusted habits of discursive second order awareness by freeing the practitioner from thetic positings. In Kūkai's language:

A mantra is suprarational; It eliminates ignorance when meditated upon and recited.[56]

b. *Mandalas*

Just as the *mantra* channels auditory intentions that aid a practitioner's understanding of the mystery of speech (sound), a *mandala* channels cognitive intentions that aid the practitioner's understanding of the mystery of mind (word). In the same way, we will see below that a *mudra* channels physical intentions that aid a practitioner's understanding of the mystery of body (reality). We have already seen the rather obvious relationship between the mystery of speech and sound; however, the relationship between the mystery of mind and word or between the mystery of body and reality is not so obvious and requires a brief explanation.

Sound, word, and reality refer to the title of one of Kūkai's most famous works — *The Meanings of Sound, Word and Reality* (*Shōji jissō gi*). In short, Kūkai instructs that practitioners ought to

meditate upon sounds, words and realities in order and in reverse order. Sound is to recite the words (syllables); word is to visualize the forms of words; and reality is to meditate on the meanings of these words.[57]

Since we have discussed the "recitation of syllables" in the *mantra* section, we may explain the above quotation by suggesting the "meditation upon sounds, words, and realities in order and reverse order" all have the similar effect of neutralizing extraneous intentions and sedimenting first order bodymind awareness. Since the relation between sound, *mantras* and the mystery of speech has been discussed above, attention must be directed toward the relation between word, *mandalas* and the mystery of mind. Likewise, the subsequent section will unpack the relation between reality, *mudras*, and the mystery of body.

The above "visualization" of the "forms of the words" refers to the five names of the Buddha, i.e., "one who speaks true-words, one who speaks real-words, one who speaks exact-words, one who speaks honest-words, and one who speaks consistent-words." Together these five words are called *Mandala*, "for the term *Mandala* possesses all the significations of these words."[58] This synthesis is accomplished by meditating upon a diagram (*mandala*) depicting a dynamic integration of the meaning of the five words. In this way, the *mandala* helps the practitioner to neutralize all extraneous intentions.

Mandalas, like *mantras*, have gained a reputation of assisting practitioners toward "suprarational" levels of experience. Yet, in the case of Japanese Buddhism, we must clarify that the transcendence of discursive reason is achieved through reflexive introspection and neutralization of thetic positings. First order bodymind awareness transcends second order bodymind awareness by bringing the experiencer into a mode of neutral presencing of the horizon wherein no individualized phenomena are given a privileged position. Because this level of awareness defies linguistic description, it can indeed be said to be "mystic" and/or "suprarational." These phrases, however, have often led interpreters of the Japanese Buddhist tradition to conclude inaccurately that Kūkai was referring to some other-worldly experience revealing a transcendental metaphysical reality. The following, for example, describes the manner in which *mandalas* assist students yet, unfortunately, gives the impression that there are many levels of reality to be penetrated:

> In meditation the *mandala* is used as a projection of the interior life, a revelation of the subjective universe to enable movement from the multiple facticity of daily life to a focused concentration and the revelation of the limitless potentialities of enlightenment.

Conversely, it can also lead to the realization of the outflowing of enlightenment to penetrate every sphere of phenomenal existence.[59]

A more accurate interpretation of the use of *mandalas* in Japanese Shingon Buddhism[60] is that they are employed to assist students to "penetrate" levels of awareness until the primordial ground of experience is itself presenced. The above quotation may be rephrased, for our own comparative interests, according to a phenomenological hermeneutic as follows:

> In meditation the *mandala* is used as a vehicle for reflexive awareness, an introspection into the most primordial mode of experiencing that arises as a result of a transference from third order bodymind awareness to focused second order bodymind awareness, and finally, reaching an awareness of the dynamic bodymind ground from which a limitless number of noetic vectors may arise. In addition, this process also leads to an awareness of the overbrimming expanded periphery which may be sedimented such that the entire phenomenal world may be presenced.

Here we have given some indication of the framework through which Kūkai's use of the *mandala* might be interpreted.

For Kūkai there are four basic kinds of *mandalas*. Yet, he says they are not separate from each other.[61] Although each *mandala* may signify a distinct aspect of reality, the importance of the *mandala* is to help the practitioner focus his concentration and thus experience directly that which the diagram symbolizes. The symbolism of the *mantra* is often glorified, e.g., in the *Diamond Peak Sutra*, and thus too much emphasis is given to the symbolic language. The student is apt to be led astray by such abstractions. The purpose of the *mandala* is to inculcate a primordial experience of the Dharmakāya (first order bodymind awareness) and not lead one toward inappropriate abstraction and metaphysical speculation (third order bodymind awareness). Kūkai emphasizes metaphorically the need to neutralize intentions which cover the horizon as given to consciousness. He says that when one perceives a *mandala* as it is, "the stains covering the mind (are) completely removed."[62] If one is able to calmly presence a *mandala* and grasp its meaning, then one has also experienced the Dharmakāya. This is possible because *mandalas*, like everything else, expound the dharma (*hosshin seppō*).

Still we must ask, exactly how does concentrating upon a *mandala* lead toward a neutral experience of the phenomenal world as it is (first order bodymind awareness)? *Mandalas* are said to symbolize and embrace the whole of existence. We have seen that in order to experience the "whole" of the horizon, one must neutralize all specific intentions which cause noematic foci to appear in a privileged manner in relation to the horizon in toto. Similarly, an experience of a *mandala* in toto is possible only if no one thing in particular is viewed. To accomplish this one begins second order concentration upon the *mandala*. Once sedimented, the single noetic vector may be neutralized and one is left with first order bodymind awareness. In the Shingon tradition it is said that one experiences the pervasive Dharmakāya "through a single object," e.g., a *mandala*. The *mandala* signifies many abstract ideas which are all inseparable. Yet, in order to experience their inseparability one must experience them in toto in a non-dual manner. Since in Shingon, concrete existence and abstract principle are one (*ji ri funi*) and things and mind are one (*busshin-ichinyo*), a *mandala* can at once symbolize abstract ideas beyond itself and yet remain a concrete representative or expression of those ideas. Accordingly, a *mandala itself* expounds the *dharma*. Kūkai preaches "all concrete things or phenomena are identical with truth" (*soku-ji-ji-shin*).[63]

In order to understand and internalize this two faceted aspect of a *mandala*, Kūkai emphasizes the need to become aware of our "original tranquility."[64] We are faced with what seems to be a circular problem. In order to understand the two faceted nature of the *mandala* we must become aware of our "original tranquility," yet the *mandala* is supposed to be the meditative tool which aids such awareness. This problem dissolves by noting that it is precisely the two faceted (concrete and abstract) nature of the *mandala* that allows itself to lead the practitioner toward "original tranquility" (first order bodymind awareness) while simultaneously symbolizing the highest religious truths of the Dharmakāya. The Dharmakāya is said to be pervasive and infinite. Meditation or focused concentration upon a "single object" (a *mandala*) that symbolizes infinity, forces one to neutralize all *particular* noetic intentions. Accordingly, the focus of concentration is dynamic and not static. Just as *mantra* recitation utilized the dynamic affect of continued sound harmonizing with the dynamic horizon, *mandala* meditation utilizes the dynamic abstract notion of infinity as a means to lead one toward a direct neutral experience of the horizon *in toto*. Both the *mantra* and the *mandala* are the focus of second order bodymind awareness. Since the single noematic object is not static but dynamic, the intention is easily neutralized as it shares the same qualities as the horizon.

A specific example will help to clarify this point. A typical *mandala* will have the symbol of Dainichi Nyorai at the center. Other symbols representing its various infinite characteristics may be arranged centrifugally and centripetally around the Nyorai. This two-fold infinite "descending" and "ascending" represents the two directions of *kōjō* and *kōge*. The practitioner may begin *concentrating* upon the infinitude of the Nyorai in a descending (*kōge*) fashion or may begin by expanding upon the infinitude of the Nyorai in an ascending (*kōjō*) fashion. Whatever ascending or descending imagery is employed, continued concentration (*toitsu ho*) or expansion (*kakudai ho*) will result in the eventual loss of the image, i.e., one can imagine X becoming only so small or so big. In either case, since infinity has no limit, both avenues of intention inculcate the same effect. When the image is lost, the single noetic focus upon it is neutralized and the practitioner is left with a neutral experience of no one thing in particular. In this way, the dynamic horizon is presenced as it is and the *mandala* has served as a *concrete* vehicle toward first order bodymind awareness as a result of its *abstract* symbolism of the infinite character of Dainichi Nyorai. Kūkai uses his own metaphors to describe this process as follows. Each *mandala*; permeating every other

> throughout the whole universe, fusing together and internalizing with one another, is in itself of vast expanse. Each one is never apart from the other so much as the spacious sky sets no barrier for the light [image] to shine therethrough.[65]

These poetic expressions of vastness all refer to the dynamic nature of meditation and the experience of the horizon. A person's noetic possibilities are innumerable and the untrained student, clinging to second or third order bodymind awareness, is accustomed to changing his noetic intentions constantly. Sustaining a single noetic vector is most difficult especially if the noematic object is static in character. Yet, if the noematic object is dynamic in nature, then the activity or energy sustaining the noetic vector will be less apt to wander, i.e., it will remain focused upon a similarly dynamic noema. For this reason it is said that "the merit of the Esoteric Buddhist meditation is in the method of meditation in action, for it mobilizes the student's total energy, preventing him from falling into drowsiness and stagnation."[66] The single noematic focus may be some imaginary dynamic phenomena which corresponds to an ascending or descending noetic vector. However, once the image can be imagined no more, the last intentional vector becomes neutralized. There is no more "from here to there," ascending or descending. There is only the presencing of the experiential horizon. In Kūkai's words:

> Away with all images
> The great meditation of void is to be our companion.[67]

Kūkai's description of the entire *mandala* process is similar but more symbolic than our phenomenological description. Initially he asks his disciples to

> Visualize: a white lotus flower with eight petals,
> (above which is a full moon disc) the size of a forearm in diameter,
> (in which is) a radiant silvery letter A.
> Unite your *dhyāna* with *prajñā* in an adamantine binding;
> Draw the quiescent *Prajñā* of the Nyorai in (your mind).

Then he explains:

> If they [the students] increase their competence in this meditation, they will finally be able to magnify it (the moon) until its circumference encompasses the entire universe [ascending *kōjō*] and its magnitude becomes as inclusive as space [descending *kōge*]. Being freely able to magnify or reduce it, they will surely come to be in possession of the all-inclusive wisdom.[68] (brackets mine)

The attainment of "all-inclusive wisdom" in the present body is the goal of Kūkai's meditative practice. Like first order awareness, it is said to be a "vision that all is undifferentiated oneness like the infinite space."[69] Such wisdom enables the student to experience directly the basis of Shingon doctrines, e.g., *hosshin seppō*, *hongaku*, *sanmitsu*, *sokushin jōbutsu*. His description of this wisdom, as a result of "unshakable concentration in the oneness of body (*dhyāna*) and mind (*prajñā*)," clearly emphasizes the important functional role of the *mandala*.[70]

c. Mudras

Like a *mantra* and *mandala*, a *mudra* is used as a vehicle to experience the phenomenal world as it is. Unlike a *mantra* and *mandala*—which aid the mind-aspect to focus, become sedimented and finally enter into first order bodymind awareness—a *mudra* is a vehicle which focuses upon the body-aspect. A *mudra* is a hand posture which, like the *mantra* and *mandala*, at once symbolizes the all-pervasive character of the Dharmakāya while being a concrete representative of the *dharma*. Once the practice of *mudra* gestures has been sedimented, it too can aid the practitioner to enter into first order bodymind awareness. *Mudras* correspond to the mystery of body and the *reality* of "sound, word, and reality." We have seen in section (b) (*Mandalas*) that, for Kūkai, "reality is to meditate on the meanings of these words [the five words for Dainichi Nyorai]." The *mudra* provides the focus for the body-aspect that symbolizes "the meaning of these words." A *mudra* is the "Body of the Dharmakāya symbolized."[71]

Like *mantras* and *mandalas*, the most important aspect of the various kinds of Shingon *mudras* are their functional role as catalysts which aid the practitioner to experience the phenomenal world as it is primordially given to consciousness. The emphasis upon the body-aspect of practice has not been emphasized thus far, but we can now see that the somatic-aspect of practice is underscored by the concept of *sokushin jōbutsu* (attaining enlightenment with this present body). Before we can begin our phenomenological analysis of exactly *how* this practice aids an individual to enter first order bodymind awareness, we will take a general look at the role of the body in Japanesse meditative practice.

Until now our description of Shingon practice has concentrated upon the various means to focus intentional noetic vectors. We have stated that when sedimentation of such practices occurs, the single noetic intention (second order bodymind awareness) can be neutralized and becomes an act which allows for a transfer into first order bodymind awareness. Our phenomenological analysis in Chapter 2 demonstrated the primordial oneness (bodymind ground) of the mind-aspect and body-aspect. Kūkai also recognized this inseparable relation and knew that concentrated practice focusing upon the body-aspect directly related to the mind-aspect and vice versa. Therefore, disciplined practice which focused upon either the mind-aspect (intentions) or body-aspect (tensions) would have a reciprocal effect upon the other. This should not be surprising to us since all types of practice in the West focus upon physical technique as well as mental concentration. Kūkai found both avenues (psychic and somatic) convenient depending upon the situation and mood of the student.

This Shingon pedagogy is consistent not only with Tibetan Esoteric Buddhist predecessors, but also with indigenous Japanese cultural characteristics that pre-date and, due in part to cultural assimilation, post-date Kūkai's lifetime of teaching. In Japanese culture, proper physical form has always been emphasized in the fine arts. *Kabuki* and *Noh* theater, tea ceremony, martial arts and calligraphy, for example, are arts which emphasize the beauty of the physical performance. It is assumed that the beautiful and exact form of the art reflects the inner calmness and serenity of the artist. Similarly a great emphasis is placed upon proper physical form in social circumstances. In each of the above instances, the person is trained until the proper form is sedimented. Proper form and its meaning are internalized psychosomatically. In this way, people may either perform their art or react properly in social circumstances in a pre-reflective (first order) manner. The point is to introduce and emphasize the very strong Japanese feeling that one's whole being (physical form and mental attitude) is so inseparably connected that one can train the mind-aspect by focusing upon the body-aspect. Indeed, this is the easiest way to train the mind-aspect since it is invisible and without shape, color, and form. The body-aspect, on the other hand, may easily be disciplined under the supervision of a master. Accordingly, even in religious practice, the body serves as a vehicle for, not a detriment to, the direct experience of the highest religious truth.

Hand postures (*mudras*) function symbolically in the same two-faceted manner as the *mandala*. Therefore, the difference upon which we must now concentrate is that the *mudra*, unlike the *mandala*, is a form made with the body. Whereas a *mandala* is a form given as a noematic focus for the noetic mind-aspect, a *mudra* is a form in need of perpetual creation by the body-aspect. The practitioner's body-aspect must at one symbolize the Dharmakāya and expound the *dharma* (hosshin seppō). Since hand postures are quite intricate, the entire body-aspect must be calm and relaxed; all tension must be neutralized. It would be most difficult to gracefully display the symbolic hand gestures if the practitioner's body-aspect were tense. In order for the hand and fingers to be relaxed the elbows must be down, shoulders must be rolled back and relaxed, and the back must be straight (in either the sitting or standing position). The entire position of the physical body must highlight the *mudra*. The posture, the visibly serene attitude, the position of the eyes, are all geared to embody and be a physical representation of the meaning of the *mudra*. Just as mind-aspect intentions are neutralized leaving only a single intention upon a *mandala* or *mantra*, body-aspect tensions are neutralized leaving only a single tension focused upon the creation of a *mudra*. Moreover, just as the last intention becomes sedimented and neutralized, opening up an awareness of the enduring presence of the body-aspect complement in *mantra* and *mandala* practice, the last tension similarly becomes sedimented and neutralized opening up an awareness of the enduring presence of the mind-aspect complement in *mudra* practice. In either form of practice, once first order bodymind awareness occurs, the practitioner directly experiences the psychosomatic (bodymind) ground which is present throughout practice.

The incantation of a *mantra*, the meditation upon a *mandala* or the formation of a *mudra* must all be done with one's entire being. When this is demonstrated, the master is given empirical evidence that the student has experienced and understands the bodymind ground. Kūkai emphasizes continuation of practice so that this most primordial mode of experience, with which the student is now familiar (first order bodymind awareness), becomes sedimented. For Kūkai, this means a continual experiential verification of the basis of Shingon doctrines.

Chapter 4

Kūkai: First Order Bodymind
Awareness as Enlightenment

In the previous chapter the analysis focused upon Kūkai's philosophical doctrines and techniques. In this chapter the phenomenological categories of first order bodymind awareness will be utilized in an effort to further clarify Kūkai's project. Specifically, these categories will help interpret his symbolic language used to describe the enlightenment experience. These expressions have often led commentators away from the experiential ground to which his phraseology refers. The hermeneutic categories will help demystify Kūkai's descriptions in a manner consistent with the experiential emphasis found in Shingon philosophy. The meaning of Kūkai's symbolic descriptions may be clarified by interpreting them from the perspective of first order bodymind awareness. In this way the close relation between Kūkai's description of the enlightenment experience and first order bodymind awareness will be exposed. It should be noted that a phenomenological hermeneutic need not be considered the only viable interpretative device. Kūkai's symbolism speaks to many ears in many contexts. The analysis presented here underscores the often overlooked empirical correlates compatable with Kūkai's rich symbolic metaphors.

1. The Neutralization of Thetic Positings

The initial phenomenological category of first order body-mind awareness to be utilized in laying bare Kūkai's paradigmatic mode of experience will be the neutralization of thetic positings. This experience is called "paradigmatic" because his philosophy is constructed from, and empirically verified by, its occurrence. Its centrality is further underscored insofar as esoteric practice is cultivated for the purpose of sedimenting this perspective. It may be argued that this paradigmatic mode of awareness is thetically neutral. Because this mode of experience is not characterized by finite intentions, it is theoretically impossible to describe accurately the experiential ground of esoteric theory and practice. To recognize this limitation is to acknowledge the role of practice guided by Mahayana faith. In contrast, the exoteric doctrine is adequately communicated through language. The latter mode of teaching relies upon second and third order bodymind awareness characterized by discursive reasoning. Language, which is characterized by thetic distinctions, is thus an inappropriate vehicle to describe authentically the thetically neutral mode of experience. If we consider the fact that the reflective use of language can only inadequately capture the full pre-reflective meaning of the experience, then we may appreciate the "secret" or "mystical" reputation of Kūkai's philosophy. Since it has often been stated, however, that (1) the "written word or letter . . .has limitations insofar as it represents a conceptualized [second or third] order notion of reality based upon human agreement" and (2) "the absolute truth can never be directly expressed in human language since it transcends the discursive reasoning that constantly divides the universe [via thetic positing],"[1] some Shingon interpreters have suggested that Kūkai's poetic descriptions refer to a mystic experience of a *transcendent* other-worldly reality. In contrast, we have seen (in Chapter 3) that Kūkai's concern is with direct experience of the phenomenal world as it is presented to consciousness. This paradigmatic (first order) experience transcends ordinary (second order) experience in a reflexive direction by neutralizing all thetic positings until a protodoxic level of awareness is realized. From this perspective, Kūkai's metaphors will be interpreted in terms of a neutral experience of the phenomenal world and not in terms of a transcendental experience of some other world. The secret or mystery of Kūkai's project is thus interpreted as referring to the difficulty of sedimenting this neutral mode of awareness.

This experience enables the practitioner to hear the non-thetic language of Dainichi Nyorai. The words of the Nyorai, the Dhar-makāya, subsequently represent individual noematic objects as abstracted from this direct first order acquaintance with the ex-periential horizon. In short, whereas the words or teachings of the Dharmakāya are presenced in a unified and complete manner *via* first order bodymind awareness, the words of humans have mean-ings which are specific, fixed and abstracted from the horizon due to intentional noetic/noematic vectors. The words of the Dhar-makāya are dynamic without restriction or limitation. Without form or letter, they can accurately "describe" the infinite, limitless, formless, unrestricted characteristics of Dainichi Nyorai. In the Shingon tradition these characteristics are not carefully guarded secrets hidden behind a veil of human language (thetic positings).[2] The veil which hides the words of the Dharmakāya (the horizon in toto) may be taken away *via* the neutralization of thetic positings. In this way, the infinite teaching of the Dharmakāya may be experienced within the limited periphery of undifferen-tiated *dharma* (things and words). For example, within the periphery of a given first order bodymind experience there may be many things that may be abstracted from the horizon in reflection. These "things," which "expound the dharma" according to the doctrine of *hosshin seppō*, are said to be the "substantial nature of the Dharma-world."[3] Since they are abstracted from the horizon in reflection, their ontological meaning is thetically bestowed subse-quent to the occurrence of the antecedent pre-reflective ex-perience. However, if we accept Kūkai's view that the paradigmatic mode of awareness empirically verifies the forementioned characteristics of the Nyorai, then we must abandon a substantial interpretation of dharma. Rather, *dharma* must be experienced directly prior to thetic ontological positings for it is only during this first order bodymind awareness that they preach the non-dual, undifferentiated character of Dainichi Nyorai.

The problem is to sediment this mode of awareness. Esoteric practices are necessary for this very difficult task, especially if the practitioner has reached adulthood. A newborn baby perceives primordially not knowing how to compartmentalize his or her ex-periences. In fact, it has been suggested that the newborn takes quite some time to simply learn the boundaries of its body as distinct from the rest of its surroundings. Primordially, the baby's identity is not yet clear; its whole world is bodymind awareness. Yet, as the baby grows, learns to compartmentalize experience, and acquires a conventional language that defines its world, it becomes more and more sedimented into second and third order bodymind awareness. In the Japanese Buddhist tradition there are many metaphors which describe this first order experience as "pure," "original," or "virgin." Thus the direction of the experience which transcends language is reflexive and approaches the most primordial mode of experience which presences the phenomenal world as it is, totally devoid of any thetic intention.

In addition we need to recognize that this awareness is innate whereas third order bodymind awareness is acquired. For this reason, Kūkai requires that his disciples cultivate, and be able to sediment at will, first order bodymind awareness *in addition to third order bodymind awareness*. This is a most important qualification which distinguishes the enlightened individual's mind from an animal or infantile mind. The enlightened adult may presence their surroundings in a neutral manner and thus be informed of the proper response to their situation. The adult, being equipped to deal with complex situations requiring second or third order awareness, is able to utilize these modes of experience as they are needed. In contrast, the infant's horizon is just beginning to accumulate a history of its own. The sum total of its experiences (perceptions, emotions, thoughts) will eventually acquire a historicity of its own and therefore allow it to presence the total horizon in a *meaningful* manner. The adult, familiar with his/her surroundings, can interpret the meaning of a situation as presenced. Hence, whereas the adult presences a meaningful horizon informed by its historicity, the infant presences a horizon just beginning to take shape. The adult has acquired additional modes of awareness that enable him/her to deal with complex situations. This knowledge does, however, become so domineering that the adult often forgets how to presence his/her surroundings. The emphasis upon attaining a childlike mind is thus an appeal to neutral presencing which, for the enlightened adult, ought to be as easily manifested as it occurs in the case of an infant who actually has no choice but to begin its experiential encounter with the phenomenal world in a neutral manner.

Below, Kūkai describes the relationship between what we have come to call first and third order awareness in his own words.

1   The bodhisattvas in the familiar stages engage
     in groundless speculations.
3   The experience of enlightenment of this mind is
     not yet genuine.
5   The One Way, unconditioned and signless, is spotless;
     It unfolds the teaching of nonduality of neither
     being nor nonbeing.
8   When both seeing and the seen are negated,
     the eternal ground of quiescence will be found;
     When all thought determinations are exhausted,
     one will meet with Dainichi Nyorai.
12 He, like vast space, knows no duality of body and mind.
     Adapting himself freely to all beings, He manifests
     himself forever and ever.[4]

By interpreting this passage phenomenologically, we will be able to clarify its meaning and significance. The "groundless speculations" (line 2) of unenlightened bodhisattvas refer to third order bodymind awareness. This mode of experiencing is ungrounded and "not yet genuine" (line 4) because speculation requires thetic abstraction and thus violates the "One Way" which is "unconditioned, signless and spotless (line 5), i.e., thetically neutral. This interpretation continues to be supported in lines 6 and 7 for neutral first order awareness "unfolds" in the manner described since nothing is thetically done. The "non-dual" horizon is presenced prior to such ontological judgments as "being" (affirmation) and "non-being" (negation). Kūkai's phenomenological sensitivity is further demonstrated by noting that the "seeing" (noesis) and "seen" (noema) are "negated" (neutralized) during the paradigmatic enlightenment experience (line 8). Once this is achieved, further characteristics can be presenced. For example, "the eternal ground of quiescence will be found" (line 9). This romanticization refers to the ever-present neutral bodymind ground at the base of non-quiescent thetic experience.

Another ramification of this mode of awareness is that one "will meet with Dainichi Nyorai" (lines 10-11). In brief, the many attributes of first order bodymind awareness described in Chapter 2 are identified with some aspect of the Nyorai himself. The Nyorai is said to be like "vast space" (line 12) — the periphery expands during this experience. He also "knows no duality of body and mind" — the bodymind ground is presenced amidst the complete horizon. Finally, he "manifests himself forever and ever" (lines 13 and 14) — the dynamic simultaneous character of that which is circumscribed by the periphery makes relative spatiotemporal distinctions based upon a fixed privileged standard impossible. This interpretation suggests that first order bodymind awareness is itself the Nyorai. That is, since the Nyorai is the personification of the Dharmakāya which expounds the *dharma*, and since one is aware of the *dharma* only when phenomena are presenced as they are primordially given to consciousness, then we may conclude that the Nyorai personifies characteristics of primordial neutral bodymind awareness and is at the same time empirically verified by them.

By describing this mode of awareness in a metaphorical rather than analytic or phenomenological manner, Kūkai succeeds in discouraging attempts to understand discursively the ground of experience. He is aware that thetic speculation, no matter how keen, can never posit abstracted noemata in such a way that they are presenced as a whole. Such a project would be similar to attempting to restore a puzzle to its condition before the individual pieces were even cut. Therefore, Kūkai attempts to lead his students to become aware of the ever-present uncut puzzle (horizon) by using poetic language to evoke first order bodymind awareness.

Since thetic experience is never capable of overcoming the rift which its occurrence, by definition, requires, Kūkai knew that discursive thinking would not enable a man to experience for himself the basis of the esoteric doctrines. He says the Dharmakāya simply can "not be predicated by a hundred negative statements or by a thousand affirmative expressions . . . .it [the Dharmakāya] defies all predications; no matter how eloquent a man may be, his speech must come to an end and his speculation must cease."[5] (brackets mine) Yet, he also acknowledges the value of discursive abstract language as "symbolic expressions of Esoteric Buddhism" and cautions that students "should not indulge in senseless speculation while clinging to the ordinary and superficial meanings of these words."[6] He rebuked those who sought to dogmatically impose (noesis) their own linguistic definitions upon their particular situations while passing them off as absolute descriptions of reality given without distortion. Consequently, he omitted experiences approximating the structure of third order bodymind awareness from the "category of authentic enlightenment" and taught that "to attain enlightenment is to know one's mind as it really is . . . the characteristic of enlightenment is like that of empty space."[7] The enlightened mind, like empty space, transcends affirming/negating positings and is characterized by an expanded periphery. In this light, we can see that Kūkai clarifies the *dharma via* first order bodymind awareness.

Kūkai's method of helping students to sediment this awareness is not limited, however, to describing characteristics like empty space. The devotee is taught to become aware of the structure of the experiential process. Here Kūkai's pedagogical project is explicitly phenomenological. In the following passage, he describes his version of the noetic/noematic aspects of experience that differentiate and distort the neutral experiential ground. He says:

> all colors, forms, and movements having to do with the working of the eyes are objects of the eyes. Those having to do with the working of sight are the objects of sight and the objects that are related to sight. Those having to do with consciousness are the objects of consciousness and objects related to consciousness. We call these the categories of differentiation. They are the expressions of patterns (*monji*), for the characteristics (which differentiate one from another) are patterns (*mon*).[8]

Appreciating these aspects of experience, the student becomes sensitive to the neutral thetic conditions necessary to sediment awareness that is like empty space. For example, the above mentioned "patterns" of thetic behavior are to be observed and studied by the students so that, presumably, they will not be inclined to become attached (affirmation) to, nor avoid (negation), them as suggested by previously cited passages. Rather, by witnessing how such "patterns" arise from a neutral ground *via* noetic/noematic relations, the practitioner empirically verifies the manner in which the myriads of intentional habits are continually created. By understanding the nature of thetic experience, the student has a clear perception of the obstacles and goal of Esoteric practice.

Kūkai says, "by entering the meditation on the Dharmakāya-Thusness, one realizes the equality, like space, of the perceiving function of mind and the object of perception."[9] The student recognizes that the "perceiving function of mind" (no-en) and "object of perception" (sho-en) refer to the complete neutralization of noetic/noematic positings. During this meditation, the pure non-privileged ground is presenced in absence of all intentional distractions. For this reason, Kūkai instructs that a Bodhisattva "advocates return to the oneness of the seeing and the seen."[10]

Alternatively, Kūkai is quick to condemn the "common people in the world" for sedimenting a mode of awareness which conceals this oneness. The habitual occurrence of thetic positing leads people to believe in their illusion that abstracted noemata possess an independent ontic status. Kūkai asserts that the common people themselves are responsible for empirically verifying their original enlightenment. The problem, he suggests, is that people cover or conceal (in the sense of Sk. samvrti) these experiences. Accordingly, Kūkai has made the following observations in different contexts:

> Sentient beings are the ones who conceal it,
> but the Buddha does not hide it from them.
> clinging to their perspective tenets, they refuse
> to advance . . .
> They do not understand the esoteric import . . .
> They are unaware of what they originally possess.
> The sea of assembly of numberless Enlightened Ones
> Is the very treasure that belongs to them all.[11]

The expression "taizen fudō" (implying to be calm and determined in one's practice), describes the frame of mind required to become aware of this "treasure." Calm and determined practice sediments the perpetual neutralization required to reflect clearly one's innate treasure. Like the calm, still surface of the ocean reflecting the moon and a flying bird, a calm determined attitude neutralizes thetic waves distorting one's perception. Just as an infinite number of waves can arise from a calm sea, an infinite number of thetic positings may arise from the complete horizon. If the ocean is left to its natural state, however, the waves become calm and the moon may be reflected clearly. In the same way, if one's mode of experience is thetically neutral, and allowed to return to its primordial state, the phenomenal world may be presenced clearly.[12]

This metaphor helps to clarify another aspect of becoming aware of one's original enlightenment. In Japanese Buddhist literature, much emphasis is placed upon "emptiness" (*kū*) and "nothingness" (*mu*). When misunderstood, this may lead practitioners to negate, rather than neutralize, thetic positings in a determined effort to become calm (Determined negation is actually a new thetic standpoint opposite affirmation.) The following analogy may help to clarify this point. Negating waves is comparable to placing one's hand on a small pond and trying to smooth out the ripples. The only consequence of such activity is to create more waves making clear reflections even more unlikely. Kūkai cautions that practitioners engaged in this kind of activity "have not reached the ultimate source of mind; they have merely blocked [negated] the illusions which exist outside the [originally neutral] Mind. They have not yet uncovered the jewels in the secret Treasury."[13] (brackets mine) The kind of emptiness refered to above is *not* a void in some transcendent world wherein there are no material objects which men can crave. Rather, since matter and emptiness are one, everything within this phenomenal world, including one's body, are the expression of the Dharmakāya. It is through the phenomenal world that the Dharmakāya expounds the *dharma* (hosshin seppō). Therefore, phenomenal entities are not to be negated but rather experienced within the undifferentiated experiential horizon wherein no specific thing has a privileged position. From this perspective, we can understand that if all phenomenal entities within our periphery are experienced totally, then this could be called an experience of no specific thing — nothingness/emptiness. Kūkai explains this as follows:

> Matter, which is not different from emptiness, unfolds itself as all phenomenal experiences; yet it is of the nature of emptiness. Emptiness, which is not different from matter, nullifies all marks of particularity; yet it is manifested as a variety of temporary beings. Thus, matter is none other than emptiness, and emptiness itself is none other than matter; all phenomenal existences are of the same structure.[14]

The avenue toward such awareness is calmness and determined neutralization. When tensions are calmed and intentions are neutralized, all delusions cease. "When the Bodhisattva hears the words 'Form is emptiness,' he relaxes his jaw in a smile, understanding them to express the meaning of perfect interpenetration."[15] In short, matter is emptiness because, during first order bodymind awareness, no specific noemata possess privileged positions within the horizon.

Most importantly, Kūkai emphasizes the positive ramifications of the neutralization of thetic positings. Once all such positings are neutralized one holds "the precious key to the secret treasury." He says:

> When the medicine of Esoteric teachings have cleared
> away the dust; the True Words open the treasury.
> When the secret treasures are suddenly displayed;
> all virtues are apparent.[16]

In the *Precious Key*, Kūkai metaphorically describes the "clearing away of dust" as the process of neutralizing thetic positings covering the phenomenal world as primordially given to consciousness. This experience of the basis of all Shingon doctrines is only contingent upon the removal of the so-called "mist," "stains" and "images" covering the primordial awareness. Each of these metaphors refers to neutralization for it is through this process that the "unhindered," "unobstructed" experience of enlightenment can be made to "function like a clean mirror."[17] Once this mode of awareness is attained the practitioner encounters the forementioned "opening" of the treasury. Our next endeavor will be to interpret phenomenologically the meaning of this opening, in which "all virtues are apparent," in terms of the expanded periphery and the direct experience of the total horizon.

2. The Expanded Periphery and Experience of the Horizon in toto

In Chapter 2 the phenomena of an expanded periphery which accompanies neutralization was described. Specifically, attention was given to the increased sensitivity of all five senses during first order bodymind awareness. Once the specific noetic vectors are neutralized and no single noema possesses a privileged position within the horizon, the borders of the periphery expand. This process allows for increased sensitivity of the entire experiential horizon. Kūkai also recognizes this characteristic in his paradigmatic mode of experience. He speaks of the experience as being "immense as space" including "the performance of all acts," i.e., the historicity of the objects and the practitioner's talents are included within the horizon. He likens the expansion of the periphery to a direct encounter with "the ground of great space (that) is the Dharmakāya Buddha."[18] Although in Chapter 2 we did not attach these metaphysical and religious connotations to first order bodymind awareness, Kūkai gives great significance to the "opening" of the periphery as the condition for increased sensitivity towards the horizon as given to consciousness. This is important when we consider the value attached to the direct experience of the horizon *in toto*. We recall from the previous section that the characteristics of this experience are personified by the Dainichi Nyorai. For example, the mutual interpenetration of the contents of the horizon, are the words of the Nyorai. Since the contents of the horizon are experienced as one, Kūkai (1) attaches value and significance to this oneness, and (2) teaches that this is synonymous with the Oneness of the Dharmakāya (Dainichi Nyorai), i.e., the Dharmakāya expounds the *dharma* through the horizon's contents.

For Kūkai, this increased sensitivity is the vehicle for religious inspiration. The mind-aspect and body-aspect are so calm, reflecting clearly that which is primordially given, that the practitioner may become aware of their originally enlightened character.[19] We need to explain the reasons why Kūkai may have equated the type of experience to which first order bodymind awareness refers, with an experience of the Dharmakāya if the Dharmakāya is all-pervasive and infinite? This problem is remedied once we realize that it is not the ontologically distinct Dharmakāya but the Dharmakāya within the horizon that is experienced in toto. The contents of the horizon (the *dharmas*) cohere in a manner that are equated with the infinite character of the Dharmakāya. The horizon experience is thus a microcosm of the macrocosmic Dharmakāya. Kūkai incorporates the idea that "the microcosmic world of unenlightened consciousness can be integrated into the macrocosmic enlightenment of Dainichi Nyorai."[20] When the horizon is presenced, no specific thing circumscribed by the periphery is distinguished. This "absence of any particular cause" is regarded as "the origin of all things," i.e., the absence of any distinction leads one to experience the origin of all distinctions—the horizon *in toto*. He goes on to suggest, as we have done in Chapter 2, that subsequent noetic vectors are products of one's own intentionality. That is, the primordially given is completely given wherein no thing presents itself independent from the whole. Kūkai says, "we should know that (predications of) all things are of mind only [noesis] and that the real feature of our mind is all-inclusive wisdom [the primordially given horizon *in toto*)."[21] (brackets mine) This all-inclusive wisdom transcends conceptualization (third order bodymind awareness) and is suprarational in the reflexive primordial sense of first order bodymind awareness. The infinite number of possible noematic foci are presented as one mutual interrelationship. In this way, the infinite character of the Dharmakāya is presented microcosmically through the oneness of *dharmas* primordially given within the horizon.

3. Dynamism and Simultaneity

In first order bodymind awareness, when no specific noetic vector occurs, there is no static noema upon which one's glance is fixed. We have seen in Chapter 2 that the experience of the horizon is thus dynamic. We have also mentioned, in connection with our discussion of *mantra* practice, that the dynamic quality of first order bodymind awareness is simulated by focusing (second order bodymind awareness) upon a noematic focus (sound) that is also dynamic in character. In addition to this dynamic character Kūkai also discusses the simultaneous character of his paradigmatic mode of experience. Accordingly, these two categories will serve to clarify his position.

In Chapter 2 our phenomenological analysis revealed the dynamic bodymind quality at the ground of all thetic experience. We noted that all mind-aspect and body-aspect activity is rooted in the dynamic manner in which the phenomenal world is presented to consciousness. We arrived at this conclusion by noting that the direct experience of the horizon is characterized by a dynamic flow of awareness which does not stop to focus upon any specific static noema. Kūkai similarly gives value and significance to this aspect of his paradigmatic mode of experience. The dynamic character of *all* experience is equated with the activity of preaching the *dharma* by the Dharmakāya through all things. In other words, the action of *hosshin seppō*, personified by the words (mystery of speech) of Dainichi Nyorai, is equated with the dynamism characteristic of the experiential horizon. Therefore, all dynamic experiences of the phenomenal world are said to reflect the dynamic, active character of the Dharmakāya. All our experiences of mind-aspect and body-aspect activity thus have religious significance for Kūkai. In the *Dainichikyō* he says, "Dainichi Nyorai always proclaims mystic verses with all actions, bodily, verbal and mental [*sanmitsu*], anywhere and anytime in the world of sentient beings."[22]

In our initial characterization of the Dharmakāya,[23] we noted that it does not refer to a static abstract principle, but encompasses the *karmakāya* (the body of action) and represents the personification of the *dharma*, i.e., Dainichi Nyorai.[24] Dainichi Nyorai, the "Great Illuminator," makes the awareness of *dharmas* available to sentient beings through the dynamic action at the basis of *all* experience. Although the dynamic activity is present in first, second, and third order bodymind awareness (as we have seen in Chapter 2), it is only directly experienced in first order bodymind awareness. For this reason Kūkai urges his students to directly experience this dynamic ground in order to verify empirically the *karmakāya*. Just as the dynamic bodymind ground of experience characterizes all experience and can be directly observed during the first order experience of the horizon, Kūkai believes that the dynamism of the Dharmakāya grounds "bodily, verbal, and mental" (*sanmitsu*) experiential activities and can be directly observed during his paradigmatic mode of experience. In this way, religious significance is given to first order bodymind awareness. Its dynamism is equated with the presence of the *karmakāya* and the mysteries of body, speech, and mind. Since the presence of the forementioned may be experientially verified, the doctrine of *hosshin seppō* may be substantiated, i.e., the practitioner becomes directly aware of the mechanics of the Dharmakāya expounding the *dharma* through all things. In other words, since we are aware of all things *via* dynamic experience, and since the dynamism of experience is equated with the presence of the Dharmakāya, Kūkai claims that we can be directly aware of all things (within the periphery) expounding the *dharma* (the words of Dainichi Nyorai and the actions of the *karmakāya*) because of the presence of the Dharmakāya.

In addition to the dynamic quality of experience, he describes his paradigmatic mode of experience in a manner parallel to the phenomenological category of simultaneity applicable to first order bodymind awareness. In Chapter 2 we noted that

> During first order bodymind awareness, past, present and future occur *simultaneously*. Since the horizon is experienced *in toto*, there is no succession of moments. There is no t1, t2, t3 into which a series of before and after may be constructed. Moreover, there is no noematic object which is given a status unique to the rest of the horizon. Once intended, a noematic object may be seen as something which stands apart; it is something capable of undergoing relative change in space and time. Spatial change is possible for a noematic object and may be observed to move across the periphery relative to the rest of the horizon. This, in turn, is possible because one is aware of specific moment (t1) in which the noema became the specific object of our attention. Once focused upon, it may acquire a history relative to the rest of the horizon, i.e., it may do X at t1, Y at t2, and Z at t3, etc. However, in first order bodymind awareness wherein the horizon is presenced *in toto*, there is no recognition of something changing relative, in space and time, to everything else. The horizon *in toto* is presenced in a simultaneous manner. Since nothing stands apart from the horizon, there is no experience of relative space and time. Only the dynamic simultaneity of the horizon is experienced as the reservoir of possible relative spatio-temporal distinctions.[25]

For Kūkai the "reservoir of possible relative spatio-temporal distinctions" is experienced as the Dharmakāya itself. The Dharmakāya expounds the *dharma via* all noemata experienced as perpetually corresponding together. In this way, no specific noema stands apart, relative to other noemata in space of time. All noemata are experienced as mutually penetrating, harmonizing, and equally expounding the *dharma*.[26] From this perspective of his paradigmatic mode of experience, as in first order bodymind awareness, the past, present and future occur simultaneously. Accordingly, all noemata (*dharma*) within the periphery, and by extension everywhere, can be experienced simultaneously, thus offering experiential verification for the spatially unobstructed and temporally immutable character of the Dharmakāya. Focusing our attention upon the temporal character of his paradigmatic mode of experience, we note that according to the Shingon tradition:

Any one period means absolute time, a period of having neither beginning nor end [a relative distinction], indeed, one and the same time. Accordingly, within this one period are all the periods of preaching by the Buddhas in the ten directions and of the past, the present and the future. This means one period in all periods; and all periods in one period.[27] (brackets mine)

Kūkai himself adds, "He [the Buddha] taught that infinite time is in one moment and that one moment is in infinite time; that one is in many and that many is in one, that is, the universal is in the particulars and the particulars are in the universal."[28] The forementioned phrases "one period of time" and "infinite time" temporally describe the mode of awareness that empirically verifies the temporal oneness (*ichiji*), and, incidently, spatial oneness (*ichijo*), of the Dharmakāya. It has been suggested that these temporal attributes of the Dharmakāya are based upon a "law of spontaneity [simultaneity]."[29] Kūkai's position contends that such a law may be empirically verified *via* a direct experience of the horizon. The contents of the horizon cohere "spontaneously" because there is no outstanding criterion by which a standard of spatial distance or temporal duration may be grounded. In short, no *standard* is thetically obtainable to give it the necessary privileged position within the horizon. In one of Kūkai's commentaries in *The Precious Key to the Secret Treasury*, he relies upon the traditional naturalistic imagery of his predecessors to explain this aspect of primordial experience as follows:

1   The King of Mind is just like the water of a lake
    whose nature is originally clear and pure.
    The purity of its functions is just like that
    of the purified particles of dust in the water.
5   Therefore, when one realizes the purity of this
    Mind, he is able to become aware that the Mind is
    originally unborn. Why? Because the Mind is
    unobtainable in time. Waves in the great ocean,
    because they come to be contingent upon causes
10 (wind, etc), have not existed before and will
    not exist later (in their identical forms). But
    the nature of the water is different. The water
    was not nonexistent when the waves came to be

contingent upon their causes, and it will not be
15   nonexistent when the waves will come to cease at
the disappearance of these causes. The King of
Mind is like this; it knows no distinction of
before and after. Since it is free from the
distinction of before and after, though its
20   functions come to be or cease to be conditioned
by the wind of the world of objects, the
essential nature of the Mind is free from
23   appearing and disappearing.[30]

This description parallels first order bodymind awareness so closely that we may interpret Kūkai's naturalistic language using the hermeneutic of our phenomenological categories. Following this procedure will enable us to pinpoint the various characteristics of Kūkai's paradigmatic mode of awareness, i.e., the "King of Mind" (line 1). To begin, this awareness is equated with the "water of a lake whose nature is originally clean and pure" (lines 1-2). The body of water itself represents the experiential horizon that is "originally pure" insofar as it occurs prior to thetic positings. In lines 3 and 4 we note that "purification" might designate the activity of neutralization which metaphorically clears "particles of dust" (thetic positings) thus laying bare the "Mind [that] is originally unborn" (lines 5-7), i.e., one becomes directly aware of the birthplace of thetic experience.

Rhetorically, Kūkai asks "why" this is the case and thus gives himself cause to proceed to describe further characteristics of this experience. It is said to be "unobtainable in time" (simultaneous) because the "waves" (thetic positings) are "contingent upon causes" (noetic intentions) and therefore have no independent ontological history of "existing before or later (in their identical forms)" (lines 7-11). In other words, the experience is characterized by simultaneity because all thetic positings are contingent upon the intentionality of the experiencer and thus have no independent ontological status acquiring a history of their own. No "identical" objective standards are given a privileged position within the sea of the horizon by which spatio-temporal measurements may be assessed. Hence, since the superficial thetic positings ("waves") never occur in an "identical" manner, being subject to the external conditions ("causes") of each situation, they are said to be "nonexistent." However, the core horizon ("water"), from which thetic positings arise, is said to be "not non-existent" (lines 12-13). This is because it remains as the ground of all experience "when the waves will come to be contingent upon their causes" (lines 13-14) and "when the waves will come to cease at the disappearance [neutralization] of these causes" (lines 15-16). The direct experience of the horizon is therefore said to be the "King of Mind" because it is the everlasting empirically verifiable ground of experience knowing "no distinctions of before and after" (lines 16-18).

In summation, we may interpret his last statement as follows: *"Since it* [the King of Mind] *is free from the distinction of before and after* [simultaneity], *though its functions* [thetic positings] *come to be and cease to be conditioned by the wind* [noesis] *of the world of objects* [noema], *the essential nature of Mind* [the horizon as it is primordially given to consciousness] *is free from appearing and disappearing* (lines 18-23). Thus, the King of Mind is described as temporarily immutable. This direct experience of dynamism and spatio-temporal simultaneity have great significance for Kūkai. These characteristics not only approximate the dynamic, eternal, and limitless character of the Dharmakāya but also offer an experiential basis for those doctrines which rely so heavily upon the existence and presence of the Dharmakāya, e.g., *hosshin seppō, hongaku, sanmitsu,* and *sokushin jōbutsu.*

4. Sedimentation and Bodymind Awareness

In Chapter 2, we described sedimentation as the psychosomatic internalization of an activity. We noted that proper and repetitive training of any specific activity may eventually allow the practitioner to neutralize unconsciously the single operative noetic vector. This in turn allows the practitioner to have experience in the mode of first order bodymind awareness while still performing the sedimented skills required by the activity. In addition, we noted that the performance of a sedimented activity during first order bodymind awareness often gives the practitioner a totally new and sensitive awareness of the performance.

For Kūkai this new awareness is religiously significant. Accordingly, he encourages his students to sediment this paradigmatic mode of experience. In fact, we have seen that this mode of experience is "paradigmatic" because it consistently yields religious insight. From a Buddhist perspective, the sedimentation of this experience may be interpreted as that which enables the practitioner to internalize basic Mahayana Buddhist beliefs, e.g., without self, nothingness, impermanence, mutual interpenetration, the avoidance of craving, and so on.[31] During practice both the mind-aspect and the body-aspect are cultivated as vehicles and constituents of first order bodymind awareness. For example, the mind-aspect is trained to *experience* the meaning of "nothingness" (*mu*) through neutralization. For such reasons, first order bodymind awareness, instead of second or third order bodymind awareness, is sedimented. Kūkai teaches that one cannot "conceptualize what defies conceptualization, that is, what is neither being nor nonbeing." He asks, "how is it possible to conceptualize what is empty?" In response he says, "to seek liberation by means of their [those who conceptualize] doctrines of nihilism, eternalism, nonbeing and being is to seek milk by milking the cow's horn."[32] Here he humorously tells us that the direction one must go to understand the basis of Shingon doctrine is reflexive, toward neutral first order bodymind awareness, and not toward conceptual third order bodymind awareness.

In accord with this reflexive emphasis, the body-aspect is neither denied nor forsaken, but is trained to aid the sedimentation of first order bodymind awareness. The *Dainichikyō* states, "Without forsaking his [the practitioner's] body, he . . . wanders on the ground of great space, and perfects the mystery of Body."[33] We have already encountered the emphasis of the body-aspect training in our discussions of *mudra*. At this time we wish to underscore Kūkai's frequent plea that the serious student practice these techniques often and sediment paradigmatic awareness. He teaches that the student of meditation should "consecrate his heart" with "mirrorlike wisdom"; "consecrate his forehead" with the "wisdom of equality" and "consecrate his mouth" with the mystic letter [*mantras*].[34] He continues to emphasize "consecration" (sedimentation) of other aspects of the body as well. In fact his works are full of such pleas as, "keep training without abandoning the body," "devote yourself to the practice of meditation," "do not annihilate the activity of body and mind," "a man must practice exclusively without interruption" and "if a man practices diligently, day and night, he will obtain the five supernatural powers," i.e., he will permanently acquire the "powers of seeing and hearing anything at a distance" [expanded periphery].[35]

To enhance the quality of cultivation, Kūkai recommends practicing *mantras*, *mandalas*, and *mudras* simultaneously. In this type of practice (*Goshin-pō*), a *mantra* is uttered while forming a *mudra* and meditating upon their meaning. This is called "[practice] with form" (*usō*). Its purpose is to sediment the skills of *mantra* recitation, *mudra* formation, and *mandala* meditation. However, we have seen that these are merely vehicles to inculcate the paradigmatic mode of experience. Kūkai's true purpose is to sediment this experience into the practitioner's daily life. When practitioners can experience in this way at will, they have succeeded in their "[practice] without form" (*musō*). Here the practitioner "accommodates and universalizes [sediments] . . . practice to daily action. . . . It is an ideal practice that makes daily actions harmonize with the actions of the Dharmakāya."[36] (brackets mine) Kūkai believed that daily practice would be the process by which an individual, in the habit of making constant thetic positings and focusing upon finite noemata, could continually relate himself to the infinitude of Dainichi Nyorai. In this way, there was no end to the paradigmatic experience of meditation cultivated in daily activities with this present body (*sokushin jōbutsu*).[37] Ultimately, the purpose of *shugyō* (cultivation) was sedimentation in daily life — *gyōshu* (meaning to train and sediment meditative experience within one's body — "*shugyōshite jibun no karada ni osameru*").

The centrality of practice and the sedimentation of first order bodymind awareness is unmistakable in the philosophy of Kūkai. We have not, however, mentioned explicitly the most important quality of this mode of experience. In Chapter 2, we specifically focused upon the role of bodymind within first order awareness. Our phenomenological analysis described the nature of bodymind as an ever-present quality in all our experience. We noted that our awareness of mind-aspects or body-aspects were actually abstractions from a primordially given bodymind. Thus far, we have merely assumed that this paradigmatic mode of experience, which we have come to equate with first order bodymind awareness, similarly shares the same bodymind ground. For further clarification attention must be given to Kūkai's view of the nature of body and mind.

In the *Precious Key*, when Kūkai describes the "glorious mind, the most secret and sacred," he wastes no time in teaching the importance of understanding the inseparability of body and mind. As in first order bodymind awareness, his paradigmatic mode of experience is grounded upon bodymind awareness. Yoshito Hakeda describes his view of body and mind as follows:

> In the Ten Stages Kūkai begins his presentation of this mind [the Glorious Mind] with the following definition: 'The glorious mind, the most secret and sacred is, ultimately, to realize one's own mind in its fountainhead and to have insight into the nature of one's own existence.' He [Kūkai] conceives man as 'body-mind' not as mind or body, nor body and mind, and holds that this body-mind is grounded in the 'Body-Mind,' the secret and sacred living Body-Mind of all, the Dharmakāya Dainichi Nyorai. His premise is that our mind in its essence is united with the Mind of Dainichi-Nyorai and that our body, so long as it is in the universe, is part of the Body of the Dainichi-Nyorai; all men as all sentient beings are particular body-mind beings participating in the Body-Mind. It is this Body-Mind that is represented in the Shingon mandalas, which describe various aspects of Dainichi Nyorai.[38] (brackets mine)

In this passage, a sentient being's body-mind is equated with the Body-Mind of Dainichi Nyorai. This, however, can be misleading unless we realize this distinction is a result of what Kūkai might call exoteric thinking. That is, an abstract distinction has been made between a man's body-mind and the Nyorai's Body-Mind. From the perspective of first order bodymind awareness, Kūkai's esoteric thinking, there is *just bodymind*. That is, one becomes aware of the bodymind ground that is always present in the horizon. Sharing the *same* position within the horizon are the objects (*dharmas*) which are the teachings (words) of the Dharmakāya. Accordingly, there are no experiential bases for such distinctions as body-mind and Body-Mind or *dharma* and *Dharma*. These are useful explanatory devices but can be misleading if interpreted as having separate experiential correlates. For example, Hakeda points out that in the work entitled "*Sokushin Jōbutsu gi*" (Attaining Enlightenment in this Present Body," "body" (*shin*) "clearly does not mean body as opposed to mind but stands for 'existence' or 'body-mind-being.'"[39] In other words, bodymind or "body-mind-being" is the most primordial experiential ground making it possible for us, subsequently, to posit thetically our existence and the existence of the Dharmakāya. Simply stated, body-mind is Body-Mind and *vice versa*. In Kūkai's words:

The Buddha Dharma is nowhere remote. It is in our mind; it is close to us. Suchness is nowhere external. If not in our body, where can it be found?[40]

Body-mind distinctions are merely explanatory devices used to instruct those fixed upon the encrusted habits of exoteric thinking (second and third order bodymind awareness). From the perspective of esoteric thinking (first order bodymind awareness), bodymind is experienced within the horizon prethetically, i.e., prior to the positing of ontological body-mind/Body-Mind distinctions.

Hakeda suggests that Kūkai's use of the character (*shin*; body) in *sokushin jōbutsu*, rather than (*shin*; mind), punctuates his thisworldly approach to Buddhism about which we keep referring. Hakeda points out,

> The choice of 'body' over the normally expected 'mind' underscores the basic character of Kūkai's religion: emphasis on direct religious experience through one's total being [bodymind] and not merely through the intellect. Kūkai required that any religious teaching withstand the test of actual meditation and of daily life.[41] (interpretative brackets mine)

Regardless of Kūkai's choice of terminology in this regard, he often cautions the student not to attach ontological significance to such distinctions as "mind" and "body." He says, positing psychophysical constituents lead one into a state of "delusion" for they are "empty" and "not real,"[42] i.e., the distinctions ultimately have no experiential correlate. The judgments of real and not real are ontological thetic positings which occur subsequent to neutral experiencing of bodymind awareness. From the perspective of first order bodymind awareness

> all diverse phenomena [thetically posited] are identical as to their constituents within [the horizon *in toto*]; all are in the state of constant transformation; no absolute [ontological] difference exists between man and nature; body and mind are non-dual; . . . mind is not necessarily higher than body.[43] (Interpretative brackets mine)

This perspective is characterized by an implicit phenomenological reduction wherein all existential judgments are suspended. Kūkai explicitly acknowledges this condition and preaches that differences exist between matter and mind [in abstraction], but in their essential nature they remain the same. Matter is no other than mind; mind, no other than matter. Without any obstruction, they are interrelated. The subject is object; the object, the subject. The seeing [noesis] is seen [noema], and the seen is seeing.[44] (Interpretative brackets mine)

Although we have concluded that during first order awareness the mutual interpenetration of bodymind is a neutral experience (in accord with our phenomenological reductions), Kūkai adheres to his religious motivations and suggests that the oneness of bodymind at the root of all experience is originally a manifestation of Dainichi Nyorai. By associating the horizon given to consciousness, with a manifestation of Dainichi Nyorai, the Nyorai is interpreted as the source of all things *we can experience*. Kūkai calls the horizon in toto, the Body-Mind of Dainichi Nyorai from which all "subject and object" (noesis and noema) distinctions emerge.[45] As a result of this interpretation, he states we are originally enlightened (*hongaku*), the Dharmakāya expounds the *dharma* (hosshin seppō), we can attain enlightenment in this present body (*sokushin jōbutsu*) and we can empirically verify each of the above. Once practitioners sediment their original experience of the horizon, then, their bodymind awareness becomes united with the Body-Mind of Dainichi Nyorai, i.e, the bodymind ground is experienced within the horizon in toto for which the Dainichi Nyorai (Body-Mind) is responsible. Kūkai describes this relation in the *Prescious Key* as follows:

When the student becomes perfected in . . . meditation, then and only then will he become the Body of the most sacred One. Then his luminous being will be the all-pervading Body and Mind . . . once the student has attained enlightenment he will be in an order where time distinctions between past, present and future are unknown. Indeed, the ordinary man's mind is like a lotus flower yet to open and the Enlightened One's Mind, like the full moon.[46]

A careful reading of this passage reveals an equation between "enlightenment" and an "order" of experience characterized by simultaneity and an expanded periphery. It is clear that these structural characteristics and the corresponding awareness of bodymind is central to Kūkai's paradigmatic mode of experience.

5. Kūkai's Descriptions of Paradigmatic Modes of Experience: A Summary

In Chapter 2 we noted that thetic neutralization was necessary for the transfer from second order bodymind awareness to first order bodymind awareness. Kūkai similarly believes that the horizon of our experience may be presenced as it is only when all thetic intellection has ceased.[47] He says:

1   The three luminous bodies – the sun, moon, and stars –
     Have been shining from the beginning in the sky.
     They may be hidden at times by mists and clouds
     Or veiled completely by smoke and dust.
5   Ignorant people thereby imagine
     That the sun and the moon came to cease to be.
     Its the same with the intrinsic Three Bodies;
     [Dharmakāya, Sambhogakāya, Nirmanakāya]
     From the beginningless beginning
10   They have been living in the space of Mind.
     Yet being covered by their illusions
     And being entangled by their defilements,
     They are unmanifest like a mirror inside a box or a gem in ore.
     Deluded people thereby may imagine
15   That they have no element of original enlightenment. . .
     Nonetheless, those intrinsic Three Bodies
     Are unperturbed without gain or loss.[48]

In the passage Kūkai suggests that even though the horizon is primordially given *in toto* and there to be presenced at the base of all experience, continual thetic positings cover a direct awareness of the horizon as it is independent of thetic intervention. Again, he metaphorically uses such expressions as "mist," "clouds," "smoke," and "dust" to represent the manner in which thetic experience covers our awareness of that which is innate. The possibility of this primordial awareness has always been present "from the beginningless beginning" (simultaneity), and can be verified anytime one's perspective ceases to be vectoral and begins to have breadth like "the space of Mind" (lines 9-12). When second or third order bodymind awareness becomes sedimented, people become "deluded" thinking "that they have no element of original enlightenment," i.e., first order bodymind awareness (lines 14-15). Kūkai concludes that even though such a feeling may prevail, that which is innate will remain "unperturbed" and thus remain available for inspection whenever a transfer into first order bodymind awareness may occur (lines 16-17).

Next we will examine another of Kūkai's descriptions of the paradigmatic mode of experience.

The sun and the moon shine forth in space and on the water,
Undisturbed by gales in the atmosphere.
Both good and evil are relative in his [Dainichi Nyorai's] preachings;
The notion of I and Thou will be erased and lost.
When the sea of our mind becomes serene through meditation
and insight,
He reveals himself unconditionally as water overflows.[49]

Our structural categories of first order bodymind awareness will help to interpret this verse into a phenomenologically meaningful system through which his description of the phenomenal aspects of enlightenment may be accurately conveyed. In the first line we find a naturalistic description of the expanded periphery (spacious sun and moon light) characteristic of presencing the horizon (water). Next, this mode of awareness is said to be maintained by continued neutralization which remains "undisturbed by gales" (thetic positings) that may suddenly arise within the "atmosphere" (experiential horizon). The third line depicts a theme that should be most familiar. The Nyorai's "preachings" are equated with the horizon itself wherein no distinctions arise as a result of the absence of a privileged standard by which a criterion for, in this case, ethical judgment ("good and evil") may be assessed. Similarly, the fourth line underscores the suspension of ontological judgments regarding self and other. As a result of the thoroughly neutral mode of this experience, it is likened to a sea of serene meditation in line 5. Finally, the dynamic overbrimming quality of this first order awareness is equated with the Nyorai's revealing himself through the environment as presenced (line 6).

This mode of experience is encouraged for if everything within the horizon shares the same position with respect to each other, then the student is not apt to be led astray from that which is primordially given, i.e., the words of the Dainichi Nyorai. The intentions behind human's words, cravings and desired effects are thus neutralized and redirected expanding the experiential periphery. In Kūkai's poetic language,

> I have realized the original unproducedness,
> Gone beyond the path of [human] words,
> Attained liberation from various faults,
> Freed myself from causes and conditions,
> And realized that voidness is like space.[50] (brackets mine)

When a person's thetic positings are neutralized, the horizon itself stands out as never before. For example, a musician may focus upon sheet music until the melody is sedimented. Having thoroughly internalized the piece of music and the skills required to play the tune, he or she may unconsciously neutralize the last intentional vector and play the tune "without thinking." At this time the musician may hear the real beauty of the piece for the first time. In the same way, Kūkai's writing is often so beautifully descriptive that it seems likely that the inspiration for his work comes from the sedimentation of a mode of experience not unlike first order bodymind awareness. For example,

> Flowers in the spring, though transient, are bright to our eyes;
> The autumnal moon reflected in serene water delights us.
> Swift summer clouds appear and disappear in deep dales.
> Heavy snow in wind—dancing maidens—seems light to the streams.[51]

Kūkai suggests that repetition and practice pave the way to sediment the paradigmatic mode of awareness. Below, he describes *mantra* practice in a manner that touches upon a variety of our phenomenological categories.

> A mantra is suprarational.
> It eliminates ignorance when meditated upon and recited.
> A single word contains a thousand truths.
> One can realize Suchness here and now.
> Walk on and on until perfect quiescence is reached.
> Go on and on until the primordial Source is penetrated.[52]

A phenomenological interpretation of each line might help to unpack some of the symbolic references.

"A mantra is suprarational."
That is the *mantra* transcends discursive third order reasoning in a reflexive direction.

"It eliminates ignorance when meditated upon and recited."
When meditated upon the sound has the affect of neutralizing all extraneous intutitions. Its dynamism harmonizes with the character of the horizon and thus leads the practitioner into a transfer from second to first order bodymind awareness.

"A single word contains a thousand truths."
The *mantra* is given so much value and significance because it helps the student to witness the ground of an infinite number of thetic positings. Moreover, the simultaneous character of the horizon allows the student to become aware of no one static "truth" (*dharma*) for all *dharmas* dynamically coalesce.

"One can realize Suchness here and now."
Realization is thus not some secret noumenal realm but rather describes the clarity of present phenomenal experience.

"Walk on and on until perfect quiescence is reached."
"Quiescence is reached" when the last single noetic vector focusing upon sound is eventually neutralized.

"Go on and on until the primordial Source is penetrated."
One must practice diligently "on and on" before the Dharmakāya (horizon *in toto* may be presented at will. At this time, experiential verification of the highest Shingon truths is possible.

Kūkai describes this experience of the Dharmakāya through the mysteries of the body, speech, and mind as follows:

> The Three Mysteries pervade the entire universe,
> Adorning gloriously the *mandala* of infinite space.
> Being painted by brushes of mountains, by ink of oceans,
> Heaven and earth are the bindings of a sutra revealing the Truth.
> Reflected in a dot are all things in the universe;
> Contained in the data of senses and mind is the sacred book.
> It is open or closed depending on how we look at it;
> Both his silence and His eloquence make incisive tongues numb.[53]

Thus we understand that the all-pervasive character of the Dharmakāya is not limited to the phenomenal world present to our consciousness. The Dharmakāya also pervades ourselves and may be
empirically verified "depending how we look at it." Yet, the
neutral quality of this experience and the pervasiveness of the
Dharmakāya make locative descriptions of "incisive tongues
numb." For this reason we have come to understand Kūkai's efforts to describe first order bodymind awareness *via* the interpretive device of phenomenological categories.

Finally, the discussion of Kūkai concludes with an analysis of
a description of the "essential nature of the World of *Dharma*"
found in the *Dainichikyō*. The Nyorai himself is said to have experienced this as follows:

1   I have realized that which is unborn;
    It is what language cannot communicate;
    It is free from all defilements;
    It transcends causality;
5   I know it is void like space;
    I have gained the wisdom to see things as they are;
7   I am free from all Darkness;
    I am ultimately real and immaculate.[54]

In line 1 the primordially given horizon is characterized as "unborn" for it is experienced prior to existential judgments. As a
mode of awareness prior to thetic distinction making, it is "free
from all defilements" (line 3). It follows that an absence of
specifiable noemata would entail a "transcendence of causality"
(line 4). That is, since a direct experience of the horizon "is void
like space" (line 5), all identifiable causes and effects are neutralized into an abode of spatial and temporal simultaneity. Having
"gained the wisdom to see things as they are" [first order bodymind awareness] (line 6), the Nyorai is thus "free from all
Darkness" (line 7), i.e., he is free from thetic positings which hide
the "ultimately real and immaculate" (line 8) "World of Dharma"
within us all.

In conclusion, I would like to again point out that the above
textual interpretations are made possible by first examining the
eidetic structure of Kūkai's paradigmatic mode of awareness. Once
the hermeneutical categories were defined, based upon our own

familiarity with fleeting instances of first order bodymind awareness (Chapter 2), we were able to analyze phenomenologically Kūkai's symbolic rhetoric describing the process of sedimenting this awareness. In this way, the experiential basis for the salient philosophical doctrines discussed in Chapter 3 should now be apparent. In the next two chapters we will employ a similar strategy. We will begin with a general description of Dōgen's main philosophical doctrines and then utilize our structural categories to achieve a more sensitive understanding of their experiential basis.

Chapter 5

Dōgen: A Descriptive Philosophy

In Chapter 5 and 6 the experiential basis for the philosophy of Zen Master Dōgen Kigen (1200-1253) will be interpreted. Chapter 5 describes, albeit anachronistically, the phenomenological tenor of Dōgen's central doctrines. Utilizing this type of hermeneutic strategy, we will focus upon the presuppositions of his philosophical framework and explore a few examplary fascicles[1] from his collection known as *Shōbōgenzō* ('correct' + 'dharma' + 'eye' + 'storehouse'; thus the "Treasury of the Correct Dharma-eye"). Like Chapter 4, Chapter 6 will utilize our phenomenological categories to describe various aspects of the experience upon which Dōgen's philosophy is grounded. Again it should be noted that the phenomenological stragegy need not be considered the *only* viable hermeneutic with which Dōgen's philosophy may be explained to a predominantly occidental audience. The shared existential-ontological orientation of Husserl's radical empiricism and Dōgen's description of experience cultivated through zazen, however, provide for complementary analyses which underscore the common denominators of their respective methodologies.

1. Introductory Background

In the previous chapter we discussed Kūkai's complex metaphysical theories and esoteric techniques arising from his paradigmatic mode of experience—first order bodymind awareness. The emphasis on cultivating an awareness of the ground of experience was reinforced in Dōgen's philosophy. Since Dōgen was one of the earliest Buddhist scholars to write in Japanese, his works became accessible within the growing Sōtō sect during the Kamakura period (1185-1333). Like Kūkai, Dōgen's philosophy was guided by experience rather than theory. This experiential perspective therefore began to emerge as a characteristic of Japanese Buddhism. Furthermore, Kamakura period Buddhists, including Dōgen developed alternatives to the esoteric rituals characteristic of Kūkai's techniques. Dōgen's contribution to demystifying practice and underscoring the experiential ground of complex Buddhist doctrines was monumental. In an effort to understand better the emphasis upon experience in Dōgen's philosophy, we will outline a few biographical details.

Tradition states that Dōgen's pursuit of enlightenment and keen awareness of the transience of all things were, in part, the result of the early loss of his parents.[2] Following the instructions of his dying mother, Dōgen renounced his aristocratic heritage and, at the age of twelve, prepared for a monastic existence. With the aid of an uncle who lived as a hermit at the foot of Kyoto's Mt. Hiei, the center of Japanese Tendai Buddhism, Dōgen was ordained by Kōen, the chief abbot of the Tendai school. At the age of thirteen Dōgen's aptitude and diligent efforts enabled him to comprehend complex Buddhist theories and rituals. Young Dōgen, however, soon encountered an apparent incongruence which he could not assimilate:

Both the exoteric and esoteric doctrines teach the primal Buddha-nature of all sentient beings. If this is so, why then do all Buddhas and Bodhisattvas arouse the longing for enlightenment and engage in ascetic practices?[3]

That is, the relationship between the theories of original enlightenment (*hongaku*) and acquired (or incipient) enlightenment (*shikaku*) achieved through cultivation seemed to be incompatible. In short, if we are originally enlightened, why do we cultivate that which is already innate? What, then, is the meaning and purpose of cultivation? The apparent inconsistency between the doctrinal teachings found in the sutras and the practical disciplines of Tendai cultivation haunted Dōgen until he left Mount Hiei in search for a resolution.

Having studied Chinese classics since the age of four, Dōgen was prepared to travel to China. Accompanied by Myozen, the abbot of Kyoto's Kennin-ji temple and successor to the Rinzai Master Eisai, Dōgen left for China in the spring of 1223. Dōgen received two important lasting impressions in China. Upon his arrival, he learned from a kitchen steward of a temple that daily work is a form of cultivation leading to enlightenment. The emphasis upon cultivation in daily life is a theme permeating Dōgen's philosophy and we shall have occasion to investigate it further below. Two years later, Dōgen learned, from his encounter with the famous Chinese Zen Master Ju-ching (Jp. Nyojō, 1163-1228), the importance of strict discipline with persistent zazen practice and that proper cultivation includes "casting off body and mind." In fact, Dōgen suddenly achieved enlightenment when he heard his master explain "In Zen, body and mind are cast off." Thereafter, casting off body and mind became the central principle of Dōgen's practice and philosophy as a whole.[4] Since Dōgen's philosophical works are based upon a description of the zazen experience, and since casting off body and mind is its goal, the "casting off of body and mind" is an important key to understanding Dōgen's philosophical positions.

2. Dissolving the Rift Between Theory and Practice

In this section we shall examine the central philosophical doctrines of Dōgen which ultimately resolved, or more accurately dissolved as we shall see below, the apparent[5] incongruence between Tendai theory and practice.

a. *Hongaku*

Dōgen was familiar with the theory of original enlightenment (*hongaku*), discussed in our previous chapters. In his important work *Bendōwa* ('to transact,' 'to negotiate' + 'way,' 'Tao' + 'topic,' 'discourse,' hence, *'Discourse on Negotiating the Way'*), Dōgen describes original enlightenment in the following manner,

> This Dharma [*hō*, "Truth"] is amply present in every person, but unless one practices, it is not manifested, unless there is realization, it is not attained. It is not a question of one or many; let loose of it and it fills your hands.[6] (brackets mine)

Dōgen emphasizes that we must "let go" of our quest for finding the Dharma within ourselves. One must neutralize the desire to find it. At this time the Dharma will "fill your hands." The Dharma is not something to be attained; it will make its presence known when the thetic desire to know it is neutralized. The Dharma is *empty* of anything specific; it can not be limited or perceived as specifiable noemata. Elsewhere in *Bendōwa*, Dōgen writes that the "workings of the mind" (thetic positings) only serve to cause the Dharma to remain hidden: "it is like being in the middle of a great ocean and saying there is no water."[7]

An important aspect of Dōgen's interpretation of *hongaku* is his emphasis that original enlightenment is not limited to sentient beings. For Dōgen, even non-sentient beings are originally enlightened.[8] (In general, it is helpful to conceive of an entire framework [the world], that is "originally enlightened." If, for pedagogical purposes, we think in this way, we are less apt to misinterpret enlightenment as either an innate, a static or a substantial entity which all beings possess. It may be more accurate to suggest that enlightenment is not something you possess but a way that you are; a way in which one interacts with one's surroundings.) In the *Shōbōgenzō* fascicle *Kobusshin* ('ancient,' 'eternal,' + 'Buddha' + 'mind,' hence *'The Mind of the Ancient Buddhas'*), Dōgen states that the eternal Buddha-mind or enlightenment is found in everything from tiles to oceans to mountains to stones. And in the fascicle *Daigo* (*'Great Realization'*) he states that although our own body and mind are originally enlightened, it is wrong to think enlightenment resides only in these places and not in others. Such I-it dualism, characteristic of second and third order bodymind awareness, only restricts one's awareness of the dharma's pervading everywhere.[9] Similarly the fascicles *Kūge* (*'Flower of Emptiness'*), and especially *Kōmyō* (*'The Light [of the Buddha]'*), emphasize the notion that there is no place between heaven and earth that Buddha-nature, and therefore original enlightenment, does not permeate.[10] (A cursory look at the many fascicle titles [*Kūge, Juki, Kōmyō, Daigo,* and *Kobusshin*] themselves reveal a sense of the central and all embracing nature of original enlightenment.)

The basis for Dōgen's emphasis on the enlightened character of all things requires further explanation. While the above metaphors of vast emptiness and pervading light express the character of original enlightenment, Dōgen cautions his readers not to attach themselves to such expressions. They are to be understood as mere symbols (not metaphysical realities) attempting to describe the *experience* of becoming concretely *aware* of original enlightenment. Using an excerpt from the fascicle *Shinjingakudō* ('body' + 'mind' + 'study' + 'way,' *'Learning [through] the Body and Mind')* as a case in point, one of Dōgen's statements may be interpreted in order to clarify the attitude required to become aware of the originally enlightened character of all things.

> There is a ground of the soil, a ground of the mind and a ground of the treasure as well. Even though they are of many kinds, it does not mean that they can not be without a ground. There should be a world with emptiness as its ground. There is a different human and celestial view with respect to the sun, moon and stars. These views of various kinds are not the same. But regardless of what it is, the view of the undivided mind puts it on one plane (unifies it).[11]

Note that the interpretative analysis below is not intended to illustrate Dōgen's "phenomenology," rather the hermeneutic is utilized to build bridges in comparative studies and help interpret Dōgen's use of metaphor and symbolism. The danger of the former procedure would surely contribute to an anachronistic vicious cycle of translation interlaced with phenomenological interpretation. In the first sentence Dōgen suggests that every perceptible entity seems to possess its own defining essence. Yet, in the next sentence he cautions, simply because there may be many instances when we could make such an assumption, it need not be the case. That is, rather than assigning (positing) specific essences for each thing, there is another perspective from which all things share a common ground—emptiness. This perspective of the "undivided mind" (first order bodymind awareness) is thus contrasted with "views of various kinds" (second and third order bodymind awareness). These latter views, casting different noetic attitudes ("human" or "celestial"), posit different noematic meanings upon, for example, "the sun, moon and stars." The view of the undivided mind on the other hand, puts all the various views on the same plane and thus unifies them. Phenomenologically speaking, experiencing from the view of the undivided mind would entail a neutralization of all intentional perspectives thus laying bare the bodymind ground within the horizon. In this way, the horizon could be perceived with no specific noemata possessing a privileged position. A non-privileged horizon could be interpreted as an experiential verification of the notion of emptiness. Finally, since this notion also depicts the sense of shared essence (ground), it is reasonable to interpret that the view called the undivided mind experientially verifies the original enlightenment which all beings equally share. Dōgen's emphasis upon the practical means of acquiring the "view of the undivided mind," which authenticates the theory of original enlightenment, leads us to a discussion of the role of practice in solving his problem of the rift between theory and practice.

b. *Shinjin datsuraku*

Shinjin datsuraku is a phrase traditionally translated as "cast off body and mind."[12] The importance of this phrase can not be underestimated. It occurs throughout *Shōbōgenzō*, works by Dōgen not included in *Shōbōgenzō*, and is most evident in *Shōbōgenzō Zuimonki* which was edited by Dōgen's disciples shortly after his death. The importance of this phrase was punctuated by Dōgen as he considered it to be the "one great matter of Zen practice for my entire life."[13] As the key to practice, it became the key to understanding Buddhist theory as well. In fact, Dōgen stated explicitly that this is all you need to understand Buddhism.

> From the first time you meet your master and receive his teaching, you have no need for either incense-offerings, homage-paying, nembutsu, penance disciplines, or silent sutra readings; only cast off body and mind in zazen.[14]

Dōgen states that he became enlightened when he heard his master Nyojō shout at a sleeping monk, "Zazen is to cast off body and mind!" Why are you sleeping?" Dōgen subsequently pro-strated himself before his master and said, "I have come here with body and mind cast off." Nyojō confirmed his enlightenment say-ing, "Now cast off body and mind!"[15]

On numerous occasions Dōgen uses the metaphor of the pole to explain casting off body and mind. One such instance is as follows:

> Students, cast aside your bodies and minds and enter fully into Buddhism. An old Master has said, 'you've climbed to the top of a hundred-foot pole. Now keep on going.' . . .Resolve to cast aside both body and mind.[16]

"Casting off," interpreted phenomenologically, is parallel to the neutralization of thetic positings. Dōgen strongly emphasizes that casting off is not a denunciation (negative positing) of body and mind. One must cast aside all thetic positings, e.g., "accepting good" and "rejecting evil."[17] To cling to any such "preconceptions"[18] or "personal views"[19] is like clutching on to the top of the pole. One must "let go with both hands and feet"[20] and this suspends all relative thinking and worldly opinions. In words reminiscent of our phenomenological *epoché*, Dōgen teaches his student not to fear the opinions of others when one has given up worldly views (the natural standpoint).[21] The monastic life is not a denunciation or negation of the world, but it allows the monk to be a community of men seeking to experience the world as it is with tensions (body) and intensions (mind) cast off. In short, Dōgen hints at neutralization, versus negation, when he says *forget* body and mind and all preconceived notions about Buddhism.

Dōgen states that understanding even the Buddhist doctrine of impermanence is contingent upon casting off body and mind. In the work entitled *Shōji* ('*Life and Death*'), Dōgen teaches neither to hate nor desire life or death. Such thetic attitudes cloud one's ability to experience life as it is, and death as it is. Moreover, one should "not attempt to measure [life and death] with your mind nor to articulate them with words."[22] Rather, Dōgen describes the neutral attitude, saying one must achieve detachment from life and death without effort or using your mind. Since this concept is at the root of other doctrines besides impermanence, we will have further occasion to examine the implications and impor-tance of casting off body and mind. At this time, we only seek to underscore the degree to which the notion of "casting off body and mind" permeated Dōgen's philosophy. Now we are prepared to discuss Dōgen's solution to the conflict between the forementioned theory and practice.

c. *Shushō ichinyo*

Shushō ichinyo ('to study, complete, cultivate, discipline' + 'proof, evidence' + 'oneness,' hence "the oneness of cultivation and authentication')[23] is a phrase which literally describes Dōgen's solution to the apparent rift between Tendai theory and practice. Casting off body and mind leads to the experiential verification that there is no distinction between cultivation (*shu*) and authentication (*shō*). Dōgen's previous assumption that these two were different led him to assume inaccurately that practice was a tool, vehicle, method, or means of achieving the end—enlightenment. The inspiration for realizing the oneness of cultivation and authentication will become clear when we remember that Dōgen's master was a strict disciplinarian. Nyojō insisted upon practicing zazen day and night. Dōgen, therefore, learned the importance of "just sitting" (*shikantaza*). Accordingly, Dōgen's zazen experience led him to the conclusion that "just sitting" is enlightenment itself. In this way, Dōgen dissolved the distinction between practice (cultivation, *shu*) and enlightenment (authentication, *shō*). Dōgen's use of the word *shō* (authentication) served to accentuate his understanding that enlightenment is continually confirmed and verified during practice itself.

In *Bendōwa*, Dōgen clarifies how his notion of *shushō* dissolves the problem which he perceived between the theory of original enlightenment and practice. He says:

Patriarchs and buddhas, who have maintained the Buddha Dharma, all have held that practice based upon proper sitting in zazen in *jijuyū* samādhi was the right path through which their enlightenment opened. . . . When even for a short period of time you sit properly in samādhi, imprinting the Buddha-seal in your three activities [deeds, words, and thought], each and everything excluding none is the Buddha-seal, and all space without exception is enlightenment.[24]

In other words, man's original enlightenment is experientially confirmed and immediately authenticated during practice itself. Accordingly, Dōgen sought to justify the principle of *shushō* by describing the *experience* of zazen, i.e., the experience of enlightenment. Kōshirō Tamaki similarly underscores this cardinal role of experience when he says, "the ultimate aim of Dōgen's practice is the realization that the absolutely formless truth is identical with the actual world of experience."[25] Dōgen's project thus takes on a phenomenologically motif[26] as he attempts to describe this "actual world" as it is primordially given to consciousness during zazen practice.

Dōgen's emphasis on casting off tensions (body) and intentions (mind) during practice arises from his sensitivity to what one might call today *phenomenological intentionality*. The contribution of thetic positings prevents Buddha-nature from being experienced directly as it is. For example, static thetic abstractions or objectifications cloud Buddha-nature as given to consciousness. In the fascicle *Genjōkōan*[27] Dōgen writes:

> The dusty world and (the Buddha way) beyond it assume many aspects, but we can see and understand them only to the extent our eye is cultivated through practice. To understand the (true) nature of all things, we must know that in addition to apparent circularity or angularity, the remaining virtue of the mountains and seas is great and inexhaustible. . . .[28]

"The dusty world" may be interpreted as the world experienced *via* second or third order bodymind awareness, i.e., the world experienced after noetic intentions have been posited. The Buddha-nature "beyond" this, refers to a reflexive transcendence[29] of this mode of awareness through cultivation. Learning to cast off thetic positings allows one to experience the horizon as it is — "the (true) nature of all things." The "apparent circularity or angularity" similarly refers to Dōgen's sensitivity to the contribution of specific intentions and the limited nature of experience. The periphery of experience may be circular, angular, small or large, depending upon the intensity of the noetic attitude.[30] Accordingly, each new perspective mirrors the meaning bestowing noesis. This interpretation seems to be substantiated when Dōgen says, "To be associated with perceptions is not the mark of realization, because the mark of realization is to be beyond [reflexive transcendence] such illusions."[31]

Consequently, Dōgen suggests that Buddha-nature can be directly experienced, thus dissolving the rift between the theory of original enlightenment and practice. Even though Buddha-nature is ever present, Dōgen urges cultivation of the proper mode of experience so that the presence of Buddha-nature will be authenticated. The following traditional *mondō*, reproduced by Dōgen, is representative of his feelings regarding this most important matter.

> As Zen master Pao-ch'ê of Ma-ku shan was fanning himself, a monk came up and said: 'The nature of wind is constancy. There is no place it does not reach. Why do you still use a fan?' Pao-ch'ê answered: 'You only know the nature of the wind is constancy. You do not know yet the meaning of it reaching every place.' The monk said: 'What is the meaning of 'there is no place it does not reach?' The master only fanned himself and bowed deeply.[32]

Just as the nature of the far reaching wind is constant, the original Buddha-nature of all things is always present. The monk's question is therefore asking why there is a need to practice (use a fan) when Buddha-nature (the wind) is constant. Pao-ch'ê's answer suggests that a breeze arises from the use of the fan precisely because the wind is constant and it is far reaching. Yet, without the fanning motion, the constancy of the wind goes unnoticed. That is, although the air is always present, its cooling affect is not felt without a fanning motion. In the same way, authentication of Buddha-nature is possible because it is ever-present and permeates all things. Yet, without cultivation, these qualities of Buddha-nature go unheeded.[33] Thus Dōgen has been able to come to terms with the question which originally inspired his religious quest. The theory of original enlightenment is true and insistence upon practice is also true. Cultivation and authentication are one and the same.

In these past three sections we have briefly examined the constituents (theory and practice) and solution (authentication-cultivation) of Dōgen's initial problem. In the next two sections we will examine two more doctrines of Dōgen's philosophy. Our purpose for including these sections is two-fold. First, each of the following doctrines parallels concepts previously examined in the philosophy of Kūkai. Therefore we will be able to establish a thread linking important trends between Kūkai and Dōgen. Second, the following sections will help to enhance our overall understanding of Dōgen's primary concerns. This will prove helpful when we begin our analysis of a few of the most illuminating fascicles within *Shōbōgenzō*.

d. *Sokushin zebutsu*

Sokushin zebutsu ('this very' + 'mind' + 'is' + Buddha,' lit. 'Mind is Buddha,' hence, '*This Very Mind is Buddha*') is the title of a fascicle in *Shōbōgenzō* and an important concept used throughout Dōgen's philosophical scheme. Like *sokushin jōbutsu* (Chapter 3), *sokushin zebutsu* emphasizes the fact that enlightenment is attained in this lifetime. Kūkai emphasizes body (*shin*) to punctuate the physicality (body-aspect) of bodymind awareness, and Dōgen emphasizes mind (*shin*) to punctuate the dynamism of neutral (mind-aspect) bodymind awareness. For Dōgen the dynamism of cultivation, i.e, the *act* of casting off body and mind, enabled the practitioner to participate in, and experience directly, impermanence. Specifically, *sokushin zebutsu* was utilized to demonstrate the futility of searching for a source of permanence within oneself. Dōgen makes it clear that the act of neutralization (casting off) eliminates any conception of a static, permanent "mind" or fixed "Buddha." In this way, Dōgen lays the groundwork for his thesis that *sokushin zebutsu* ('this very mind is Buddha') refers to the *act* of experiencing in an authentic manner. The act of cultivation authenticates the Buddhist doctrine of impermanence, i.e., that there is nothing substantial to seek in oneself or in Buddhahood.

The dynamic activity of neutralization itself places the practitioner into a mode of experience (first order) wherein the dynamism of the horizon is experienced directly. This action allows one to presence the "acting Buddha" (*gyōbutsu*)[34] which pervades all things. As was noted in our analysis of Kūkai, this paradigmatic mode of experiencing requires neutralization of tensions and intentions. As a result, the emphasis upon mind is not to be interpreted as separate from body any more than cultivation can be separated from authentication. For example in *Bendōwa*,

Dōgen emphasizes that "this very mind is Buddha" is dependent upon "cultivation."[35] In short, the *Mind of Buddha* is discovered only during the dynamic activity of *attaining* it.

In the fascicles *Sokushin zebutsu* and *Bendōwa*, Dōgen specifically emphasizes this dynamic character of attaining the Mind of Buddha in order to dispel the *Senika* heresy (*sennigedō*)[36] advocating a permanent self:

> Only through the transmission from patriarch to patriarch has 'this very mind is Buddha' been fully realized and practiced. There is hearing, practicing and authenticating. . . . There is the wall of the mind, but it has never been muddy water and it has never been constructed. Thoroughly examine 'this very mind is Buddha' and every variation of this idea. This kind of thorough investigation is precisely 'this very mind is Buddha' and advancing this is the true transmission of 'this very mind is Buddha.'[37]

The thrust of Dōgen's argument is intended to accentuate the *dynamic process* of manifesting an awareness to the fact that 'this very mind is Buddha.' Since 'this very mind is Buddha' is itself a dynamic mode of awareness, any heretical notion of permanence is simultaneously dispelled. From this quotation we can recognize that 'this very mind' of ours, which is engaged in hearing, seeing, and practicing, etc., is in an active, primordially given state ("it has never been constructed" or thetically intended). Dōgen suggests that if this natural process of experience were to cease, our awareness would become muddy like stagnant water. This would, however, be undesirable for our primordially given, dynamic experience ought to be "advanced" according to Dōgen. We have observed that the dynamic character of experience is most obvious during first order bodymind awareness. It is during this mode of awareness, when all thetic positings are neutralized, that the dynamic ground of subsequent noetic glances is presenced. Accordingly, the dynamism of "this very mind" ('this very' referring to the most simple, most primordial condition of awareness), which is said to be equivalent to a Buddha's experience, most clearly approximates the structure of first order bodymind awareness.

It is noteworthy that in his summary of *Sokushin zebutsu*, Dōgen places his emphasis upon the need to achieve the mode of experience in which "this very mind is Buddha" is not separated from cultivation and authentication. He says, "to not yet have aroused the mind, cultivated, authenticated it and achieved enlightenment is not 'this very mind is Buddha.'" "If," he continues, "for even one instant one were to cultivate and authenticate the aroused mind, it would be 'this very mind is Buddha.'"[38]

e. *Hosshin seppō*

We will recall from Chapter 3 that *hosshin seppō* means "The Dharmakāya expounds the *dharma*." This term refers to an experience wherein every thing we experience (*hosshin*) is teaching, expounding or explaining (*setsu*) the dharma (*hō*). Hence, the third Buddha-body (Dharmakāya) expounds the truth (*dharma*) by manifesting itself immanently within every thing. Like Kūkai, Dōgen believes this *dharma* permeates all sentient and non-sentient beings. Indeed, we have already seen this to be the case in our discussion of *hongaku*. We noted that in the fascicles *Kobutsushin*, *Jippō*, *Kōmyō*, *Daigo* and *Juki*, Dōgen especially emphasized the Buddha-nature or dharma-nature that is originally inherent in all things. Like Kūkai, Dōgen also believed that since *dharma*-nature permeates the self, all aspects of the self must be cultivated in order to bring about self-awareness of this innate *dharma*. In this regard he says:

> Students of the Way must each *reflect upon themselves*. To reflect upon your own body is to reflect on how you should behave with your own body and mind. The correct rules for the use of *body*, *speech*, and *mind* can be seen in the actions of the Buddhas who have come before.[39] (italics mine)

This passage includes three important points. We notice that, like Kūkai, Dōgen recognizes that "body, speech and mind" are aspects of the self that must be cultivated in order to *act* in the manner of a Buddha. We may ask, how does a Buddha act? Here Dōgen hints that "reflection upon oneself" is the key to self-awareness of the innate *dharma*. This reflexive look is the *action* of a Buddha. Consequently, the *dharma* within oneself is not a *thing* but a thing-as-experienced. To summarize the three points: First, body, speech, and mind must be cultivated to *act* as a Buddha. Second, introspection is the first act that the student must perform, i.e., reflexive self-awareness informs the student of the structure of experience including thetic positings, neutralization, and the horizon *in toto*. And finally, *dharmas* are not things hidden from us, but are things-as-experienced (they are things experienced as-they-are free from thetic tainting). The latter notion of *dharma* as a thing-as-experienced that is the distinguishing act of a Buddha is most important and requires further explanation.

Dōgen is not speculating metaphysically about any hidden *dharma*-reality. Rather, Dōgen's dominant experiential standpoint leads him to conclude that *dharmas* have been erroneously conceptualized in the past. Our above interpretations may seem far-fetched unless one considers Dōgen's habit of using metaphorical expressions which, at time, sound quasi-metaphysical. Although these statements by Dōgen have often been interpreted as such, it may be suggested that these passages are actually *descriptive* statements about experience.[40] Kasulis maintains that Dōgen's reference to

> Kegon (Ch. Hua-yen) and Tendai (Ch. T'ien-t'ai) statements about the interpretation of *dharmas*, for example, are not statements about 'things' but rather are statements about 'things-as-experienced.' In other words, the expressions of those schools are not metaphysical at all; rather they are descriptions of human experience.[41]

By acknowledging explicitly the phenomenological perspective of our hermeneutic utilized throughout, it may be added that the "interpretation of the *dharmas*" is a description of the equal or non-privileged position of things-as-experienced prior to ontic judgments during the act of cultivation (first order bodymind awareness).

From this perspective we may interpret that when Dōgen describes metaphorically the pervasive character of the *Dharmakāya* and says "the entire universe [*jippō*] is the Buddha-land,"[42] he refers to the mode of experience (cultivation) wherein things are experienced as they are (authentication), independent of thetic positings. Insofar as one can experience this way anywhere, the "entire universe," as it is primordially given to consciousness, may be experienced microcosmically.[43] The Dharmakāya pervades all things equally but it is authenticated as the totality of all things experienced as they are independent of thetic impairment. It may be inconsistent to suggest that for Dōgen knowledge of the Dharmakāya requires omnniscient or omnipresent knowledge (as opposed to other Mahayana philosophers). Just as we can not experience the entire universe that is the Buddha-land at once, we can not experience the totality of the *dharma* (the Dharmakāya) at once. Yet, when we consider the finite periphery of experience, the meaning of *dharma* (individual things experienced as they are) may be experienced microcosmically. The full force of the meaning of the Dharmakāya, for Dōgen may be known without positing an inconsistent speculative metaphysical theory or mystic vision upon an otherwise radically empirical Buddhist thinker.

In defense of this interpretation of *dharma*, the following statements by Dōgen are suggested for consideration:

> The ocean speaks and mountains have tongues—that is the everyday speech of Buddha. . . . If you can speak and hear such words you will be one who truly comprehends the entire universe.[44]

When the ocean, mountain or whatever is experienced as it is, its primordial, untainted *dharma* nature "speaks" to the viewer. When the experiencer is equally united within the horizon, then one can "hear" or presence the *dharma* nature shared by all the constituents. By extension, the primordial nature of the "entire universe" is presenced as it is as well.

At this stage, we are prepared to examine the most important fascicle of *Shōbōgenzō*. Our study of the fascicle *Genjōkōan* will help us to further understand the mode of experience that Dōgen finds paradigmatic for "hearing" the "everyday speech of Buddha," i.e., experiencing things-as-they-are. The analysis of *Genjōkōan* will be preceded by a brief introduction concerning the philosophical proejct of *Shōbōgenzō*.

3. The Descriptive Project of Shōbōgenzō

Shōbōgenzō is a collection of Dōgen's discourses, given orally or written, from 1231 until his death in 1253. The phenomenological rigor of *Shōbōgenzō* is characterized by Dōgen's argumentation based on reference to everyday experience. Dōgen's foremost intention in *Shōbōgenzō* is to describe the most primordial mode of experience in which the world is presented to consciousness. He is concerned with describing faithfully a mode of experience void of unjustified presuppositions, metaphysical conceptualizations, ontological presuppositions or any other impairment to an authentic neutral encounter with the world. Dōgen's philosophical acumen in this regard is shrewd and rigorous. He aspires toward the highest philosophical standards, seeking to ground all tenets upon primordially given experiential evidence. As we have seen in Kūkai's philosophy, Dōgen seeks to transcend ordinary levels of discourse, often tainted by hidden presuppositions, by describing levels of awareness more thetically primordial. This quest leads him to describe ordinary experiences to which his audience can relate. In general each fascicle concentrates upon the nature of a specific aspect of experience, e.g., its contextual framework, temporal dimension, and so on.

This appeal to direct present experience was intended to justify his insistence upon the cultivation of zazen. To accomplish this task, Dōgen interlaced concrete and poetic images, pushing the language to its most expressive levels. Dōgen sought to break the encrusted habits of his readers' thinking and to evoke the paradigmatic mode of experience through the use of symbolic yet everyday nuances.[45] This method utilized in *Shōbōgenzō* arose as a result of Dōgen's previous unsuccessful attempts to communicate what we have come to call a "transfer" from second or third bodymind awareness to first order bodymind awareness.[46] Specifically, Dōgen abandons his initial attempts to describe how to perform zazen (*Fukanzazengi*) and to justify its prominent role in the history of Buddhist practice (*Bendōwa*) in favor of his technique in *Shōbōgenzō* of justifying zazen by describing the *experience* of zazen itself. The attempt to describe this mode of experience is most apparent in the first fascicle of *Shōbōgenzō* entitled *Genjōkōan*.[47]

a. *Genjōkōan*

The term *genjōkōan* ('present, existing, manifest' + 'become, do, perform, fulfill' + 'public' + 'proposition, opinion') is usually divided into two terms *genjō* (becoming present, presencing) and *kōan* (a paradoxical riddle given to students as the focus of

meditative practice in the Rinzai Zen tradition).[48] Adopting the
verbal form "presencing," we can interpret etymologically *genjōkōan* as the "presencing koan." More importantly however, this
interpretation is consistent with, and underscores, Dōgen's
philosophical intentions. Dōgen's foremost concern is to describe
the nature of experience as it is given *here and now* to consciousness. He seeks to suspend all thetic positings and thus allows
primordially given phenomena to be "presenced as-they-are." In
keeping with Dōgen's emphasis upon the oneness of cultivation-
authentication, the active verbal form of "presencing things-as-
they-are" reflects accurately Dōgen's use of the term as an activity.
In this way, presencing things-as-they-are describes the act of
cultivation-authentication which is itself the *kōan*.

The activity can be considered a different sort of *kōan* in the
sense that Dōgen is not concerned with "solving" a single paradoxical riddle, as is the case in traditional Rinzai practice, but seeks to
describe the mode of experience which allows one to be fully aware
of all situational contexts (*jisetsu*), especially those instructive contexts between Master and student. For Dōgen, when presencing
things-as-they-are, the student will give the accurate descriptive
response to the Master and thus "resolve" all *kōans*. The solution
therefore is not to be understood in a means-end context but, as we
have seen in the case of cultivation-authentication, as a mode of
experiential presencing wherein one is completely involved in the
dynamic and non-privileged character of the situation. From
another perspective this mode of experiencing may be considered a
kōan in that "it implies an attempt to do something that must not
be willfullly 'attempted.'"[49] In other words, one can not posit an
affirmative thetic intention, nor attempt to negate all intentions
for, in either case, the neutral mode of presencing things-as-they-
are is violated. In short, the "presencing *kōan*" (*genjōkōan*) will be
translated as "presencing things-as-they-are."

The theme of the fascicle *Genjōkōan* is to presence things-as-
they-are and the entire situation or occasion (*jisetsu*) as it is *in
toto*. The subsequent fascicles in *Shōbōgenzō* reiterate this theme
and thus encourage practitioners to transcend thetic judgments
concerning given occasions. For example in *Tsuki* Dōgen says not
to become attached to discursive thinking but "accept the drifting
clouds and moving boat as-they-are; advance beyond limited
ideas."[50] To impose one's own "limited ideas" and pass judgment
upon another is as foolish as a fish who seeks to fly after mastering

the water or a bird seeking to swim after mastering the air.[51] To be a reflection of one's own situation, versus reflecting the situation as it is given, is a sign of a narrow periphery and limited understanding. One must presence spontaneously his or her own situation and act accordingly. Dōgen explains:

> To master the Buddha way is to master oneself,
> To master oneself is to forget oneself,
> To forget oneself is to realize the myriads of dharmas,
> To realize the myriads of dharmas is to cast off one's body
>   and mind, and the body and mind of others.[52]

In this way "mastering oneself" requires forgetting I-it distinctions. Once such thetic distinctions are neutralized, the "myriads of dharmas" (things-as-experienced) are presented to consciousness. Ultimately, this is achieved by casting off body and mind of *self and other*. Again, the centrality of *shinjin datsuraku* is reinforced through a discussion of *genjōkōan*. Investigating a few ideas within the fascicle *Shinjingakudō* (*Learning [through] the Body and Mind]*) will help us to clarify Dōgen's specific ideas regarding casting off the body-aspect and mind-aspect in the quest to presence things-as-they-are.

b. *Shinjingakudō*

In the fascicle *Shinjingakudō* ('body' + 'mind' + 'study' + 'way,' hence *Learning [through] the Body and Mind*), Dōgen concentrates upon describing the inseparability of bodymind. Although he discusses the body-aspect and the mind-aspect individually, he prefaces his explanations by stating that each aspect represents a focus of concentration for the purposes of learning. Dōgen begins his analysis by discussing "learning through the mind." He says that diligent study may bring about an awareness of three states of mind — *kobutsushin* ("the eternal Buddha-mind"), *heijōshin* ("everyday mind"), and *sangai isshin* ("universal mind"). Yet, as we shall see below, each "mind" represents a description of a different aspect of the same "mind" — *hotsubodaishin* (*hotsu*, 'departure, radiate, start from' + *bodaishin*, 'devout disposition,' 'aspiration for Buddhahood'; this term is interpreted, not translated, as "learning through the mind." (This interpretation captures the notion that *hotsubodaishin* is the key term signifying the mind-aspect portion of *shinjingakudō* (learning [through] the body and mind). Using this term, Dōgen accentuates the *activity* of experiencing the Buddha-mind. He says harmonizing cultivation and authentication will lead one to the source of all the above minds, *hotsubodaishin*. Specifically he states:

> Even if the true enlightened mind has not yet arisen, you should study the dharma of the Buddha and the patriarchs who have previously given rise to the enlightened mind. It is the *hotsubodaishin*, every bit of the pure mind, the mind of past Buddhas, the ordinary mind, the one mind of the three worlds.[53]

Experiencing with this mind (mode of awareness) will bring the practitioner into a direct simultaneous encounter with *kobutsushin*, *heijōshin* and *sangai isshin*.

Dōgen describes this unifying character of "learning through the mind" as follows:

> These [sun, moon, and stars] are already mind. Are they inside or outside of it [mind], coming or going? . . . Coming and going is simply one or two thoughts of mind. And one thought or two thoughts are one mountain, river and great earth or two mountains, rivers and the great earth. Since things like mountains, rivers and the great earth are neither existent nor non-existent, they are neither big nor small. . . . You should decisively accept in faith that learning through the mind means regular practice of personally studying this kind of mind.[54]

There are a number of characteristics of learning through mind that may be interpreted from the passage above. Dōgen instructs that it is wrong to assume that things ("sun, moon and stars") exist either inside (idealism) or outside (materialism) this mind (mode of awareness). To make such ontic judgments are merely thetic acts which are reducible to "one thought" or "two thoughts." Dōgen also acknowledges that for each noetic act (one thought), there is a corresponding noematic meaning (one mountain). In addition, he says that from the perspective of learning through the mind, each of these possible objects of perception, are viewed as noemata, i.e., they are presenced as neither existing nor non-existing. More importantly, however, is his contention that even mountains, from this perspective, are not big or small. Phenomenologically speaking, this may be interpreted as presencing the mountain, river and great earth from a first order perspective. That is, only during this mode of awareness is the horizon presenced in such a manner that all potential noemata share a non-privileged position. Accordingly, no relative distinctions (big or small) can be assessed. There is no fixed (privileged) standard by which such judgments could be ascertained. Dōgen concludes this passage by suggesting that this perspective ought to be "regularly practiced" (sedimented). It would seem like a viable interpretation to suggest that "learning through the mind" reflects the condition of the mind-aspect during first order bodymind awareness. The mind-aspect (intensions) are thetically neutral allowing for the occurrence of a mode of experience structurally consistent with Dōgen's description above.

Similarly, Dōgen utilizes another term which describes the condition of the body-aspect (tensions) during first order body-mind awareness. He says that "learning through the mind" must be united with "learning through the body" (*shinjitsunintai*, 'truth' + 'reality' + 'human body,' literally, 'the real human body'). (Again, this interpretation is intended to reflect Dōgen's use of the term as representative of the body-aspect portion of *shinjingakudō* (learn-ing [through] the body and mind)). Learning through the body is said to be the "goal of Buddhist practice."[55] That is, to embody, internalize or sediment this paradigmatic mode of perpetual casting off, is to presence things-as-they-are throughout daily life. Again it is the on-going activity of neutralization itself that con-cerns Dōgen. Whereas *hotsubodaishin* refers to the dynamic activi-ty of the mind-aspect, *shinjitsunintai* is concerned with the dynamic activity of the body-aspect.

Dōgen describes an interesting characteristic of learning through the body as follows: "You at this moment and I at this moment are persons (which) are true human bodies exhausting the entire world."[56] Here Dogen emphasizes his contention that we are all capable of becoming aware of our Buddha-nature here and now. This awareness need not take aeons of time (*kalpas*) for there are certain to be moments along the way where each individual may study, practice and authenticate his or her originally enlightened character. An interesting paradox emerges in this statement which requires a closer examination. Learning through the body can be attained immediately "at this moment." Yet, at the same time, learning throught the body also "exhausts the entire world." In order to clarify this present yet all-pervasive feature of this experience we will turn to another of Dōgen's fascicles, *Uji*. This procuedure will enable us to expose the temporal character of *shinjitsunintai*.

c. *Uji*

Uji, which usually means "at a certain time," is interpreted by Dōgen as "being-time." For Dōgen, "*uji* means that time itself is being and each being is a time."[57] This rather unorthodox interpretation is intended to describe our direct experience of time. Analyzing this theory of time will serve three main purposes. First, as we have mentioned above, understanding the experiential mode of *shinjitsunintai* requires that we grasp the "present" yet "all-pervasive" aspects of sedimented enlightened experience. We will see that the paradox arises only from our presupposition that time is linear. That is, we assume that a present ("now") experience must be different from a temporal duration of experience that "exhausts the entire world." Second, Dōgen's denial of the usual linear sense of before and after will further clarify the idea of cultivation-authentication wherein a means-end relationship is rejected. Finally, an investigation of Dōgen's description of time-as-experienced will set the ground work for our phenomenological analysis (Chapter 6) of the temporal aspect of Dogen's paradigmatic mode of experience.

To begin, let us examine how Dōgen arrives at the notion of "being-time." Typically, Dōgen begins his fascicle *Uji* by challenging us to observe reflexively our experience. We notice that "for each thing (being) in experience, there is a time; for each time, there is a thing (being)."[58] Or, from another perspective, for each thing-as-experienced (dharma), there is a time; for each time, there is a thing-as-experienced (dharma). In either case, the practice of presencing illuminates an awareness of being (things-as-experienced/*dharma*) in time, hence "being-time." Since time itself is being and being itself is time, authentication of things-as-experienced occurs *at the same time* there is cultivation. Cultivation itself is authentication and authentication itself is cultivation. Dōgen describes this "temporal-aspect"[59] of presencing as follows:

Just when you arrive at the perspective on everything's being just as it is, a blade of grass *is* a phenomenon: to comprehend the phenomenon is not to comprehend 'the phenomenon' and to comprehend the blade of grass is not to comprehend 'the blade of grass.' Since this is nothing other than time's authentically being as

> it is, all beings-times (*uji*) are the whole of time, and each particular blade of grass as well as each phenomenon is a time. All of being, the whole universe, is within time as specific times. Isn't all of being and the whole universe included in this time? Contemplate this for awhile.[60]

To grasp the temporal-aspect of presencing Dōgen asks us to first enter the mode of experiencing things-as-they-are (*genjōkōan*). At this stage he says "a blade of grass is a phenomenon." Our phenomenological perspective helps us to recognize that Dōgen is referring to the blade of grass as it appears within the horizon (the phenomenon). Like first order bodymind awareness, presencing things-as-they-are describes a condition wherein all noetic vectors, e.g., toward a blade of grass, are neutralized. Therefore, when Dōgen suggests that to "comprehend a blade of grass is not to comprehend 'the blade of grass' he implies that to comprehend a blade of grass as it is within the horizon, is not to *intend* 'the blade of grass' as a privileged noematic focus. Once the horizon is presenced in this neutral manner Dōgen says that "this is nothing other than time's authentically being as it is." Here all beings are times such that each particular thing within the horizon, e.g., a blade of grass, is a time. The presencing of all the blades of grass in toto is what Dōgen calls "the whole of time." If one specific thing were a noema, then it would appear to accumulate a linear temporal history with respect to the background horizon. This linear notion of time, however, arises from one's own thetic positing. When one presences things-as-they-are, one recognizes that the horizon is the whole of time. Dōgen thus asks us to contemplate the fact that experience confirms the notion that "all of being (individual beings in toto) . . . is within (the whole of) time as specific times."

The notion of linear time as flying from the past, through the present, towards the future thus appears to be abstracted from concrete experiences of being-time. To think that time flies away is to separate ourselves from time-as-experienced. Dōgen asserts that time appears to fly away only if there is a "gap (between oneself and time)."[61] However, the primordial experience of presencing verifies that a pine tree or a piece of bamboo, experienced as a phenomenon, is time.

These phenomena, depicting the primordial giveness of the whole of time, may be reflected upon according to two acceptable perspectives for Dōgen. In each case, the individual presences the situation and acts; thus the perspective and experiential periphery is dictated by the occasion (*jisetsu*) and not one's self. In the first case, the occasion is likely to call for concentrated effort and a narrow periphery. Dōgen uses the example of climbing a mountain wherein time is presenced as "right now" (*nikon or nikon no ima*). This term does not refer to the theory of moments in which the present aspect is continually reaffirmed. To the contrary, "right now" is intended to underscore the individual's immersion in experience as it is given to consciousness. The project of climbing the mountain thus consumes one to the point that the experience of being and time (being-time) is limited to the confines of the limited periphery of the project at hand. In the second instance, our awareness may be governed by a totally different occasion (*jisetsu*). In the beginning of *Uji*, Dōgen likens being-time to being on the highest mountain top. Being on the top of a mountain is an entirely different situation than climbing one. Rather than being immersed in the project of climbing, one can sit back, as it were, relax and enjoy the view. While presencing this situation one would respond with an expanded periphery that Dōgen calls *keireki* or *kyōryaku* (ranging). "Ranging" refers to the non-directional, continuing, and connected aspect of time wherein an entire range of mountains (beings-times), for example, may be presenced in toto.

At this point, we can appreciate Dōgen's assertions with respect to *shinjitsunintai*. The sedimented enlightenment experience occurring "at this moment," yet "exhausting the entire universe," refers to the two basic responses an individual presencing one's situation may undertake—*nikon* or *kyōryaku*. Although neither perspective is more primary, each is an authentic reflection of the temporal mode of experience stimulated by the situation. In either case, there is no abstract notion of time divorced from the experiential situation. Applying what we have learned to cultivation-authentication, we realize that the cultivation experience is not a means toward future authentication of the *dharma*. Rather, cultivation occurs at the same time as the authentication of things-as-experienced (*dharma*). Finally, with respect to our third purpose for the preceding analysis of *Uji*, we have laid the groundwork for an analysis of being-time using our phenomenological categories in Chapter 6. In conclusion, we may add that the description of the temporal-aspect of the enlightenment experience serves to underscore the full and overbrimming character of presencing things-as-they-are. The entire experiential horizon, presenting *dharma* (things-as-experienced) to consciousness, occurs "right now" and fills the "range" of our periphery.

The last fascicle to be examined is called *Kaiizanmai*. It is particularly relevant to our phenomenological study as it is in this fascicle that Dōgen explicitly enumerates the relationship between body and mind-as-experienced during cultivation. Thus far, we have reiterated the importance and centrality of casting off body and mind (*shinjin datsuraku*) in the sense of neutralizing body-aspect tensions and mind-aspect intentions. We have not yet, however, acknowledged Dōgen's description of their mutual interpenetration as bodymind.

d. *Kaiinzanmai*

Kaiinzanmai[62] ('sea, ocean' + 'seal, imprint' + 'self-effacement, concentration, meditation (samadhi),' hence 'Ocean Imprint Meditation') is a term which traditionally names Shakyamuni Buddha's highest form of experiential insight. The title itself depicts a mode of awareness wherein the *dharma* is imprinted (sedimented) within and reflected by one's self as clearly as if it were an image cast by a quiet sea. Dōgen calls *kaiinzanmai* a mode of experience, which, when cultivated, "is a time for preaching and authenticating [the *dharma*]."[63] In other words, *kaiinzanmai* names the meditative mode of experiencing cultivation-authentication. Metaphorically, Dōgen describes this experiential condition as one which "breaks through the chain [of delusions]" (thetic positings). He says this process of "clearing away . . . is like all rivers confluently flowing [back] into the great ocean",[64] i.e., all things-as-experienced give up their privileged noematic status thus appearing to "flow back" (return) to a mutual non-privileged status amidst the experiential horizon.

Dōgen specifically begins to focus upon the relationship between "clearing away" and the body and mind. "Clearing away and breaking through" may be interpreted as referring to the neutralization of thetic positings as well as casting off body and mind. He says:

In the honorable words of Shakyamuni, "This body is synthesized merely by means of numerous dharmas. At the time of generation only dharmas are generated, and at the time of extinction, only dharmas become extinct. [Therefore] when dharmas are generated one does not say that an 'I' is generated. [Likewise] when dharmas become extinct, one does not say that an 'I' becomes extinct. Earlier thoughts and later thoughts do not depend on each other, nor do they oppose each other. This is called the samadhi of oceanic reflection.[65]

Accordingly, if, for example, the body and mind are posited as separate entities, they are "generated" as abstractions (body-aspect, mind-aspect). Once this separation is "generated" (affirmative thetic positing) or "extinguished" (negative thetic positing), even in the form of a hidden presupposition, the groundwork is set for the arising of "later thoughts" (thetic positings) creating a more explicit gap between noesis and noema, "they oppose each other." Consequently, if the body and mind are cast off, it appears as though the groundwork for additional thetic positings is simultaneously cast off. Our point is that Dōgen's emphasis upon *shinjin datsuraku* appears to be, in part, stimulated by his contention that positing a distinction between body and mind is the initial, sometimes hidden, presupposition which precedes the more obvious forms of intentionality, e.g., when noematic foci appear as visual "things-as-experienced" or receptors of noetic vectors.

Dōgen metaphorically describes this phenomenon by saying, "suddenly a fire starts."[66] He explains that things suddenly (thetically) appear as distinct from one another and arise from a ground that is itself distinctionless. If no *dharmas* (things-as-experienced) thetically "arise" with a privileged position with respect to the rest of the horizon, then the relative distinction between the forementioned earlier and later thoughts would be eliminated. In this regard, the structure of the ocean imprint meditation shares a basic feature of first order bodymind awareness — simultaneity. Given a non-privileged horizon, no temporal distinctions regarding "earlier" or "later" thoughts could arise (there is no privileged standard to serve as a criterion for such temporal judgments). In Dōgen's words:

The very temporal fruition of the samadhi of oceanic reflection is a temporal fruition [brought forth] 'solely by means of all dharmas,' and is an expression 'solely by means of all dharmas.' At a time like this, we say that 'the body is composed.' This body is nothing but an aspect of one unity which is composed of dharmas. Do not regard this body merely as an aspect of the composed but rather regard it as being composed of all dharmas. What I mean by 'this body' is a body that is synthesized [of all dharmas].[67]

The body, therefore, as "an aspect of one unity" [bodymind], is presenced within the horizon as a whole. Bodymind appears as sharing the non-privileged horizon wherein "all dharmas" are presenced equally.

In this way, casting off body and mind undercuts the foundation for thetic intentions. The presence of a thetically separated body and mind covers the bodymind ground allowing for the possibility of more obvious forms of separation amidst the horizon, viz., noetic/noematic distinctions. It must be remembered, however, that Dōgen is not speaking of any metaphysical separation of body and mind. He merely describes thetic separation that appears as an initial doxic modality that prepares for a transition from first order awareness, where the bodymind ground is experienced directly within the horizon, to second order awareness where the bodymind ground is hidden by thetic intervention. The ocean imprint texperience, like first order bodymind awareness, names the mode of experience which verifies implicitly the presence of bodymind inseparability at base of all experience. Dōgen describes this primordial mode of awareness as follows:

A temporal situation of the extinct 'I' is not-saying and a temporal situation of the generated 'I' is not-saying, even though both are the birth of not-saying, they are not the same death of not-saying. It is already an extinction of earlier dharmas and that of later dharmas. It is the dharmas' earlier and later thoughts. Being-dharmas is of earlier and later dharmas, and is of earlier and later thoughts. Non-dependence is being-dharmas and non-opposition is being-dharmas. If you can make [dharmas] non-dependent, and non-opposed, it would be a near perfect expression [dotoku].[68]

This quotation reveals a vivid description of a mode of awareness which neatly parallels the phenomenological structure of first order bodymind awareness. First, the beginning of this passage reinforces our previous phenomenological interpretation of the temporal structure of the ocean imprint experience. When all thetic positings have been "extinguished" the experiencer is left presencing the simultaneity of an entire experiential horizon characterized by "non-dependence" and "non-opposition." Dōgen then suggests that this mode of awareness arises when all thoughts (noesis) and all *dharmas* (noemata, things-as-experienced) disappear (are neutralized). When this occurs, the *dharmas* are presenced as "non-dependent" and "non-opposing." In other words, all *dharma* are experienced as sharing equally a non-privileged horizon. In conclusion, Dōgen offers a rare explicit statement equating the forementioned characteristics with those of a "near perfect expression."

In the remainder of the *Kaiinzanmai* fascicle, Dōgen continues to describe the condition wherein the awareness of body-mind is authenticated. This project entails further development of the "high level of detachment" in which the horizon itself becomes presenced *in toto*. Briefly summarizing Dōgen's method, he equates everyday actions, e.g., "reaching for a pillow at night," and various formulations of "non-attachment" with *kaiinzanmai*.[69] In addition, he systematically equates cultivation, non-attachment, authentication, and presencing, together. In this way the meaning of *kaiinzanmai* is communication. In short, the "imprint" of *dharma* is reflected in a "sea" of non-discrimination. Or, perhaps more accurately, *kaiinzanmai* is a "printless print" characteristic of the non-privileged ocean. Once experienced, bodymind awareness reveals itself as the product of casting off separate notions of body and mind.

Chapter 6

Dōgen: First Order Bodymind
Awareness as Enlightenment

In this chapter the paradigmatic mode of experience cultivated in Zen meditation (zazen) will be analyzed. We will begin by outlining characteristics of the actual technique of zazen practice and subsequently apply our phenomenological categories to further lay bare this mode of awareness. Since Dōgen's justification and defense of zazen is largely a descriptive endeavor, at least in *Shōbōgenzō*, a similarly descriptive phenomenological analysis may provide an appropriate vehicle to clarify Dōgen's work. A phenomenological hermeneutic will help to tie together a number of issues related to our topic. First, the relationship between Sōtō Zen philosophy, as described in Chapter 5, and zazen awareness will be clarified. Second, insofar as zazen awareness is considered to be the paradigmatic mode of experience which acts as a mutual referent between theory and practice in Sōtō Zen philosophy, a phenomenology of zazan awareness is particularly appropriate. Third, in Chapter 5 it was suggested that understanding casting off body and mind (*shinjin datsuraku*) may provide a key to understanding the ground of Dōgen's philosophical positions. A phenomenological analysis of this practice will enhance our understanding of this important activity. Recall that Dōgen himself exclaimed, "students, cast aside your bodies and minds and enter fully into Buddhism." Finally, a phenomenological analysis of zazen awareness (the act of casting off body and mind) will help to focus our study upon the bodymind ground that appears to be so central to the Sōtō tradition that it is often presupposed and is in need of explicit articulation.

In *Bendōwa* and *Fukanzazengi* Dōgen is emphatic in his defense of "just sitting" (*shikantaza*) in order to sediment the mode of zazen awareness. Unlike Kūkai, for example, who returned from China loaded with *sutras, mandalas*, incense, and so on, Dōgen advocated, above all others, the importance of one form of cultivation—zazen. He says, "Sanzen is body and mind being cast off. It is attained only in singleminded sitting [*shikantaza*]."[1] In addition, Dōgen was skeptical about the power of discursive reasoning to being about enlightenment:

> You should . . . cease from practice based on intellectual understanding, pursuing words and following after speech, and learn from the backward step that turns your light inwardly to illuminate yourself. Body and mind of themselves will drop away, and your original face will be manifest. If you want to attain suchness, you should practice suchness without delay.[2]

Here we witness what we might anachronistically refer to as Dōgen's reflexive phenomenological attitude. This "inward" examination of experience awakens one to the bodymind ground of all experience. Once this is recognized, the propensity to posit a separate body and mind is seen as an inauthentic representation of bodymind awareness. Hence, body and mind seem to "drop away of themselves." Thus the "original face" in which the self shares an equal, non-privileged, position amidst one's experiential horizon is presented.

Our analysis will begin with a section focusing upon Dōgen's specific instructions concerning the "technique" of cultivating zazen awareness. The remainder of the chapter will, in effect, phenomenologically analyze this technique as well as Dōgen's descriptive accounts of the various aspects of zazen awareness.

1. The Technique of Cultivating Zazen Awareness

To begin, let us turn to Dōgen's account of how to perform zazen. After we have reproduced this famous description, we will utilize it to help explain the relationship between the said technique and first order bodymind awareness.

> For sanzen [in this particular case, a synonym for zazen], a quiet room is suitable. Eat and drink moderately. Cast aside all involvements and cease all affairs. Do not think good or bad. Do not administer pros and cons. Cease all movements of the conscious mind, the gauging of all thoughts and views. Have no designs on becoming a Buddha. (Sanzen) has nothing whatsoever to do with sitting or lying down.

> At the site of your regular sitting, spread out a thick matting and place a cushion above it. Sit either in the full-lotus or half-lotus position. In the full-lotus position, you first place your right foot on your left thigh and your left foot on your right thigh. In the half-lotus, you may simply press your left foot against your right thigh. You should have your robes and belt loosely bound and arranged in order. Then place your right hand on your left leg and your left palm (facing upwards) on your right palm, thumb-tips touching. Thus sit upright in correct bodily posture, neither inclining to the left nor to the right, neither leaning forward or backward. Be sure your eyes are on a plane with your shoulders and your nose in line with your navel. Place your tongue against the front roof of your mouth, with teeth and lips both shut. Your eyes should always remain open, and you should breath gently through your nose. Once you have adjusted your posture, take a deep breath, inhale and exhale, rock your body right and left and settle into a steady immobile sitting position. Think of not-thinking. How do you think of not-thinking? Without thinking.* This in itself is the essential art of zazen.

> The zazen I speak of is not learning meditation. It is simply the Dharma-gate of repose and bliss, the cultivation-authentication* of totally culminated enlightenment. It is the presencing of things-as-they-are.[3]

The conditions described above prepare the practitioner to experience directly first order bodymind awareness. Each step is designed to aid the process of neutralizing body-aspect tensions and mind-aspect intentions. Once the practitioner enters this mode of awareness, the presencing of things-as-they-are occurs and the forementioned philosophical theories are recognized as being mutually referent to the practice. Dōgen begins his account seeking moderation in all phases of cultivating zazen awareness. The room is to be familiar and quiet. Familiarity is important, for if the occasion (*jisetsu*) is one in which the student is "familiar" (due to the historicity included in the meaning of the horizon), then he or she will feel comfortable and the actual operations of experience will become much more evident. For example, in Chapter 2, we noted that musicians and athletes are very "familiar" with the "occasion" of performing their particular skills. When the transfer from second to first order bodymind awareness occurs, the familiar horizon is presenced as never before. Yet, since this horizon is indeed familiar, that which is most striking is the *new* mode of experience itself. The aspects of this experience, e.g., extended periphery, dynamism, simultaneity, and bodymind ground, are recognized more fully if the horizon is one with which the student is most familiar. The same relation holds with the practice of zazen. Familiar and quiet surroundings lend themselves to an environment in which subtle differences in one's mode of awareness are most recognizable.

The next few sentences reiterate the need to neutralize all affirmative and negative thetic intentions. This is a main theme to which Dōgen frequently alludes. We will therefore postpone our discussion of this important theme until we can discuss it at length in our next session.

The last statement at the end of the first paragraph and the bulk of the second paragraph may seem paradoxical without further explanation. Dōgen says, "*Sanzen* has nothing whatever to do with sitting" and then carefully describes the do's and don'ts of proper sitting technique. Strictly speaking, proper zazen is an attitude; a mode of awareness (presencing) and not a meditative technique or posture. Cultivation is authentication when one presences things-as-they-are and is not contingent upon the practitioner's activity. Although cultivation-authentication is not limited to sitting in a full-lotus position, it is possible to explain how this technique aids the novice to become aware of the occurrence of first order bodymind awareness.

Performing the correct posture is a form of *shinjitsunintai* (lit. true human body, interpreted in Chapter 5 as "learning through the body-aspect"). The important point to remember in this regard is that, for Dōgen, since the body and mind are verified experientially as one, then any effort focused upon the body-aspect will have a direct affect upon the mind-aspect. Correct posture has such an affect. Any physical tension or impairment of the physiological functions inevitably affects mind-aspect intentions and thus diminishes the possibility of a direct awareness of presencing things-as-they-are. In Dōgen's words, "It [the goal of practice] should be a body sitting crosslegged [full-lotus posture]. It should be a mind sitting crosslegged. It should be a body and mind cast off sitting crosslegged."[4] Therefore, when a student asks "is the Way attained via the body or mind?" he answers, "the Way is attained through the body."[5] Yet we must understand that this is because "the Buddha Dharma from the first preaches that body and mind are not two, that substance and form are not two."[6] Consequently, Dōgen instructs:

With an upright body [full lotus], the mind is easily rectified. In upright sitting the mind does not grow slothful. With an upright mind and right thought, mental activity is concentrated right before you. If the mind strays, if the body starts to waver, you put them to rest and into your command again. If you wish to realize samadhi, if you wish to enter samadhi, put all your wandering thoughts and various discords and disorders to rest. Practice in this way and you will enter into realization of the King of Samadhis Samadhi.[7]

In sum, proper sitting can help the practitioner to become aware of the original bodymind ground of all modes of experience.

Dōgen also makes explicit the purpose of *shikantaza* ("just sitting") and zazen awareness. *Shikantaza* is a discipline intended to aid the practitioner to become aware and cultivate zazen awareness, i.e., presencing things-as-they-are (first order bodymind awareness). To experience regularly a mode of awareness in which "body and mind are cast off," Dōgen says, "we must protect and uphold the mind, thought, and perceptions and examine exhaustively all thoughts and views of this attainment."[8] This, then, is our task. By thoroughly examining the various aspects of this experience, we will become better acquainted with Dōgen's emphasis upon applying zazen awareness, cultivated during *shikantaza*, to daily life. For example, zazen awareness must be maintained during the four bodily attitudes (*shi-igi*), viz., moving, standing, sitting and lying down.[9] In this way, the student internalizes this mode of experience in body and mind. *Jijuyū* ('oneself' + 'receives' + 'uses') samadhi refers to this mode of sedimented awareness in which presencing things-as-they-are is "realized and sustained."[10]

The specific affects of proper posture upon first order body-mind awareness are as follows. Dōgen describes the correct posture as "immovable."[11] To sit "immovably" means that physiologically the weight of one's body must settle about two-and-a-half inches below the navel. This physiological center lies at the base of the pelvic girdle which supports the weight of the entire upper body. When all tensions and intensions, such as anger which causes tension in the upper body, are neutralized, the weight of the upper body naturally settles to this physiological center and we sit "immovable." Furthermore, Dōgen instructs "rock your body right and left and *settle* into a steady, immovable sitting position." Here "settle" refers to both the body and mind. By focusing one's single second order noetic intention upon the vertex/fulcrum of this rocking movement, one's mind-aspect intention becomes focused upon the physiological center of the body-aspect.[12] Thus body-aspect and mind-aspect are systematically joined in preparation for first order bodymind awareness. Relaxed and full breathing issues from this lower region. When intentions and tensions are neutralized one's breath "settles" in this area. For this reason Dōgen instructs "take a deep breath, inhale and exhale." Becoming aware of the repetitions of one's breath serves to neutralize extraneous thetic intentions. Thus, if one follows Dōgen's instructions concerning posture, one can cultivate a mode of awareness in which most body-aspect tensions and mind-aspect intentions are neutralized (by focusing a single noetic intention upon the physiological center of the body). Accordingly, numerous qualities of first order bodymind awareness have been systematically implanted making the transition from second to first order awareness more natural.

There is one final point regarding zazen technique which is most noteworthy. We have emphasized throughout that for Kūkai and Dōgen enlightenment is not an other-worldly, transcendental experience. Rather, we have seen that enlightenment is rooted in this phenomenal world. For this reason Dogen requests that the practitioner's "eyes should always remain open." Presencing things-as-they-are requires that all one's senses be acutely aware and sensitive (expanded periphery) to the present situation (*jisetsu*). Illustrative examples of calm yet aware sitting can be seen through Japanese temple artwork. The statues of Buddha within the temple always depict a serene state and soft body. In the

Japanese meditative tradition the phrase *jigen onyō* ('merciful eyes' + 'kindly face,' hence 'merciful eyes and gentle body') describes this calm yet alert state of the Buddha who presences things-as-they-are. In contrast, the phrase *nio-zen* (meaning sitting in zazen with a tense abdomen and staring eyes) describes the fierce appearance of the statues of the temple guards (*niōmon*) which are forever situated outside the temple never being permitted to enter the serenity of the temple itself. The peaceful face of the Buddha with eyes open thus reflects a mode of expanded awareness, whereas the angry faces of temple guardians reflect a single-minded intention of protection which is narrow and thus does not entitle them to enter the gates of the temple. Accordingly, Dōgen encourages zazen practitioners to open their eyes and all senses. He often suggest that students set their eyes on that which is immediately present in order to impel his students to neutralize extraneous intentions and presence the immediate situation in an alert manner. This technique once again elicits a characteristic of first order bodymind awareness—the expanded periphery.

Having concluded our discussion of the relation between the physiological technique of zazen and first order bodymind awareness, we will move on to explore further the relation between the physiological technique of zazen and first order bodymind awareness.

2. *Hishiryō* and Thetic Neutralization

Referring once again to our lengthy quotation from *Fukan-zazengi*, Dōgen says:

> Cast aside all involvements and cease all affairs. Do not think of good or bad. Do not administer pros and cons. Cease all movements of the conscious mind, the gauging of all thoughts and views. . . . Think of not-thinking. How do you think of not-thinking? Without thinking. This in itself is the essential art of zazen.

The first three sentences are readily recognizable as examples of the neutralization of thetic positings to which we keep referring. In the second section of this quotation, however, Dōgen explicitly refers to "without thinking" (*hishiryō*) which is a technical term paralleling our contemporary phenomenological category of "neutralization." Just as "neutralization" has been seen to reflexively transcend both affirmative and negative thetic intentions, "without thinking" (*hishiryō*) reflexively transcends both "thinking" (*shiryō*) and "not thinking" (*fushiryō*). "Thinking" (*shiryō*) is used by Dōgen to represent affirmative thetic positings. "Not-thinking" (*fushiryō*), of course, designates the denial of thinking and is itself a negative thetic positing. Therefore to represent the mode of neutral prescencing, which transcends thetic judgments and frees attachment to body-aspects and mind-aspects, Dōgen uses the term "without thinking."

Although *hishiryō* has been alternatively translated as "non-thinking" and "super-thinking," I believe "without thinking"[13] most accurately conveys Dōgen's intentions regarding intentionality. In his fascicle *Zazenshin*, Dōgen calls this mode of awareness one which is "crystal clear"[14] and thus describes another familiar characteristic of presencing things-as-they-are and first order bodymind awareness. Since "without thinking" describes the neutral ground of subsequent affirmative (*shiryō*) or negative (*fushiryō*) thetic positings, it describes the most primordially given mode of enlightened consciousness with which we are already most familiar. Dōgen summarizes the importance of this mode of awareness in the following manner:

> The act of shaving the head and donning black robes is precisely converting the mind, illuminating the mind. Leaving the city and entering the mountains is going out from and entering one mind. Entering in a mountain is to think of not-thinking, leaving the world is without thinking.[15]

"Without thinking" (*hishiryō*) can be interpreted as a synonym for "presencing things as-they-are" (*genjōkōan*). The difference in meaning parallels the relationship between "thetic neutralization" and "first order bodymind awareness." In both instances the former term is the more specific and describes the thetic operation characteristic of the more general second term.

Dōgen uses the concept of "without thinking" as a touchstone for further clarification of other aspects of zazen awareness. This should be familiar to us, since, in Chapter 2, we described thetic neutralization as the prerequisite necessary for a direct awareness of the horizon and its accompanying characteristics, viz., an expanded periphery, dynamism, simultaneity, and bodymind awareness. In discussions of the self and zazen awareness, Dōgen says, "to learn one's self is to forget one's self" or "to learn one's self is to master one's self." By neutralizing or "forgetting" one's self-as-posited, the self-as-primordially-experienced issues forth and is thus "mastered." Hence, "to forget one's self is to be confirmed by all dharmas. . . ." Since *dharmas* are "things-as-experienced," our own *dharma*-nature is discovered when the self-as-experienced is presenced amidst the horizon in toto. Here we see the use of "without thinking" (forgetting) as a touchstone for presencing the horizon wherein all *dharmas* are authenticated. Accordingly Dōgen continues, "To be confirmed by all dharmas is to effect the casting off of one's body and mind. . . ." In this way, "without thinking," like thetic neutralization, is a prerequisite necessary for a direct awareness of the horizon and its accompanying characteristics, e.g., authentication of *dharmas* (things-as-experienced), casting off body and mind, authenticating one's original Buddha-nature, presencing the occasion (*jisetsu*) which "answers" koans, and so forth.[16]

The awareness of "without thinking" is authenticated in the same manner as complete thetic neutralization. In Chapter 2, we noted that when all noetic vectors are neutralized, the experiential periphery begins to expand. Rather than focusing upon a single static noematic focus, one's awareness permeates the horizon as a whole. Thetic experience consequently differs from neutral experience in that the former mode of awareness points toward its noematic focus and the latter mode of awareness permeates the experiential horizon. For Dōgen, the occurrence of "without thinking" is authenticated in a similar manner. The following quotation is illustrative of such authentication.

When the Dharma is still not fully realized in man's body and mind, he thinks it is already sufficient. When the Dharma is fully present in his body and mind, he thinks there is some insufficiency. For example, boarding a boat and sailing out to the midst of a mountainless sea, we look around and see no other aspect but the circle of the sea. Yet this great ocean is not circular, nor is it four-sided. It's remaining virtue is exhaustible.[17]

In the first sentence, Dōgen says the *dharma* is not authenticated when one "thinks it is already sufficient," i.e., when one perceives it in a static, privileged manner. In this case the *dharma* only appears to be grasped. Dōgen then states that when the *dharma* is truly authenticated, it appears to be "insufficient"; it appears to be quite illusive, defying noetic/noematic compartmentalization. Dōgen illustrates this metaphorically by stating that the "insufficient" experience is like being in the midst of the ocean. Here seeing "no aspect but the circle of sea" refers to presencing the horizon *in toto*. In contrast to a "sufficient" noetic/noematic experience, this "insufficient" mode of pervasive presencing is authenticated by its ability to point beyond itself. In the midst of the sea even though one's experiential periphery appears to be circular, one is aware that this is an "insufficient" account of the ocean's (*dharma's*) "inexhaustible" nature. In other words, accompanying the awareness of an expanded periphery, is an awareness of the "insufficiency" of our experience to presence the "inexhaustible" totality of *dharma*—the Dharmakāya. Similarly, Dōgen says that Buddha-nature, being inexhaustible, cannot be at once experienced in its entirety.[18] Authentic awakening to the Buddhanature within the experiential periphery points beyond our finite perceptions. At this stage, we can understand that the "insufficiency" characteristic of "without thinking" points to the infinite abode of possible experience. In this way, both thetic neutralization and "without thinking" are authenticated *via* the presence of an expanded periphery that points beyond itself.

This important concept can become even more clear if we recall Dōgen's metaphor of the flagpole in Chapter 5. "Without thinking" describes the mode of not clinging to the flagpole representative of spiritual attainment. To continue to climb the flagpole, reach the top, and strive even beyond the pole is to "forget" the pole and its finite stature. This step away from the security of the flagpole is to enter into an experiential abode which "points beyond itself" toward infinity. The practitioner realizes that enlightenment is not a thing to possess or posit. Rather, it is a process of the continual cultivation of presencing the world as-it-is primordially given, yet, at the same time, experiencing a feeling of insufficiency motivating the individual to continue the presencing process. The presencing of thing-as-experienced (*dharma*) is thus never complete and points beyond itself to the infinitude of the Dharmakāya. In the fascicle *Kannon* ('*The Bodhisattva of Compassion*') Dōgen illustrates this insufficient characteristic of "without thinking."

In Ungan's saying 'Daihi Bodhisattva uses numerous hands and eyes,' the expression 'numerous' does not mean only 84,000 hands and eyes, and it certainly does not mean numbers like 12 or 32 or 33. 'Numerous' means 'innumerable'. An expression such as 'numerous' is beyond the limits of a given classification. And since it is already beyond the limits of a given classification, it should further be limited beyond the boundless. The number of uses of 'numerous' should be examined in this way.[19]

Hence, we recognize that the infinite qualities of *Kannon*, represented by his many hands and eyes, are never completely presenced. Dōgen suggests that it is not enough to know that *Kannon* is all-pervasive. One must also be aware that our finite experiential periphery points to, but never grasps, *Kannon's* totality. Recognizing this, one frees himself from the attachment of being conscious of a *thing* called "Buddha-nature" or "enlightenment." Stepping beyond the flagpole entails a transfer from sufficient second order positing (clinging to the flagpole) to the insufficiency of first order bodymind awareness. Consequently, "enlightenment" is recognized as a *mode of continued awareness*. Insufficient awareness moves beyond its incomplete nature, and is not a static group of truths to be treasured. In Dōgen's words, "When buddhas are genuinely buddhas there is no need for them to be conscious that they are buddhas. Yet they are realized buddhas, and thus continue to realize buddha."[20]

It is natural that we have been led into a discussion of the expanded periphery and horizon by our attempt to describe the relation between Dōgen's "without thinking" and thetic neutralization. This is, of course, due to the fact that the expanded periphery and horizon are merely phenomenological categories describing various discernible aspects of "without thinking" (zazen awareness) and first order bodymind awareness.

3. The Expanded Periphery, Horizon In Toto and Zazen Awareness

Above, we have mentioned that the feeling of "insufficiency" authenticates "without thinking." We noticed that this feeling arises due to the presence of an expanded periphery which points beyond itself. Because there is no single noetic vector to channel one's awareness, this "pointing" must be recognized as a metaphorical gesture applicable to the heightened sensitivity of all our perceptions. However, we must remember that even though the experiential periphery is expanded, it is still a mode of presencing a finite number of dharmas. The universal Dharmakāya may be presenced in a special sense; however, this ought not be interpreted as a mode of awareness in which the consciousness of the Sōtō practitioner becomes universally omnipresent or omniscient.

For example, Dōgen explains:

> Seeing forms and hearing sounds with their [enlightened ones'] body and mind as one, they make them intimately their own and fully know them; but it is not like a reflection in a mirror, or like the moon and the water. When they realize one side, the other side is dark.[21]

This is a rare instance when Dōgen clarifies that although presencing things-as-they-are allows one to become aware of things-as-experienced (*dharmas*) as clear as a "reflection in a mirror," it *does not* mean that the totality of the Dharmakāya is also presenced. Rather, what lies beyond the immediate experiential periphery is "darkness." This is precisely the reason why the mode of "without thinking" is "insufficient." Therefore, even though one "sees forms," "hears sounds," and is aware of bodymind oneness "fully," while presencing with an expanded periphery, one only experiences a microcosm of *dharma*.

This point is not intended to demean or secularize the enlightenment experience but merely to clarify the common mistaken notion that the whole of reality is experienced during enlightenment. This interpretation arises from such passages as below:

> Man attaining enlightenment is like the reflection of the moon on the water. The moon does not get wet, the water is not broken. For all the breadth and vastness of its light, it rests upon a small patch of water. Both the whole moon and the sky in its entirety come to rest in a single dewdrop of grass, in a mere drop of water. Enlightenment does not destroy man anymore than the moon breaks a hole in the water. Man does not obstruct enlightenment any more than the drop of dew obstructs the moon and the heavens.[22]

A common yet mistaken interpretation is as follows: By presencing a single dewdrop in an unobstructed manner, in which neither man nor object possesses a privileged position within the horizon, the totality of *dharmas* may be experienced. This follows from assuming that if the entire moon is perfectly reflected in a single dewdrop, then the totality of *dharmas* must be able to be known through correct observation of the dewdrop. Once again this incorrectly assumes that enlightenment is some body of truths or secrets that transcends finite presencing. This passage actually serves to underscore the authenticity of the microcosmic awareness of things-as-experienced within the limits of the periphery. Within the periphery, the *quality* of presencing is pure, unobstructed and ensures that things-as-experienced (*dharmas*) are witnessed as they are primordially given to consciousness. However, the *quantity* of all *dharmas* are not presenced at this time. If this were true, enlightenment would become something which transcends the act of presencing things-as-they-are. It would become static and quantitatively sufficient. Rather, presencing is qualitatively accurate and quantitatively insufficient. This insufficiency points beyond itself and motivates the practitioner to sediment this experience into his daily life. The dewdrop is merely a metaphor for the whole body of truth—the Dharmakāya. The dewdrop, reflecting all things clearly, becomes a mirror or authentic microcosm of the macrocosm of *dharmas* surrounding it. The quality of presencing one's situation (*jisetsu*) is complete yet the quantity of *dharmas* presenced is sufficient and therefore remains dynamic, not static.

Dōgen utilizes the entire fascicle *Ikkamyōju* ('One Bright Pearl', another metaphor for the Dharmakāya) to explain this notion of presencing as a qualitatively accurate reflection of things-as-experienced and a quantitatively limited reflection of *dharmas* as a whole. The title itself signifies that microcosmic presencing is equivalent to the act of enlightenment itself. Presencing is like a single "bright pearl" that is quantitatively small yet qualitatively valuable. Dōgen describes each thing-as-experienced (*dharma*) as a bright pearl which authenticates the mode of enlightened awareness. In fact, Dōgen says this "bright pearl is the Eye of the True Law" designated by the word, "*Shōbōgenzō.*"

Like Kūkai, Dōgen acknowledges explicitly that bodymind awareness arises during a state in which the periphery is expanded and the horizon is presenced *in toto*. Dōgen acknowledges that presencing the horizon means that no specific thing has a privileged position with respect to the rest of the horizon. He says the "undivided mind" is not characterized by big or small, one thought or two thoughts, known or not known, existent or non-existent, obtained or not obtained, enlightenment or non-enlightenment.[23] In addition, he recognizes other familiar characteristics of the horizon when he says that "When you authenticate emptiness, there is neither affirming nor non-affirming."[24] Interpreting phenomenologically, one might say that the horizon is presenced in a non-privileged manner wherein all affirmative and negative thetic positings are neutralized. Dōgen's explicit statements regarding the occurrence of an expanded periphery during the mode of presencing are no less striking. In his work before Shōbōgenzō, throughout the Shōbōgenzō period and even within the works edited after Dōgen's death, there are many references to alert states of awareness in which sights, sounds, and smells issue forth for the first time in a crystal clear manner.[25]

Such heightened states of awareness might be encouraged since their occurrence authenticates, in phenomenological language, the complete neutralization of all noetic vectors. This state of awareness is in itself valuable as it makes the Zen practitioner acutely aware of the difference between neutral experience and thetic experience. After presencing a mode of primordial expanded awareness, the process of how the size of the experiential periphery is directly determined by one's thetic involvement within the context of the situation is made clear. Henceforth, the practitioner is able to see how hidden suppositions introduce thetic delusions which prohibit the presencing of things-as-they-are. A thorough acquaintance with presencing the complete horizon also helps the Zen practitioner to understand what suppositions are "proper" and thus included within the horizon. We may recall that the historicity of a situation is included within the horizon which is primordially given to consciousness. Accordingly, if the situation is presenced and the discursive, musical, or athletic sedimented skills are required, then the individual is free to utilize any mode of awareness deemed appropriate. Understanding the situation as given, therefore, helps the practitioner to distinguish between the given and the projected aspects of a situation. In this way, the manner in which past experiences affect the present situation is clarified. The enlightened person is one who can presence the situation as given and the unenlightened person is one who posits his own situation.[26]

Thus far our phenomenological categories, descriptive of various aspects of first order bodymind awareness, have helped to unpack various aspects of zazen awareness. We have suggested that Dōgen's description of zazen awareness includes viable counterparts to the hermeneutic categories of our phenomenological analysis. The next category of "dynamism" is no exception. In Chapter 2 we saw dynamism to be a characteristic of first order bodymind awareness. In section 4, which follows, we will see that it is also an aspect of zazen awareness. Like first order bodymind awareness, we will see that Dōgen insists that dynamism not only describes accurately the zazen mode of awareness but also is empirically verified by a direct experience of a dynamic horizon.

4. Dynamism and Zazen Awareness

Dōgen's experiential, or even phenomenological, approach to Buddhism calls for experiential verification of all Buddhist doctrines. One of the most characteristically Buddhist doctrines is that of *impermanence*. For Dōgen this doctrine is verified experientially during zazen awareness. Since we are already familiar with the nature of dynamism in first order bodymind awareness, we will utilize our knowledge of this category to describe phenomenologically the dynamic aspect of zazen awareness, the authentication of impermanence.

In no uncertain terms Dōgen says, "Impermanence is a fact before our eyes."[27] On another occasion he says, "If our vision is true, *activity* will be seen to function naturally in physical objects and our understanding of phenomena will be complete." (italics mine)[28] "True vision" suggests zazen awareness. "Activity" and "impermanence" may therefore be interpreted as aspects of phenomena primordially given to consciousness within the horizon. This dynamic activity is, in part, responsible for the "insufficient" aspect of zazen awareness. Yet, presencing a state of constant flux is itself to be valued (given the existential ontological suppositions of Dōgen's radical empiricism). First, it is a paradigmatic mode of experience because it authenticates the proper mode of zazan awareness, and second, it describes faithfully another aspect of the horizon as it is primordially given. For these reasons Dōgen instructs:

'Life is the manifestation of the total dynamism: death is a manifestation of the total dynamism.' You should clarify and penetrate this utterance in practice. What you must penetrate is this: although the principle of 'life is the manifestation of the total dynamism' covers all the world and all space, without concern for beginnings or endings, not only does it hinder [any] 'life as the manifestation of the total dynamism,' it does not even hinder [any] 'death as the manifestation of the total dynamism.'[29]

Here Dōgen is most explicit with respect to the dynamic characteristic of zazen awareness. When abstract concepts like life and death are neutralized, the practitioner simply presences a dynamic non-privileged horizon wherein neither *spatial* (this experience is said to "cover all the world") nor *temporal* (relative distinctions such as "life" and "death" require a second order privileged criterion according to which temporal judgments may be posited) characterizations are applicable. Without fixed or static positings, there are no obstacles to hinder one's awareness of "total dynamism." Dōgen describes the procedure for presencing this non-privileged, dynamic horizon as follows:

When you simply release and forget both your body and your mind and throw yourself into the house of the Buddha, and when functioning comes from the direction of the Buddha and you go in accord with it, then with no strength needed and no thought expended, freed from birth and death, you become Buddha. Then there can be no obstacle in any man's mind.[30]

Interpreting phenomenologically, neutralizing the mind-aspect (intentions) and body-aspect (tensions) frees oneself of all obstacles and thus allows one to presence the "functioning" (dynamism) at the base of all experience.

Positing some thing as permanent (creating an "obstacle") is a ramification of one's own intentions during second order bodymind awareness. Dōgen does not, therefore, deny the appearance of permanence but merely states that it is a by-product of one's own thetic intervention:

When a man goes off in a boat and looks back to see the shoreline, he mistakenly thinks the shore is moving. If he keeps his eyes closely on his boat, he realizes it is the boat that is advancing. In like manner, when a person [tries to] discern and affirm the myriad dharmas with a confused conception of [his own] body and mind, he mistakenly thinks his own mind and his own nature are permanent. If he makes all his daily deeds intimately his own and returns within himself, the reason that the myriad dharmas are without self will become clear to him.[31]

First, Dōgen explains that positing the shoreline or boat as noematic foci leads to different conclusions. Recognizing that the fault of the situation must be in something that approximates the act of thetic positing itself, Dōgen states that the boatman must "return within himself" and, according to our vocabularly, neutralize the proto-thetic positing of all subsequent thetic positing, viz., the initial thetic distinction between "his own mind and his own body." The mind-aspect and body-aspect, we may recall, are merely abstractions of primordial bodymind awareness. Recognizing this aspect of experience, the boatman becomes aware of the "myriad dharmas" (without a privileged position) and thus, "the reason that the myriad dharmas are without self will become clear to him."

At this juncture we will address ourselves to how Dōgen aids practitioners to become specifically aware of the dynamic nature of the horizon. In each chapter thus far, we have encountered instances of practitioners simulating aspects of the experience they are attempting to achieve. For example, Kūkai uses *mantras*, *mudras*, and *mandalas* as dynamic noematic foci in order to inculcate patterns of behavior so similar to first order bodymind awareness that the transfer from second order awareness to first order bodymind awareness is minimal. In Chapter 2, we noted that athletes and musicians sediment their skills so well that they learn to perform their respective activities without conscious thetic intention. Similarly in Section 1 of this chapter, we alluded to various aspects of zazen technique which act as a catalyst for the achievement of zazen awareness, e.g., correct posture leads to tension and intention neutralization, open eyes aid the practitioner to remain alert, expand their periphery and presence the situation before them etc.

In this regard, it is interesting to note that, in the Sōtō tradition, after the period of sitting is terminated, the rocking motion that initiates a session of sitting[32] is repeated in reverse order from small arches to large ones.[33] This practice is intended to remind the practitioner to maintain this dynamic and alert mode of awareness in daily life. In this way, the technique once again helps to inculcate the sediment zazen awareness. Retaining a keen awareness and expanded periphery enables practitioners to go about their daily monastic chores free of thetic intervention. *If a situation calls for a specific skill to be performed, then the arising of thetic interventions required to successfully complete the skill are taken as a spontaneous reaction to presencing the situation as it is primordially given.* In this way, the practitioner lives a harmonious existence with his environment by presencing things-as-they-are and responding appropriately. Such alert behavior requires that the "mind" of the zazen practitioner be as dynamic as the presenced situation.[34] One's self (bodymind) must be presented as within the horizon.

Indeed, all aspects of zazen awareness discussed thus far have been seen to be dynamic activities. We have encountered *genjōkōan* (presencing things-as-they-are), *sokushin-zebutsu* (this very mind is Buddha), *shinjin datsuraku* (casting off body and mind), and Dōgen's interpretation of *dharma* as things-as-experienced. Zazan awareness itself is the mode of enlightened experience. Dōgen says, "When we say 'a man of Great Enlightenment' it refers to someone who does not *possess* enlightenment from the beginning, or attains it from some other place and keeps it hidden."[35] Enlightenment is therefore not a static thing or dogma to possess, crave, covet or hide. Rather, it is an *activity* to be sedimented and a manner of being. Even when sedimented, enlightenment is insufficient, dynamic, and a sort of pure over-brimming potentiality that changes and harmonizes with the emptiness of *dharmas*. Speaking on behalf of a "man of Great Enlightenment" Dōgen writes:

> My wisdom increases more and more because there is nothing in my mind for anything to attach to. I just move in my own original Way. My daily fare consists of manifesting the Original Buddhist Way. This Way is free and dynamic.[36]

Accordingly, Dōgen not only describes the mode of awareness that verifies empirically the doctrine of impermanence, he also preaches that "great Enlightenment" itself "is the *daily activity* of Buddhas. . . . To become a Buddha is to have the enlightenment of Buddha: dynamic, living enlightenment."[37]

Applying our next phenomenological category will help us to describe and interpret some of the philosophical beliefs which arise as a ramification of direct experiential verification of impermanence. Our discussion of "simultaneity" will expose further the reasons why impermanence (dynamism) is experienced as it is, why cultivation and authentication occur simultaneously, and how the distinctive features of *kaiinzanmai* occur.

5. Simultaneity and Zazen Awareness

From our discussion of being-time (*uji*) in Chapter 5, we are already familiar with the two acceptable temporal responses to a situation described by Dōgen. Both *nikon* (right now) and *kyōryaku* (ranging) dispel the notion of a linear or momentary theory of time. Whereas the former entails a narrow periphery and immersion into a situation, e.g., climbing a mountain, the latter entails an extended periphery and a distant observance of the whole range of phenomena within a situation, e.g., surveying a mountainous landscape from atop the highest peak. In each instance however, the temporal-aspect of *uji* is the same. Regardless of the size of the periphery, the continuity of time in each instance is not uniformily directional, i.e., "the future ranges into the past, as well as past into present and present into present."[38] Presencing the "axis of the confluence of events"[39] occurs during both *nikon* and *kyōryaku* perspectives. This axis in which past, present and future interpenetrate can be accurately described *via* our phenomenological category of simultaneity.

Equating the temporal-aspect (*uji*) of zazen awareness with the temporal-aspect(simultaneity) of first order bodymind awareness will help us to better understand a few of the implications of dynamism discussed above. Dōgen believes that when one directly experiences impermanence he should understand that "the entire universe is filled with the totality of life." He ought to understand that "enlightenment means . . . full, free activity." And, he ought to recognize that "Life is the total activity of life; death is the total activity of death."[40] Our familiarity with the nature of simultaneity will help us to understand how these statements arise as ramifications of zazen awareness. This procedure is possible because the temporal-aspect of zazen awareness (*uji*) is one of simultaneity.

To begin, we may recall that during first order bodymind awareness the horizon is presenced in toto precisely because no specific thing has a privileged position that could set it spatially nor temporally apart from the rest of the horizon. Dōgen implies that the same situation occurs during zazen awareness. Life and death are presenced simultaneously. Neither can be seen as relative terms with respect to the other simply because they can never be juxtaposed within the complete horizon. Since neither life nor death is presenced as privileged with respect to the other, one only experiences that "life is the total activity of life" and "death is the total activity of death." Whether the temporal perspective is "right now" or "ranging," there is no privileged moment by which relative temporal distinctions, such as life-aspect and death-aspect, can be made. Dōgen actually describes the simultaneous character of life and death himself when he says, "These two dimensions are not opposed; they exist together in one universal experience. They are not concerned with conceptions of time and space."[41]

If we were to draw the implications of presencing all temporal and spatial events in this manner, then we would have to conclude that not only is there not a linear temporal progression from life to death, but also all other apparent temporal changes and comparisons would be seen to be inauthentic. The reason for this is that any change or comparison requires a fixed (privileged) standard by which relative alterations can be made. If no such standard is posited then all relative distinctions such as life and death become reduced to the zazen mode of presencing in which life is life and death is death. The following represents one of Dōgen's descriptions of such an occurrence.

Once firewood turns to ash, the ash cannot turn back to being firewood. Still, one should not take the view that it is ashes *afterward* and firewood *before*. He should realize that although firewood is at the dharma-stage of firewood, and that this is possessed of before and after, the firewood is beyond before and after. Ashes are in the stage of ashes, and possess before and after. Just as firewood does not revert to firewood once it has turned to ashes, man does does not return to life after his death.[42]

During zazen awareness, one presences the simultaneity of all *dharmas* (things-as-experienced) within the horizon. Firewood-as-experienced occurs in time (*uji*). Each is a *dharma* presenced as it is primordially given to consciousness. There is no posited privileged standard present by which to assess relative temporal and/or spatial changes.

Dōgen describes this mode of awareness as "unobtainable" (*shinfukatoku*—'mind' + 'not' + 'obtainable,' lit. the mind, unobtainable) because any attempt to label even this experience would imply some outside criterion by which it is distinguished from other modes of awareness. He says that this "unobtainable" or perhaps "undefinable" mode of awareness defies past, present, future or any other spatio-temporal lable. Nevertheless, it is this unobtainable mode of awareness which the zazen practitioner must utilize in daily life.[43] Again one of our hermeneutic categories has helped to interpret, in relation to its experiential context, a mystical-sounding notion. Zazen awareness is not unobtainable or undefinable because it transcends spatial and temporal distinctions and entails some other-worldly mystic experience. Rather, zazen awareness is undefinable because it undercuts the thetic positing of a privileged standard by which temporal and spatial change is measured.[44]

If we turn our attention to this simultaneous character of zazan awareness, we can better understand why Dōgen taught that cultivation and authentication occur at the same time. Dōgen is famous for stating that enlightenment need not be some glorious treasure at the end of the long road of years of disciplined study. For Dōgen cultivation is authentication whenever zazen awareness occurs. He says, "when even for a short time you sit properly in samadhi . . . all space without exception is enlightenment."[45] The reason that this is so is because time is not experienced as directional. It is experienced as *nikon* (right now) and *kyōryaku* (ranging) which are two perspectives of *uji* (being-time). Neither of these perspectives allows for any means-ends conception of time. Enlightenment, therefore, is not something which necessarily occurs only after many years of practice, i.e., from a novice level, to an intermediate level, and finally to an advanced stage of meditative practice. The temporal sequence of means-ends, where one intention is usually fixed on some fictitious goal (or the measurement of progress) runs antithetical to an interpretation of time as *nikon* (right now) or *kyōryaku* (ranging). Dōgen says,

"Enlightenment is the natural activity of the 'everyday mind' and occurs at any time."[46] Whenever one experiences the mode of zazen awareness, temporal distinctions are cast off. In this way, the act of cultivation is authentication in time.

We may also interpret simultaneity as the distinguishing feature of *kaiinzanmai* (see Chapter 5). *Kaiinzanmai* names the mode of awareness that is like an "ocean imprint." The experiential horizon is presenced with all components sharing a non-privileged position. In Chapter 5 we noticed that the proto or *Ur*-thetic positing of an abstract mind-aspect and body-aspect paves the way for all subsequent distinctions. These positings may be likened to a turbulent effect upon the surface of the "ocean" (horizon in toto). The discovery of the simultaneous character of zazen awareness serves to underscore the primordially given *non-privileged* dynamism within the horizon. *Kaiinzanmai* names this primordially given, non-privileged, dynamic bodymind awareness at the base of thetic experience. This simultaneous aspect of *kaiinzanmai* is described as follows: "when body and mind emerge the elements [within the horizon] are unified and time and existence function together." (interpretive brackets mine)[47] That is, when bodymind awareness occurs, simultaneity occurs, and the components within the horizon "function together" in a non-privileged manner. The ground-aspect of bodymind awareness is further punctuated by Dōgen when he continues to say that this underlying spatio-temporal unity (simultaneity) is presenced only when body and mind are presenced. Thus, our investigation has again pointed toward the position that bodymind awareness lays at the base of zazen awareness. When the body-aspect and mind-aspect are cast off, bodymind awareness presents itself.

The next phase of the analysis requires that we pull together the emphasis upon bodymind awareness by examining Dōgen's most explicit discussions concerning the role of body and mind within his overall project. Although we have already addressed ourselves to Dōgen's explicit instructions regarding *shinjin dat-suraku* (casting off body and mind), we presently seek to understand this, and other forementioned philosophical doctrines, in light of his goals as a practicing Zen master. In Chapter 5 we claimed that understanding casting off body and mind is a key to understanding the ground of Dōgen's philosophical positions. Our preceding discussions have demonstrated that casting off body and mind is a prerequisite to presencing the neutral, expanded, dynamic and simultaneous aspects of zazen awareness. Each of these particular aspects is authenticated when bodymind awareness presents itself within the total horizon. As we move forward we must examine the relationship between the role of casting off body and mind as the ground of Dōgen's philosophical tenets and the role of first order bodymind awareness (zazen awareness) as the paradigmatic mode of experiencing which Dōgen, as a Zen master, wishes to impress upon his disciples.

6. Sedimentation and First Order Bodymind Awareness

For Dōgen, undertaking a monastic existence is for the sole purpose of sedimenting first order bodymind awareness. This underscores Dōgen's own intentions or predelections concerning the proper environment for serious spiritual cultivation. Since the monastic life is one encouraged by various teachings east and west, it is important to acknowledge explicitly Dōgen's own attitude toward such disciplined practice. Monastic habituation or sedimentation may, at first glance, appear out of sink with his theory of original enlightenment (*hongaku*). Recall however that this sort of observation is rooted, in a more traditional epistemic frame of reference that places a rift between theory and practice; the same apparently inexplicable rift that sent Dōgen to China. Dōgen's resolution, we recall, underscores the oneness of cultivation and authentication (*shushō ichinyo*). There is no means-ends relation between theory and practice. Dōgen says that the disciple must transcend reflexively the "mind of analysis," (second and third order bodymind awareness). Dōgen exhorts, "When you begin to study the Buddhist Way, your mind must undergo a conversion."[48] Dōgen's goal is nothing short of continual perception of the Buddha-mind. For example, attaining *sokushin zebutsu* ("this very mind is Buddha") is a mode of awareness that must be sedimented into one's everyday life. Simple activities such as drinking tea and eating rice must be performed with the same mode of awareness as sitting in zazen. The "three activities" (deeds, words, and thoughts) of human life must all be governed by nothing more than presencing the immediate situation-as-it-is.[49] Experiencing in this way will allow the situation to spontaneously inform the practitioner when a thetic response to achieve a goal or accomplish a task is appropriate. It is Dōgen's wish that the monastic student sediment the mode of awareness that will enable him to presence any situation in this manner.

Dōgen's experiences with a kitchen master of a monastery in China were articulated into a central part of his teaching. In short, Dōgen learned that everyday acts were zazen and that all of one's actions were an expression of one's mode of awareness. The actions of an enlightened person thus reflect the immediate situation. The actions of enlightened people reflect their own situations imposed upon the environment. The Zen master, unable to presence a student's thoughts, must therefore be extremely sensitive to the actions of his disciple. It is for this reason many traditional *kōans* and *mondōs* describe situations in which master and students are involved in a series of unusual actions. In most cases, the master is attempting to communicate, through his actions, the principles of a mode of experience not unlike first order bodymind awareness.

Consequently, the daily chores of the monastic student are extremely important for they provide the familiar setting which becomes sedimented. Just as musicians or athletes rehearse their skills over and over again (thus enabling them to eventually perform without thetic intention), the monastic student performs his daily chores again and again so that eventually they are conducted without thinking. When this occurs, the practitioner may presence directly the various aspects of this experience which stand out amidst a familiar horizon. The following passage containing the metaphor of the rice is most illustrative of this phenomenon.

> When you are sick of rice, you know its true taste; when you have had too much rice, you become sick of it; after knowing its taste, you become sick of rice; and after you are tired of it you can taste it.[50]

When one eats rice again and again, it becomes a sedimented activity. Initially, one goes through a period of disliking rice which is dominated by negative thetic intentions. Finally, one gives up disliking it and accepts the monastic diet. This neutralization opens up a mode of first order bodymind awareness. The expanded periphery and alert senses enable one to truly *taste* the rice, perhaps for the first time. Once all thetic judgments regarding hunger, sickness, likes and dislikes are neutralized, the actual taste of the rice may be presenced.

The reason that Dōgen's method of instruction focuses upon such daily activities is that concentrating upon the body-aspect is a much more productive method of teaching. The somatic responses of students (tension, shape, color, form) can be presenced as a reflection of mind-aspect intensions. When one's daily activities are performed, the master can authenticate the degree to which bodymind awareness has been sedimented. The frequent encounters between master and student within the familiar monastery grounds enhance the student's ability to sediment zazen awareness. In addition, the student may observe the master's conduct in a variety of situations within the familiar surroundings. Although it is true that Dōgen states that a lay person and master encounter the same mode of first order bodymind awareness, he is *extremely* supportive of the need for a serious student to enter a monastery. In his opinion, there is no other way to sediment such awareness.[51] It should also be noted that this emphasis upon monastic sedimentation is not universally accepted amongst Zen Buddhist sects in Japan. The common denominators lie not in the style of external monastic life but in cultivating a mode of awareness which is authentic to one's situation, allowing for spontaneous responsiveness to others, words (*kōans*) or things-as-experienced (*dharmas*).

The monastic life makes it possible for students to detach themselves from an environment in which second and third order bodymind awareness is sedimented. The public's engrained habits of positing the body-aspect, mind-aspect and linear time, are thus avoided. Dōgen explains the need for this type of continuous practice as follows:

In the great Way of the Buddha patriarchs there is always a supreme continuous practice which is the Way without beginning or end. Arousing the thought of enlightenment, practice, bodhi, and nirvana have not the slightest break, but are continuous practice which goes on forever. Therefore, it is neither one's own effort nor someone else's effort; it is pure, and continuous practice which transcends the opposition of self and others. . . . It is this way because continuous practice is not dominated by any other thing. This kind of continuous practice which reveals continuous practice is nothing more than our continuous practice now. The immediate 'now' of continuous practice is not something which existed . . . from before. The time called 'now' is not born from continuous practice. The time when continuous practice is manifested is what we call 'now.'[52]

Here we see Dōgen's notion of continuous practice linked to two aspects of zazen awareness discussed previously. First, Dōgen explains continuous practice as continuous without thinking. No intentional effort is ever posited. One merely responds to the situation as it is given and thus allows the impetus for action to be dictated by the horizon in toto. This requires undivided attention upon the horizon. Such continuous attention is most easily sedimented at a monastery where positing distinctions such as self and other may be systematically neutralized. The second aspect of zazen awareness which Dōgen links to continuous practice is simultaneity. Dōgen emphasizes that in order to sediment the mode of awareness in which being-time (*uji*) is continually experienced, one must detach oneself from the habituated abstract conception of linear time. Again, sedimenting a mode of total immersion into one's environment in which being-time is continuously experienced as *nikon* "right now" or *kyōryaku* ("ranging"), is most easily achieved in the monastic setting. Monastic life does not share the same presuppositions as public life. Stereotyped conceptions of time and space, self and other, good and bad, etc., that are common among lay people are abandoned in the monastery. In this way, a small group of people form their own community in which continuous practice of zazen awareness is the norm. It is important to remember that the monastic life does not offer a setting to receive mystic secrets. Rather, the primordial mode of awareness, shared by Zen master and lay people alike, is merely sedimented through monastic training. In short, whereas the public at large has sedimented second and third order bodymind awareness, the monastic community seeks to sediment the most primordial mode of experience — first order bodymind awareness.

If, for Dōgen, Japanese Buddhist monastic life is geared to sediment zazen awareness, i.e., first order bodymind awareness, and if zazen awareness (1) is the mode of experience that authenticates empirically Dōgen's philosophical tenets, and (2) occurs when body and mind are cast off and the bodymind ground is presenced, then we may infer that Japanese Sōtō Buddhism is rooted in presencing the primordial bodymind ground within the total horizon. Our inference is confirmed by Dōgen's instructions regarding the first and foremost teaching of Buddha.

> You should know that the Buddha Dharma from the first preaches that body and mind are not two . . . this is equally known in India and China, and there can be no doubt about it. . . . You should give this deep deliberation; the Buddha Dharma has always maintained the oneness of body and mind.[53]

Continuing this line of reasoning we may suggest the following: if body and mind are originally one and are innate in everyone (as we learned through our discussion of *hongaku* and *hosshin seppō*), and if this original oneness is presented during everyday activities of lay persons and disciples alike, then presencing the bodymind ground at the base of all experience seems to arise out of *doing nothing*. That is, enlightenment does not mean attaining or possessing some *thing* new. To the contrary, enlightenment is the *activity* of being constantly aware, through everyday actions, of the innate bodymind ground within the horizon. Again our reasoning is substantiated by Dōgen's statements below.

> Everyone is endowed with body and mind, though their actions inevitably vary, being either weak or strong, brave or cowardly. It is through the daily actions of our body and mind, however, that we directly become enlightened. This is known as realization of the Way. There is no need to change our existing body and mind, for the direct realization of the Way simply means to become enlightened through training under a true Zen master. To do this is neither to be bound by old viewpoints nor create new ones; it is simply to realize the Way. . . .It is through our body and mind that we are able to practice the Way.[54]

Since bodymind oneness is always present at the root of our experience, Dōgen says that enlightenment occurs without effort and without thinking. The Way is realizing what is given primordially to consciousness. Hence, nothing is "new," "there is no need to change our existing body and mind," nor is there any reason to believe in the doctrines of Buddhism based upon "old viewpoints." All that is worth knowing is given innately and can be empirically authenticated constantly "through training [sedimentation] under a true Zen master."

It follows that our experience is fundamentally, in the sense of its eidetic structure, not different from a Zen master's. The difference lies in the frequency and ramifications of experiencing *via* the mode of first order bodymind awareness. Whereas the lay person posits his or her own presuppositions and conceptualizations upon the given situation, the Zen master presences the given situation and its eidetic experiential structure. Each has the "equipment" to experience in either the first, second or third order mode. The Zen master exercises an option to sediment presencing rather than positing. The lay person, on the other hand, chooses to posit their own affective notions regarding time, space, self, existence, and so on. The Zen master thus gives greater value and significance to presencing-things-as-they-are originally devoid of thetic intervention. Dōgen says that when the body and mind are cast off, "your original face will be manifest."[55] If we phenomenologically interpret this original face as representative of a primordial level of awareness, then we may suggest that presencing this original face necessitates a direct experience of the horizon in toto in which the neutral, expanded, dynamic, simultaneous and bodymind aspects are authenticated.

We may conclude that our phenomenological categories help to faithfully articulate the components of Dōgen's "undefinable" or "unobtainable" mode of awareness. We have seen that once all distinctions are neutralized and first order bodymind awareness is activated, many of Dōgen's philosophical tenets may be verified. The practitioner must directly witness the horizon and thus become acquainted with the various aspects of first order bodymind awareness. Finally Dōgen's empirical or phenomenological approach can be seen as a ramification of his belief that enlightenment consists of becoming aware of the primordially given aspects of that which enables us to have knowledge of the world around us, viz., experience. Dōgen's reproduction of the following kōan in his fascicle *Kōku* ('Universal Emptiness') [representing the horizon in toto] underscores exactly where the "secrets" of enlightenment are to be found.

Zen Master Shakyō Ezō once asked Zen Master Seidō Chizō, who was Shakyō's senior, 'Do you know how to comprehend universal emptiness?' 'Of course,' Seido answered. 'How?' Shakyō wanted to know. Seidō grasped a handful of air. 'Aha! You don't know how to grasp it then!' Shakyō exclaimed. Seidō challenged Shakyō to show him universal emptiness. Shakyō grabbed Seidō's nose and yanked it until he cried out in pain, 'Now I've got it!' Seidō said. 'Yes, now you know what it is,' Shakyō agreed.[56]

Chapter 7

Phenomenology and Japanese Buddhist Philosophy

In this final chapter I will define the boundaries of this philosophical project and work towards an understanding of the relation between philosophy and culture. Our application of Western phenomenological techniques to Japanese Buddhism gives us a unique opportunity to assess *critically* the legitimacy of our interpretation and the prospects for similar cross-cultural studies. The need to articulate the parameters of our study is necessary since one is tempted to disregard cultural nuances and draw only superficially justifiable conclusions.

There are three major areas of investigation about which we could make greater claims than are warranted. First, we might exhort that a phenomenological interpretation is the best way for Westerners to become familiar with Japanese Buddhism. If the limitations of this method are not specified, however, then we are apt to grossly distort the justifiable points which this hermeneutic enables us to observe. Moreover, there are many other hermeneutic avenues that may also be beneficially employed as bridges for cross-cultural comparative studies. Husserl's own presupposition that the phenomenological method is a "descriptive" enterprise happens to be most compatible with this particular study which focuses upon the descriptive character of Kūkai's and Dōgen's philosophy. The shared existential or ontological orientation of Husserl, Kūkai and Dōgen also underscores some basic common denominators. Without these common philosophical orientations — sympathies with radical empiricism, reflexive methodologies and so on — the appropriateness, accuracy and success of this particular cross-cultural pairing would certainly be diminished. Self-criticism of our use of Husserl's hermeneutic in this context is necessary and follows below. A critical appraisal of all *other* possible methodologies (East and West) exceeds the boundaries of this most limited project.

The second area of investigation about which we might claim greater authority than is warranted concerns the clarification of common themes in Japanese Buddhist philosophy. We might claim that our study has unveiled a thread linking important themes between Kūkai and Dōgen which subsequently became further engrained as distinguishing features of Japanese Buddhism. Such claims are, however, grossly in error without acknowledging the important differences between Shingon and Sōtō theory and practice. As mentioned previously, these differences require consideration of social, psychological, political, and historical areas of inquiry which lay beyond the limited boundaries of transcendental phenomenological application.

The third precautionary note concerns the notion that one might boast that our efforts have at last solved the perennial problem of mind-body dualism when in fact this dualism has merely been shown to be philosophically non-existent, in its classical occidental formulation, in a culture that gives greater value and significance to a mode of experience wherein the mind-body fissure rarely arises (bodymind). The analyses contained within this study suggest that cultural or philosophical stereotypes East and West largely distort issues which require subtle and sensitive study. Attempts to define the character traits of Oriental and Occidental philosophy inevitably become oversimplified, as exceptions to the proposed definitions can always be discovered. Accordingly, the explication of the eidetic structure of consciousness becomes most important in an effort to build cross-cultural bridges. Once the overall philosophical orientation, including the assumed presuppositions, of a particular philosopher or school of philosophy become clarified, one may discover complementary thinkers East and West that may give value and significance to similar modes of experience. Whether the mode of experience is intuitive, emotive, discursive, or reflective, a discussion of the shared *a priori* structure may serve to expose an important link, albeit an axiomatic one within the phenomenological *epoché*, with which to ground comparative studies. In this way, many different sorts of philosophical endeavor can become "ours." One's own experiential horizon is thus opened up to sensitively understand perspectives that would only arise from embracing presuppositions that one would otherwise not accept. In an effort to define the legitimate scope of such an enterprise, the advantages and limitations of this method will be critically reviewed below.

1. An Appraisal of Our Method

To begin, we must acknowledge that we have used phenomenology to help articulate the structure of the mode of experience to which Kūkai's and Dōgen's version of enlightenment refers. We are not claiming that either of these masters are phenomenologists. The method has, however, been particularly useful in these two cases because their philosophical doctrines are grounded in practice and experiential verification. Phenomenology, as a method of textual interpretation, is appropriate to cross-cultural studies because of its emphasis upon description of the eidetic experiential structures independent of cultural differences. Although people of various cultures share the same fundamental experiential structures, the way in which these experiences are articulated and valued may vary appreciably. A central experiential concern for Japanese Buddhism may be so peripheral to our own concerns that it is ignored philosophically and uncultivated as an ideal in everyday life. For this reason, we articulated (Chapter 2) those fleeting cases of first order bodymind awareness to which little philosophical attention has been given in the Occident. Yet, by acknowledging the presence and structure of this experience, and then explaining why and how it can become a sedimented mode of experience, our method has helped relate our own experience to another cultural setting with which we have had little or no contact. Consequently, our phenomenological interpretation has been a useful instrument for laying bare the structure of experience and thereby exposing patterns of culturally dependent behavior. Furthermore, since the structure of experience is shared, we can *identify* our own fleeting first order bodymind experiences, then *imagine*[1] the condition of sedimenting this awareness, and finally become more familiar with the eidetic characteristics of a new perspective that gives the greatest value and significance to pre-reflective experience.

Given this new perspective, one might be in an improved position to explain the legitimate and illegitimate bases for the labels attributed to Northeast Asian Buddhist philosophy. Specifically, let us briefly examine frequent characterizations that Japanese Buddhist philosophy is alogical, mystical and secretive. We have seen that Kūkai and Dōgen are very logical and methodical in their methods of instruction. Each method is designed to effect the eidetic structure of first order bodymind awareness thus enabling the practitioner to experience a dynamic neutral mode of pre-reflective presencing. This perspective may seem alogical only in the sense that the mode of experience which is valued happens to be non-discursive. In spite of this, one may still argue that if one's goal is to presence the situation as it is primordially given to consciousness, then the most rational thing to do is to cultivate a non-discursive (non-thetic) mode of awareness. Similarly, Kūkai and Dōgen are not mystical since they give the greatest significance to presencing what is before our very eyes. They are mystical only in the sense that they are obliged to say "Look!" or speak metaphorically, for the mode of awareness they are attempting to inculcate defies an accurate linguistic description.

The import of the phenomenological exegesis of Kūkai's and Dōgen's texts may be seen in this light. Husserl's emphasis upon intentionality, albeit under the powerful influence of Brentano, assists the interpreter of texts to be cognizant of the meaning-bestowing features of consciousness. There is however a fine line here that one must acknowledge. On the one hand the interpreter of texts may wade through the powerful symbolism of Kūkai's and Dōgen's writing by remaining constantly aware of their posited theories (noemata) as indicators or "transcendental clues" to help understand the author's intentions (meaning-bestowing noesis).[2] Here phenomenological exegesis may help one to penetrate reflexively an approximation of the intent of the author and thus become closer to the intended meaning of metaphors, similes and so on. On the other hand, one must acknowledge the danger of reading into the texts false intentions. This problem affects translators to a limited extent and exegesis to an even greater extent. In this study the phenomenological exegesis or critical commentary upon the text has been employed with every effort to remain consistent with the theories embraced by Kūkai (Chapter 3) and Dōgen (Chapter 5). Consequently, Chapters 3 and 5 serve as "transcendental clues" for the textual interpretation in Chapters 4 and 6, respectively. As with any hermeneutical technique every precaution must be taken to ensure that the textual interpretation is *consistent* with the overall philosophical project, theories and orientation of the author(s).

Finally, Kūkai and Dōgen are not secretive since each dedicated himself to a life of teaching, writing and spreading their gospel, as it were. Yet, there are a few warranted reasons that explain the secretive nature of the Shingon and Sōtō traditions. As mentioned previously, the monastic life is purposefully dissimilar to the lay community. Oftentimes there is a feeling that the public would not understand the way of esoteric thinking, daily regimentation, or spiritual exercises which characterize monastic existence. Because of this disparity between lay and monastic life, the community of monks retain a special bond of common experience that is cultivated, nurtured and shared by no outsiders. Therefore, many aspects of monastic life and spiritual cultivation remain a secret to those who may misunderstand their true meaning, relevance and special significance. Those individuals, who are practitioners commited to twenty-four hour a day cultivation, are emersed into a supportive context (*jisetsu*) where the full force of the activity of psychosomatic sedimentation and understanding occurs.

We may legitimately conclude that our phenomenological interpretation has enabled us to articulate the structure of the enlightenment experience described by two key Japanese Buddhist figures. It should be noted that simply because the eidetic structure of this mode of awareness is made available to us, we have not secularized Japanese Buddhist religious experience. To the contrary, our method is limited to outlining the structure of the experience upon which important philosophical doctrines are based. Therefore, it cannot verify whether or not the *content* of these experiences actually authenticates the existence of, for example, the Dharmakāya. Similarly, our study cannot prescribe whether or not one ought to cultivate a certain mode of bodymind awareness in favor of another. We have, however, described the fact that Kūkai and Dōgen cultivate first order bodymind awareness because they give value and significance to presencing their situation as primordially given. Here the existential or ontological presuppositions of these thinkers are acknowledged explicitly.

Even though our method of interpretation has enabled us to understand how the habituation of thetic positings affect neutral presencing, it is doubtful that we will now be able to penetrate the mysteries of *sedimented* first order bodymind awareness. At best we may now be sensitive to the reasons why Japanese Buddhist philosophy and religion have heretofore seemed distant to many Western observers. A culture whose recent intellectual history has given paradigmatic significance to second and third order bodymind awareness would naturally react to Shingon and Sōtō monastic life and religious practices with some bewilderment. Although there is a monastic tradition associated with the Judeo-Christian culture, the ascetic life is usually interpreted as one steeped in conspicuous religiosity or pious activity that is directed towards an *other-worldly* transcendental figure. The monastic life within the Shingon and Sōtō schools is focused upon perceiving the truths ever-present in the authentic apprehension of the phenomenal world of things themselves. Occidental readers may suggest that the disciplines of Japanese Buddhist practice are alogical and mystical simply on the basis that they cannot be sufficiently understood *via* the third order techniques of discursive reasoning. The fact that we have gained some appreciation for the disciplines and techniques required to sediment first order bodymind awareness does not therefore imply that we have in any way secularized the enlightenment experience. Again, our insight is limited to exposing the structure and not the content of the enlightenment experience. As mentioned in Chapter 6, sedimenting this mode of awareness requires an environment wherein the thetic habits of second and third order awareness are methodically neutralized. Enlightenment, as a process of continual presencing, cannot be attained through the mere knowledge of its structure. In this way, our investigation has not secularized the Japanese Buddhist religious experience. To the contrary, the focus of the study has been an exercise in hermeneutics of a specific kind. By highlighting various structural features of consciousness a transcendental bridge has been suggested. This bridge offers a set of a priori common denominators upon which interpreters of philosophical texts may rely. This particular method of interpretation is not the *only* viable one. As mentioned in Chapter 1, I am hardly in a position to make such a claim. Nevertheless, the procedure is not without significant *prima facie* support when one again considers the shared reflexive philosophical orientation of Kūkai, Dōgen and Husserl. The overall consistency of the phenomenological exegesis provides further support in underscoring the close relationship between Shingon and Sōtō theory as "transcendental clue" and practice as empirical authentication of theories as-experienced or as-meant.

2. The Relation Between Philosophy and Culture Revisited

In Chapter 1 a few points were mentioned concerning the relation between philosophy and culture. Summarizing briefly, it was stated that different cultures attach different values to particular modes of experience and thus produce distinctive, perhaps even culturally dependent, philosophical systems. The observation that different people cultivate different paradigmatic modes of experience does not imply that one tradition is somehow more rational in their methods of investigation in the pursuit of Truth. The "place" *where* Truth is presupposed "to be" or "act" significantly predetermines the type of epistemic mode of awareness that will be given the greatest value and significance. If Truth is presupposed to exist in a metaphysical world, then an appropriate epistemic mode of awareness will be cultivated at the expense of others. As Plato suggested in the *Phaedo*, the *psyché* is given the greatest epistemic value, and therefore should be cultivated, as it is that aspect of our being which is capable of ascertaining the non-spatial, perfect and eternal objects of knowledge known as "the forms." The body, therefore, is seen as a hindrance to the *psyché*. The body need not become an important focus of our attention. In fact it is due to human beings' somatic existence and incarnation that they are forced to recall objects of knowledge that were once known with greater clarity when the soul was free from the body.

Similarly, the Indo-European connection is revealed when one considers the *Upanisadic* doctrine of *maya* (illusion). That this phenomenal world is illusory and does not reflect Ultimate Reality suggests that the truely enlightened, one who has attained spiritual liberation (*Moksha*), perceives reality from a unique perspective. To understand the oneness of *Atman* and *Brahman* (*tat tvam asi*) requires a particular mode of consciousness wherein the oneness of all things is authenticated. The particular epistemological mode of experience to be cultivated is once again consistent with the metaphysical doctrine that Truth resides in a noumenal realm distinct from the phenomenal realm of *maya*. Even if Truth does not reside in an other-wordly place, as some Upanisadic interpreters have suggested, and instead reflects a unique noetic mode of perceiving the phenomenal realm in which the veil of *maya* is removed, then the corresponding relationship between epistemology and metaphysics is retained.

If we acknowledge this correspondence, then it encourages us to look first at the metaphysical presuppositions regarding Truth. Once the so-called "place" and character of Truth is laid bare, then understanding the rationale of cultivating certain epistemological modes of experience, designed to bring one closer to an understanding of Truth, become clarified. Since Kūkai and Dōgen perceive Truth to be in all things (Dharmakāya), including all sentient beings (Buddha-nature), then the radical reflexivity of their practices may be seen as being rational and consistent with their respective philosophical presuppositions. Practices designed to effect first order bodymind awareness reflect a rationale designed to allow the practitioner to authenticate the Truth of one's primordial being. This relationship would not therefore be *structurally* dissimiliar to Plato's emphasis upon the *psyché* and recollection, Nietzsche's emphasis upon creating and power (*machen* and *Macht* respectively) or Lao Tzu's emphasis upon *wu-wei* (non-action) as a guiding principle that imitates the character of the *Tao*.

Another point concerning the relation between philosophy and culture follows from this observation. Distinctive philosophical orientations at the axiomatic level suggest that the "first principles" or uncritically accepted presuppositions will significantly set a mood and context for subsequent philosophical endeavors within that system. This implies that a range of philosophical creativity will be severely limited within an acceptable range of speculation. Even an axiomatic position espousing great breadth of vision itself becomes a posited position within which subsequent thinking acquires meaning. The axiomatic presuppositions thus set the context, periphery, and experiential horizon within which all other speculative and creative activity take place. The meaning and historicity within the horizon of a particular philosophical framework is thus constructed and sedimented. The rare genius of Hegel's "hero" and Nietzsche's *übermensch* describe individuals with the strength and vision to transcend the *status quo*. Nevertheless, their respective metapositions are still bound and defined by the background of their habituated experiential horizons staged by time, place and their individual lived histories. The imposing influences of an individual person's or culture's axiomatic presuppositions are not mentioned in support of some sort of philosophical determinism. Rather, their tremendous import is simply underscored by the employment of a reflexive phenomenological methodology. Explicitly acknowledging the influence of culturally distinctive presuppositions concerning space, time, Truth and so on serve to clarify pedagogical hurdles in comparative studies. Husserl's *Cartesian Meditations* and *Crisis*, Heidegger's *Being and Time*, Watsuji's *Fudo* (Climate) and *Rinri* (Ethics) and the post-modern works of literary critics exemplified by Foucoult and Derrida reflect the efforts of just a few who have, in their own way, already argued this point in detail. The philosophical axioms of any system provide the cornerstones. The subsequently derived theorems of building blocks are thus, in many ways, given a predetermined orientation from the beginning. East or West the a priori *structural* arena of philosophical activity is shared. The actual noematic content and corresponding noetic attitude constitute the distinctive features of unique philosophical perspectives.

A specific example may help to clarify the forementioned theme. Given a specified philosophical structure, complete with presuppositions that favor paradigmatic modes of consciousness in the pursuit of Truth, certain philosophical and practical (in the sense of *praxis*) problems are more or less predetermined. Some philosophical methods East and West tend to value experiences (second and third order bodymind awareness) which tend to separate mind-aspects and body-aspects whereas Kūkai and Dōgen tend to stress experiences wherein bodymind is presenced within the non-privileged horizon (first order bodymind awareness). By comparing the paradigmatic modes of meditation accepted by the former — speculation, reflection, contemplation, reverie, fantasy and abstraction—with the paradigmatic modes of meditation in Shingon and Sōtō Buddhist schools, cultivation (*shugyō*) of neutral presencing, the origin of mind-body dualism and bodymind experience become clear. In Platonic, Cartesian and Sāmkhyan mind-body dualism, for example, mind-aspects and body-aspects have been habitually abstracted from the horizon of lived experience. Sedimentation of such an abstraction has led some philosophers to assume that minds and bodies are ontologically independent. Our present introspections have enabled us to examine a different orientation based upon an axiomatic apprehension of radical empiricism. By moving rigorously in a reflexive direction, an acknowledged axiomatic first principle of phenomenological inquiry, the primordial bodymind experience cultivated by certain Japanese Buddhist practical methods has been clarified as a viable alternative to dualist suppositions.

Given these distinctive perspectives about mind and body, we must recognize that subsequent philosophical activity reflects the original perspective. If through habitual abstraction we assume that the mind and body are ontologically distinct, then all of our efforts are channeled into demonstrating to others that this is experientially verifiable. If it is assumed by theologians, scientists and philosophers that the mind and body are originally two, then the perennial "mind-body problem" is to explain their interaction. If, on the other hand, individuals claim that bodymind is experienced as a unity within the neutral experiential horizon, then their problem is to explain how to sediment this primordial mode of awareness. In both cases, the problem to be solved is conditioned by the original philosophical structure. Whether we seek to explain body and mind interaction or authenticate primordial bodymind experience, we can best understand each project by investigating phenomenologically the structure out of which each initially arose. By assessing the value and significance given to different modes of awareness within the structure, the origin of the problems themselves can best be interpreted.

One further point follows from the above. The possible strategies for solving problems arising from distinctive philosophical structures are just as distinctive as the origin of the problems themselves. Hence, attempts to overcome mind-body dualism East and West tend to rely on the same modes of meditation that force the problem to arise repeatedly. Similarly, avenues for overcoming the problems associated with cultivating bodymind experiences, for the purpose of enlightenment, tend to rely on the same modes of meditation which inspired the value and significance attached to neutral bodymind experiences originally. The net result is that the forementioned problems remain problems as long as the reasons for their initial evolution remain a mystery. Specifically, if discursive reasoning is utilized exclusively to explain how an ontologically separate mind and body interact, then the problem of interaction is continually perpetuated because discursive thinking itself helps to create the abstract bifurcation. The problem is circular and self-perpetuating; it is a snake swallowing its tail. The motivation to continue the effort to solve the mystery of interaction is ever-present simply because our everyday experience informs us that the mind and body must somehow interact. The theoretician asks, "if the mind and body are ontologically distinct, when do they seem to interact so closely?" The answer, perhaps, is that the bodymind ground is at the base of all human experience and gives one the impression that mind and body must interact. In spite of this impression, the bodymind ground remains unnoticed due to constant thetic intervention. The persistent use of thetic modes of awareness (second and third order) to explain mind and body interaction, continues to channel the individual's attention toward various privileged noemata. This approach prohibits the individual from a direct awareness of the non-privileged horizon wherein bodymind awareness is presenced.

Conversely, the Shingon or Sōtō practitioner asks, "if the mind and body are one, why do they sometimes seem to be working against each other?" Or, "if they are one and I am originally enlightened, why must I practice diligently to become enlightened?" In response to the former question we may suggest that the mind-aspect and body-aspect appear at times to be separate due to a multiplicity of conflicting thetic positings. The Buddhist master demands practice because, although one is originally enlightened, the student must authenticate his enlightenment by directly experiencing bodymind oneness and sedimenting this mode of awareness. The practitioner's problem is to realize that which is already present. One's motivation to continue practice arises from an everyday acquaintance with first order bodymind awareness. One is aware that a unique mode of presencing is there to be sedimented. In one's efforts to become aware of that which is innate, however, one has created a strong attachment that must be neutralized before one's authentication is complete. In other words, one has created a noetic attitude (desire) for an imagined noema (the ability to sediment this mode of presencing) about which there may be many preconceived notions. Total neutralization *cannot be achieved with one eye upon the goal.*

Finally, it must be stated that giving value to certain modes of awareness significantly color *culturally dependent* philosophical structures. As a result, even culturally predetermined problems may arise. If a collective societal experiential horizon emerges complete with a sense of shared meaning and historicity, then collectively relying upon the same valued modes of awareness to solve shared problems only serves to perpetuate and recreate them. A careful analysis of the origin of the problems themselves serves as a useful strategy when attempting to understand accurately the development of philosophical issues within their own intellectual climate. This procedure serves to lay bare alternative approaches to traditional philosophical issues. In this study, new perspectives have been offered in order to at least challenge the traditional manner in which mind-body dualism has been posed. With respect to two schools of Japanese Buddhism, we have similarly offered a new perspective by demonstrating the use of phenomenological methods of interpretation as a vehicle to help us identify with modes of experience uncultivated by dualistic philosophic techniques. In short, the relationship between philosophy and culture is so intertwined that we must consider the distinctive structures of experience before passing judgment upon one culture's thinking while using the criteria of another.

3. Phenomenology and Japanese Philosophy

The empirical spirit of Japanese philosophy lends itself to phenomenological analysis and interpretation. This commitment to experiential verification has enabled our phenomenological analysis to arrive at a new perspective through which we can better understand two schools of Japanese Buddhist philosophy. We recall that the sedimentation of first order bodymind awareness authenticates the theoretical doctrines of Shingon and Sōtō Buddhist schools. In this way, sedimentation may be viewed as the distinguishing feature of the religious life of the practitioner. If we adopt the perspective that Chapters 3 and 5 describe the theoretical doctrines of the Shingon and Sōtō schools respectively, and Chapters 4 and 6 describe the manner in which first order bodymind awareness authenticates these doctrines, then we may suggest that the relation between Japanese philosophy and Japanese religion is also clarified in this context. Whereas the theoretical doctrines reflect the philosophical persuasion of the schools, the practical disciplines for sedimenting first order bodymind awareness reflect the religious life of the student. Religious enlightenment therefore implies experiential authentication of the meaning of the theoretical doctrines through the sedimentation of first order awareness in daily life. For this reason, monastic life is dedicated to creating an atmosphere wherein first order bodymind awareness may be sedimented in the form predicated by that system.

The seat of Shingon and Sōtō spiritual life is thus within this very body. By continually neutralizing intentions and tensions one becomes one's own vehicle[3] through which the enlightened mode of awareness is eventually sedimented. In this way, both the body-aspect and mind-aspect become essential in the quest to verify the bodymind ground at the base of all experience. In Dōgen's terms, "the Way is attained surely with the body."[4] This quest to sediment first order bodymind awareness — *via mantras, mandalas, mudras,* or *zazen* — distinguishes the philosophical study of the doctrine from religious authentication of their meaning-as-experienced. Dōgen accentuates the central role of bodymind awareness in religious life when he says:

You should consider carefully that the Buddha-dharma has always maintained the thesis of the non-dual oneness of body and mind. Nevertheless, how can it be possible that while this body is born and dissolves, mind alone departs from body and escapes from arising and perishing? If there is a time when they are not, the Buddhist teaching must be false indeed. . . . you should see the truth that as all the Buddhas of the past, present and future are awakened and practice the Way, they do not leave out our bodies and minds. To doubt this is already to slander them. As we reflect quietly upon this matter, it seems quite reasonable that our bodies and minds enact the Way and our desire for enlightenment is awakened truly with Buddhas of the three periods.[5]

The awareness of bodymind is thus tantamount to the sedimentation of an enlightened mode of experience. Cultivating first order bodymind awareness allows the practitioner to live a religious life and understand the experiential correlates of the philosophical doctrines. In short, by presencing the phenomenal world as it is given primordially to consciousness, the practitioner can react to the situation rather than situating his reactions by imposing his own presuppositions upon the environment.

We may conclude by underscoring our thesis that presencing in this way is cultivated by sedimenting first order bodymind awareness. Since the greatest value and significance is given to this mode of awareness, it becomes the object of philosophical investigation and the goal of religious life. Recognizing this, our analysis has worked to better understand the structure of first order bodymind awareness. This, in turn, has enabled us to clarify the relation between the philosophical doctrines and the specific categories of the religious experience to which they refer. As mentioned previously, our study does not purport to secularize this experience. The method employed has only allowed us to define the phenomenological categories of enlightened experience. In an effort to make these categories more meaningful, our study began with an examination of fleeting first order experiences to which we can all relate. In subsequent chapters, we were able to describe the major doctrines of Shingon-shu and Sōtō-shu in order to make explicit the manner in which the various structural categories of the enlightenment experience could conceivably authenticate theoretical doctrines of a similar structure. By making the distinctive philosophical structure of Kūkai and Dōgen *ours via* a phenomenological interpretation, it has been possible to work toward a clarification of the meaning of their philosophy.

In his essay "Philosophy and the Crisis of European Man,"[6] Husserl describes the urgent crisis of his day, as one which enclosed, or even trapped, philosophical endeavor in a vicious circle operating wholly within the natural standpoint. Modern philosophy and science, he said, had become steeped in naturalism and objectivism. Husserl's now famous remedy out of this crisis called for a "heroism of reason that will definitely overcome naturalism."[7] This sort of reason is a Socratic use of reason and is championed by a transcendental phenomenology that is capable of penetrating and examining critically the unchallenged axioms upon which modern philosophy and science has been presupposed. I mention this essay in closing because I believe that while Husserl makes evident his lack of knowledge about the *content* of the myriad forms of non-western philosophies,[8] he does, quite typically, provide a wealth of information concerning the *methodological* requirements to ground the discipline of comparative philosophy itself. His critique of the crisis of European culture predicts not only the horrors of fanaticism brewing on the continent but also the consequences of violating a fundamental axiomatic truth concerning individual finitude and fallibility. When humans aspire to the infinite knowledge of the gods and, thinking they are absolutely certain, turn their ideas into static dogmatism, they violate the human spirit of wonder, creativity and freedom. Against the background of engrained beliefs that had become sedimented into the collective consciousness of European intelligentsia, Husserl concluded that the critical Socratic philosopher must carry the responsibility of seeking out the ideological common denominators and bridges that unite all mankind. He writes:

> Thus the philosopher must always have as his purpose to master the true and full sense of philosophy, the totality of its infinite horizons. No one line of knowledge, no individual truth must be absolutized.[9]

In this spirit I tolerate and even welcome criticism designed to expose the failings of this study and thus prepare the way for better and more accurate methods of cross-cultural interpretation.

Notes

Preface

1. The term "bodymind" is used to denote oneness between body and mind. The absence of the hyphen signifies that body and mind, in the Japanese philosophical tradition, is not interpreted as two things that are very closely interconnected. On the contrary, bodymind is to be interpreted as originally one. The choice of "bodymind," instead of "mind-body," reflects the order in which these terms are usually written in Japanese (*shin shin*, 'bodymind').

2. *Shugyō* is a term which refers to all aspects of "cultivation." It is appropriate to Buddhist disciplines such as zazen as well as cultivation in various distinctive Japanese art forms, e.g., calligraphy, painting and martial arts.

3. Yoshito S. Hakeda, *Kūkai: Major Works* (New York: Columbia University Press, 1972), p. 220.

Chapter 1

1. Edmund Husserl, *Phenomenology and the Crisis of Philosophy*, trans. Quentin Lauer (New York: Harper & Row), pp. 134-135.

2. Euthyphro, a religious seer and legal expert in ancient Athens, is characterized in Plato's dialogue *The Euthyphro* as one who at first appears quite confident about his own understanding of piety. However,

after Socrates' probing questions and cross examination, it becomes evident that Euthyphro has not appropriately considered the far-reaching implications of his inchoate ideas.

3. All section listings refer to Edmund Husserl's *Ideas I*, trans. W.R. Boyce-Gibson (New York: Macmillan, 1941).

4. Hee-Jin Kim, *Dōgen Kigen—Mystical Realist* (Tucson, The University of Arizona Press), p. 2.

5. Yoshiniro Nitta and Hirotaka Tatematsu, ed., *Analecta Husserliana: The Yearbook of Phenomenological Research*, Vol. VIII, *Japanese Phenomenology* (Dordrecht, Holland/Boston/London: D. Reidel Publishing Co., 1979), pp. 5-6. This observation about Japanese philosophy has also been reiterated by Hajimi Nakamura in his two volume work *The History of the Development of Japanese Thought* (Tokyo: Japan Cultural Society, 1969).

6. David L. Hall, *Eros and Irony: A Prelude to Philosophical Anarchy* (Albany: The State University of New York Press, 1982), p. 41.

7. I am reminded of Einstein's "democracy of observers" metaphor.

8. Edmund Husserl, *The Crisis of European Sciences and Transcendental Phenomenology*, trans. David Carr (Evanston, Northwestern University Press, 1970), p. 32.

9. *Ibid.*, p. 65, c.f., p. 37.

10. *Ibid.*, pp. 34-35.

11. This principle was first proposed by Niels Bohr in 1923. It is called the "Correspondence Principle." The issue of correspondence is an important one because it serves to remind us that our particular vantage point within the universe, amidst the relatively large and slow moving bodies depicted in the figure, is not absolute. The a priori eidetic structure about which Husserl speaks can not be known with apodictic certainty because even these essences are immanently intuited within a specific range of speed and size. Consider the fact that relativistic and quantum effects are *not* part of our everyday lives. The very large and very small sizes of two physical constants, the speed of light ($c = 2.997925 \times 10^8$ m/s) and Planck's constant ($h = 6.62613 \times 10^{-34} J \times s$), help explain this phenomenon. Relativistic effects such as length contraction and time dilation depend explicitly on the ratio of the relative velocity to the speed of light.
Consider, for example, the following mathematical formula for length contraction:

$$L = L_0 \ \sqrt{1 - (v/c)^2}$$

L = Length of object (along direction of motion) as seen by an observer who sees the object moving at speed v.
L_0 = Length of object (along direction of motion) as seen by an observer who sees the object at rest.
  c = speed of light

This mathematical equation states that moving objects, observed from a position at rest, will appear shorter. Note that as the ratio of v/c becomes very small the effect vanishes mathematically. In a like manner consider the fact that the speed of sound is much slower than the speed of light. Thus when observing even the fastest jet planes one does not experience relativistic effects that are easily measurable using Plank's constant (a very small number). Similarly, the pendulum on a Grandfather clock could be changed by millions of allowed measurable values and yet we could not perceive a change in the arch of the swing. In short, within the limits of our everyday life, we can not "see" quantum effects because the quantum of change is too small to observe.

By reflecting upon some of these simple lessons of physics, I want to argue that the so called a priori eidetic structure of human consciousness must also be examined within a system of specifiable limitations. This structure evolves and is therefore an appropriate reflection of our time and place within the universe. Phenomenologists who attempt to lay bare the eidetic structure of transcendental consciousness must also tolerate a degree of certainty that falls short of Husserlian apodicticity. Just as the common sense world was thought to be adequately explained by Newtonian physics (not admitting quantum or relativistic effects), perspectives and problems arising from the natural standpoint were thought to be adequately explained, albeit erroneously from Husserl's position, by traditional philosophical theories (not admitting transcendental effects). Husserl's phenomenological *epoché* however opens a "new region of being," a new "transcendental" perspective that is as radical and revolutionary for philosophy as Einsteinian relativity was for classical physics. The important point here is that while revolutionary movements are usually, and appropriately it seems to me, accompanied by a feeling of suspense and wonder and openendedness, Husserl's radical suspension of the natural standpoint infers at times that at last the core of our conscious being will be objectively, immanently and apodictically made present to us. Husserl allows for a feeling of openendedness with respect to the multiplicity, in fact infinite variety, of modes of meaning-bestowing acts, but it seems unwarranted that his philosophical revolution also claim an absolute apodictic grounding of the structure of consciousness, and ultimately, the axioms upon which the sciences and philosophy will be based.

12. 10^{25}m, the upper limit of this predicament, reflects approximately the distance light has traveled during the life of the universe . (Calculation based upon an estimate of 18 billion years).

13. It is a fundamental fact of nature that the parameters that describe the location and motion of a particle can not all be known simultaneously to an arbitrary degree of certainty. The Heisenburg Uncertainty Principle expresses this fact in mathematical terms as:

$$\Delta E \Delta t \geq \frac{h}{2\pi} \text{ and } \Delta p \Delta x \geq \frac{h}{2\pi};$$

E = energy

t = time

p = momentum of particle

Since $\Delta p = m\Delta v$, then we can also express this relation as:

x = position of particle

m = mass

$$\Delta p \Delta x = m\Delta v \Delta x \geq \frac{h}{2\pi}$$

v = velocity

6.62618×10^{-34}

h = Planck's constant
     J × s

Specifically this statement means that measurement of a particle's position to an accuracy of (ΔX) will result in an uncontrolable and unpredictable disturbance of the system. This disturbance will result in an indeterminacy of velocity (ΔV) for a particle of mass (m) given by the derivation of the equation above. Thus one must measure a particle's velocity in accordance with a specifiable minimum uncertainty—a fundamental epistemic limit that describes the maximum precision possible for determining accurately a particle's velocity. Note that a particle with a large mass would have a small uncertainty. Under the same circumstances a particle with a small mass would have a much larger uncertainty. Electrons, which play a critical role in thought and perception, have a very small mass. (*See* n. 10 for a more complete description of the import of Plank's constant in this context.)

14. Rudolf Carnap, *Philosophical Foundations of Physics* (New York: Basic Books), pp. 287–288.

15. Husserl's recognition of the importance of measurement is underscored in the *Crisis*, pp. 36–39, 66. *See also* Jacob Brownowski, *A Sense of the Future* (Cambridge, Massachusetts: The MIT Press), pp. 227–228 and David W. Hall, *Eros and Irony*, p. 137.

Chapter 2

1. My use of the phenomenological term "primordial" throughout shall refer to occuring first in a temporal sequence. Therefore if X is primordially given to our consciousness, then it is experienced as it is prior to subsequent thetic intentions, e.g., regarding its ontological order, ethical status or aesthetic status. Husserl's various use of the terms *"Originäritat"* and *"Originär,"* which have been translated as "primordiality" and "primordial" may be found in the Analytical Index (p. 430) W.R. Boyce Gibson's translation of Husserl's *Ideas I: General Introduction to Pure Phenomenology* (London: Collier-MacMillan, Ltd., 1962).

2. *See* Edmund Husserl, *Ideas I: General Introduction to Pure Phenomenology*, trans. W.R. Boyce Gibson (London: Collier-Macmillan ltd., 196), ch. 10, no. 111.

3. The use of the term "mind" is not related to any metaphysical concept, e.g., the Greek *psyché*. Such metaphysical concepts lie outside the phenomenological field of investigation.

4. By the term "periphery" I mean the scope of one's experiential awareness, i.e., the background area within which the noema is circumscribed.

5. A similar conclusion could be reached by following Nāgârjuna's *reductio ad absurdum* arguments (*Mūlamadhyamakārikās*) applied to the concepts mind and body. The terms body and mind can be seen as empty (Sk., *śūnya*) (Jp. *kū*) since they are relational and have no independent, verifiable referents. Similarly, Nietzsche would argue that such terms as "body" and "mind" are mere interpretations that have, through history, erroneously acquired an assumed independent ontological status. Roger Ames, in his "The Meaning of Body in Classical Chinese Philosophy," ms. (forthcoming in *International Philosophical Quarterly*), points out that Nietzsche identifies the separation of mind and body into a rigid dualism as one of the "tremendous blunders" of Western philosophical reflection. In Nietzsche's own words,

They despised the body: they left it out of the account: they treated it as an enemy.

W. Kaufman (trans.) *The Will to Power* (New York: Random House, 1968), p. 131.

6. *See* Roger Ames, "The Meaning of Body in Classical Chinese Philosophy," m.s., p. 3 (forthcoming *International Philosophical Quarterly*). For an insightful and fully developed discussion of the "dualism"/"polarity" distinction see David L. Hall, *Eros and Irony*.

7. The "horizon" of an experience includes the content and meaning of everything within the experiential periphery. The meaning of the horizon also includes the accompanying assumptions that one may bring to his/her experience as a result of the historicity of the noemata and the familiarity of the experience with the environmental conditions (Jp. *jisetsu*).

8. By "privileged" I mean that the noematic focus is singled out as the focal point within the horizon. Therefore, first order bodymind awareness is also characterized by a horizon in which no noematic foci have a privileged position with respect to any other component within the horizon. In this mode of awareness all components within the horizon share equally a non-privileged noematic status.

9. An account of a thetically neutral mode of experience is acknowledged by Edmund Husserl in his *Ideas I*, ch. 10, section 109, entitled "Neutrality-Modification."

10. These abstract classifications are not intended to imply an implicit value judgment. The use of the terms "first," "second," and "third" merely denote the chronological order by which our experience unfolds from the most simple to subsequent complex thoughts. We may have easily employed the terms "primary," "secondary," and "tertiary," respectively, if it were not for their cumbersomeness. Our future concentration upon first order bodymind merely reflects the value and significance given this primary neutral mode of awareness emphasized by Kūkai and Dōgen.

11. The phenomenologist ideally attempts to remain presuppositionless. However, the phenomenologist must acknowledge his quest for the primordially given first principles of a specified field of inquiry. Moreover, we must acknowledge that a reflexive study of experience assumes that eidetic essences are best discovered via this approach (*see* critique of this aspect of Husserl's method in Chapter 1).

12. "*Proto-doxa*" and "*Ur-doxa*" designate the ground of all doxic modifications. *Proto-doxa* and *Ur-doxa* are experienced apodictically.

13. See David L. Hall, *Eros and Irony: A Prelude to Philosophical Anarchism* (Albany, N.Y.: State University Press of New York, 1982), pp. 19–20 for a brief discussion of A.N. Whitehead and Jean-Paul Sartre

who arrived at similar positions, with respect to the constitutive function of imagination, independently.

14. To "presence" is to "be aware," without any doxic modifications, of the horizon of experience. It is the condition of being aware of the non-privileged horizon in toto granted by the neutralization of all thetic positings *via* a second reduction.

15. "Presencing" is the active verb form of presence. Therefore, we may presence the horizon as it is through an act of presencing.

16. The metaphor of a stream is purposely intended to bring to mind many other philosophers East and West (Lao Tzu, Hui-nêng (Jp. Enō), William James, Henri Bergson, Nishida Kitarō, Jean-Paul Sartre) who have analagously relied upon a form of pre-reflective experience in order to describe their ontological and existential predilections typified by spontaneous, dynamic presencing.

17. The terms "declare" and "reveal" refer to the manner in which Being, for Heidegger, becomes un-hidden (*a-letheia*).

18. Don Ihde, *Experimental Phenomenology* (New York: 1977), p. 37.

19. "Place" (Gk. *Topos*), (Jp. *Basho*) refers to a region; it designates an area of space.

20. A "normal" periphery may perhaps be best defined by an example. When we are engaged in an activity which requires attention, even if we have performed the activity many times previously, we may refer to this situation as one requiring a normal periphery. When crossing a street we must first look each way to determine whether or not it is safe to proceed. If cars are in the distance we proceed forward to the opposite curb while remaining alert for any change in traffic. We are able to at once walk forward, monitor the speed of approaching vehicles and remain alert. Anytime we are actively involved in such a situation we are able to best participate by being attentive. The normal periphery therefore refers to the degree of attention required for one to successfully participate in a situation while remaining alert to any change within the situation.

21. Although the significance of this statement includes references beyond the scope of this limited project, it is noteworthy to at least suggest the obvious parallels in accord with the advancements made by twentieth century physicists. As technological advances enable us to gather information about our universe, our experiential periphery and horizon become significantly altered. Just as Galileo's efforts metaphorically expanded the size of the known universe a hundred thou-

sand times, so do the efforts of contemporary physicists help us to understand the relative momentum, energy, position and time of phenomena occurring within the "periphery" of classical physics, astrophysics, relativity physics and quantum physics.

22. Similarly, the magnitudes of the routine constants (below) used by physicists today were either so small or so large that their tremendous importance went undetected until sufficiently sensitive instrumentation was developed to confirm (or falsify) their influence. The constants were unknown at one time because the "periphery" of the scientific community did not yet include knowledge of their influence upon the common sense world (*see* Chapter 1), c.f., ch. 1, n. 10.

Speed of light	$c = 2.9979 \times 10^8$ m/s
Planck's constant	$h = 6.62618 \times 10^{-34}$ J $\times$ s
Mass of electron	$M_e = 9.10953 \times 10^{-31}$ kg
Charge of electron	$e = 1.60219 \times 10^{-19}$ C

23. This particularly useful definition was found in *Webster's New Collegiate Dictionary* (Springfield, Mass.: G. and C. Merriam C., 1973), p. 67.

24. The term "cultivation" (Jp. *shugyō*) will designate practice and training. Cultivation refers to the process of internalizing particular acts of experience which allow the horizon in toto, or horizon and noemata, to be presenced as primordially given to consciousness. Examples of assiduous experiences which may be cultivated may include: (1) the mode of experience required for a professional baseball player to consistently observe the rotation of a high speed pitch; (2) the mode of experience enabling a conductor to hear a single instrument amidst an entire orchestra; or perhaps, (3) the trained mode of experience which allows a dining connoisseur to detect slight changes in seasoning.

25. I first became introduced to this term reading Peter L. Berger and Thomas Luckman, *The Social Construction of Reality* (Garden City, N.Y.: Doubleday and Co., Inc., 1966), p. 63. Berger and Luckman note, on p. 182, that "the term 'sedimentation' is derived from Edmund Husserl. It was first used by Schultz in a sociological context." I have defined this term myself and used it for our phenomenological purposes throughout this book.

26. "Transitional" experiences shall refer to acts of moving from second order to first order bodymind awareness. This is achieved by neutralizing the single intention characteristic of second order experience. This entails the unconscious application of the *second reduction* of the noesis/noema intentional distinction.

Chapter 3

1. Alicia and Daigan Matsunaga, *Foundation of Japanese Buddhism*, vol. I (The Aristocratic Age) (Los Angeles-Tokyo: Buddhist Books International, 1976), pp. 171, 1972. For an additional insightful discussion of Kūkai's personal history see Yoshita S. Hakeda, trans., *Kūkai: Major Works* (New York: Columbia University Press, 1972), pp. 1-60.

2. Yasuo Yuasa, "Religious Tradition in Japan" (from the manuscript of a lecture on "National Culture and World Peace" delivered at Seoul, Korea, 1976), p. 8.

3. Matsunaga, *Foundation*, vol. I, p. 180.

4. Dharmakāya as Mahāvairocana is one of the three Buddha bodies (trikāya): Dharmakāya, Sambhoghakāya and Nirmānakāya. For a more detailed discussion of the relationships within the *Trikāya* theory see Hakeda, *Kūkai: Major Works*, p. 84, 151; Hisao Inagaki, trans., *Kūkai's Principle of Attaining Buddhahood with the Present Body* (Ryukoku Translation Pamphlet Series 4) (Kyoto: Ryukoku Translation Center, Ryukoku University, 1975), p. 25; Alicia and Daigan Matsunaga, *Foundation of Japanese Buddhism*, vol. II (The Mass Movement: Kamakura & Muromachi Periods) (Los Angeles-Tokyo: Buddhist Books International, 1976), p. 52; Shozui Makoto Toganoo, *Mikkyō Bunka*, "The Symbol-System of Shingon Buddhism (2)" (Koyasan: The Esoteric Buddhist society, Dec. 1971), p. 53.

5. A good summary of this distinction is found in Matsunaga, *Foundation* vol. I, pp. 182-183.

6. *Ibid.*; see also Hakeda, *Kūkai: Major Works*. p. 265; Kōshirō Tamaki, *Philosophical Studies of Japan*, vol. XI, "On the Fundamental Idea Underlying Japanese Buddhism" (Tokyo: Japan Society for the Promotion of Science, 1975), pp. 24-25.

7. Thomas P. Kasulis (from an unpublished manuscript of a lecture delivered at the Honolulu Concert Hall, Honolulu, April 1978).

8. Matsunaga, *Foundation*, vol. I, p. 100.

9. Matsunaga, *Foundation*, vol. II, p. 156; Hakuju Ui, *Philosophical Studies of Japan*, vol. I, "A Study of Japanese Tendai Buddhism" (Tokyo: Japan Society for the Promotion of Science, 1959), pp. 70-71.

10. Hakeda, *Kūkai: Major Works*, p. 78. Throughout this study I shall be quoting extensively from Hakeda, however, I have taken the

liberty to substitute the Japanese term *"Nyorai"* for *Tathagata* and *"Dainichi Nyorai"* for *Mahāvairocana*. This substitution is designed to accommodate those who are more familiar with Japanese Buddhist terminology.

11. Tamaki, *Philosophical Studies of Japan*, vol. XI, p. 26.

12. de Bary, William T., et al., *Sources of Japanese Tradition* (New York and London: Columbia University Press, 1971), p. 141; Ui, *Philosophical Studies of Japan*, vol. I, p. 36-37; Tamaki, *Philosophical Studies of Japan*, vol. XI, p. 26.

13. Hakeda, *Kūkai: Major Works*, pp. 77, 235. (For two fine etymological analyses of *kaji*, see Inagaki, *Kūkai's Principle*, pp. 11-12, 27-28; Shozui Makoto Toganoo, *Mikkyō Bunka*, "The Symbol-Symstem of Shingon Buddhism (3)" (Koyasan: The Esoteric Buddhist Society, June 1972), pp. 74-79.

14. Hakeda, *Kūkai: Major Works*, p. 234; Toganoo, *Mikkyō Bunka* (3), p. 65, 78-79.

15. Inagaki, *Kūkai's Principle*, pp. 11-12; Toganoo, *Mikkyō Bunka* (3), p. 68.

16. Yuasa, "Religious Tradition," pp. 9-10, Toganoo, *Mikkyō Bunka* (3), p. 64.

17. Hakeda, *Kūkai: Major Works*, p. 237; Inagaki, *Kūkai's Principle*, p. 24; Toganoo, *Mikkyō Bunka* (3), pp. 76-77.

18. Hakeda, *Kūkai: Major Works*, p. 235.

19. Inagaki, *Kūkai's Principle*, p. 18. The source of the following discussion is Inagakis' translation of *Sokushin Jōbutsu*, especially pp. 12, 13, 18, 23-24, 28.

20. That is, *Mahā maṇḍala*, *Samaya maṇḍala*, *Dharma maṇḍala*, and *Karma maṇḍala*.

21. Inagaki, *Kūkai's Principle*, pp. 18, 24, 28.

22. *Ibid.*, p. 18.

23. *Ibid.*, pp. 12-13.

24. Matsunaga, *Foundation*, vol. II, p. 156.

25. Hakeda, *Kūkai: Major Works*, p. 6. Our qualifying statement within the brackets of this quotation suggest that Kūkai was "one of the" first but not the first in Japan to uphold the doctrine of *hongaku*. For example, Prince Shotoku (574-622 A.D.) upheld such a view over 100 years

before Kūkai's birth. *See* Hajime Nakamura, *A History of the Development of Japanese Thought* from A.D. 592 to 1868 vol. I (Tokyo: Japan Cultural Society, 1969), p. 18.

26. Hakeda, *Kūkai: Major Works*, p. 86; *see also* Ui, *Philosophical Studies of Japan*, vol. I, ppl. 57 – 59, 62, 63.

27. Hakeda, *Kūkai: Major Works*, p. 218.

28. *Ibid.*, p. 219.

29. Yuasa, "Religious Tradition," p. 10.

30. Tamaki, *Philosophical Studies of Japan*, vol. XI, p. 26.

31. Hakeda, *Kūkai: Major Works*, p. 263.

32. *Ibid.*, p. 152.

33. Ui, *Philosophical Studies of Japan*, vol. I, pp. 36-37, 72-73; de Bary, *Sources*, p. 143. For an explanation of the phenomenal character of Japanese Buddhism see Hajime Nakamura, *Ways of Thinking of Eastern Peoples* (Honolulu: The University Press of Hawaii, 1974), and *A History of the Development of Japanese Thought*, vol. I and II (Tokyo, Japan Cultural Society, 1969).

34. Ui, *Philosophical Studies of Japan*, vol. I, pp. 43-49.

35. *Ibid.*, p. 72. The meaning of this quotation is intended to be applicable to the Tendai tradition in general.

36. Shozui Makoto Toganoo, *Mikkyō Bunka*, "The Symbol-System of Shingon Buddhism (4)" (Koyasan: The Esoteric Buddhist Society, March 1973), p. 85.

37. Hakeda, *Kūkai: Major Works*, p. ?56.

38. *Ibid.*

39. *Ibid.*, p. 245.

40. *Ibid.*, p. 154.

41. Toganoo, *Mikkyō Bunka* (3), p. 65; *see also* Hakeda, *Kūkai: Major Works*, p. 98.

42. Toganoo, *Mikkyō Bunka* (3), p. 64. Other vehicles which Kūkai believes "produce great results" are art and dance (see also Inagaki, *Kūkai's Principle*, p. 22).

43. Hakeda, *Kūkai: Major Works*, pp. 230-231.

44. Toganoo, *Mikkyō Bunka* (3), p. 76; Inagaki, *Kūkai's Principle*, p. 11.

45. Toganoo, *Mikkyō Bunka* (3), p. 77.

46. Toganoo, *Mikkyō Bunka*, "The Symbol-System of Shingon Buddhism" (1) (Koyasan: The Esoteric Buddhist Society, Sept. 1971), p. 74. For an excellent history of the use of *mantras*, *mandalas* and *mudras* see the Toganoo Series, *Mikkyō Bunka*, "The Symbol-System of Shingon Buddhism (1), (2), (3), (4).

47. Inagaki, *Kūkai's Principle*, p. 17; *see also* Toganoo, *Mikkyō Bunka* (2), p. 57.

48. Junjiro Takakusu, *The Essentials of Buddhist Philosophy* (Westport, Conn.: Greenwood Press, Publishers, 1976), p. 142.

49. Toganoo, *Mikkyō Bunka* (2), pp. 56-57, 72; *see also* Hakeda, *Kūkai: Major Works*, pp. 241-242.

50. Hakeda, *Kūkai: Major Works*, pp. 247, 249-250; Ui, *Philosophical Studies of Japan*, vol. I, p. 38.

51. Toganoo, *Mikkyō Bunka* (3), pp. 74-75.

52. Inagaki, *Kūkai's Principle*, p. 20; Hakeda, *Kūkai's Major Works*, pp. 236, 239, 240-241; Tamaki, *Philosophical Studies of Japan*, vol. XI, p. 26. Kūkai gives examples of exactly what sounds have what referents in nature. Each sound is an "expressive symbol" of some thing in the phenomenal world. These sounds also share the same reality as that to which they refer. Kūkai says that sounds and the contents of the phenomenal world are vibrations. Kūkai describes this relationship as follows:

> The five great elements [earth, water, fire, wind, space] of sentient beings and nonsentient beings are endowed with (the power of producing) vibrations and sounds, for no sounds are independent of the great five elements; these are the original substance, and the sounds or vibrations are their functions. Hakeda, *Kūkai: Major Works*, p. 240 (brackets mine).

It may be concluded that such metaphysical speculation arose as an effort to explain the relation between sound and its apparent kinship to the horizon of experience. That is, sound is dynamic and is thus helpful in inculcating the mode of experience that allows the practitioner to presence the dynamic horizon. Kūkai's esoteric predecessors may not have understood that sound is a mere vehicle for the type of experience to which first order bodymind awareness refers. Rather, sound became associated with some mystic property which leads one to an experience wherein all things appear as one (in the horizon in toto).

Abstract verbal symbols are often used to express the highest state of religious experience, e.g., *mu* (nothingness) or *satori* (enlightenment).

"Mantras or poetic words are symbols that have the power to *evoke* and sustain deeply *moving* forms of experience" (italics added). Toganoo, *Mikkyō Bunka* (3), p. 69, quoting John A. Hutchinson, *Paths of Faith* (New York: McGraw-Hill Co., 1969), p. 6. However, the Esoteric Buddhist tradition, to which Kūkai is an heir, equates the dynamism of the sound or symbol with that which it evokes, viz., dynamic "moving" experiences. Accordingly, sounds are said to be the mystery of speech or the voice of Dainichi Nyorai which are as much an aspect of the Dharmakāya as the contents of the horizon. Hakeda, *Kūkai: Major Works*, p. 239. Indeed in practice, sounds are a part of the horizon experienced in toto.

53. Toganoo, *Mikkyō Bunka* (3), p. 74.

54. Hakeda, *Kūkai: Major Works*, pp. 218, 219, 249 (brackets mine). (*See* n. 52 for an explanation of "A" sound as representative of Dainichi Nyorai.)

55. *Ibid.*, p. 242.

56. *Ibid.*, p. 79.

57. *Ibid.*, p. 235.

58. Toganoo, *Mikkyō Bunka* (3), p. 74.

59. Matsunaga, *Foundation*, vol. I, p. 184.

60. For example see Inagaki, *Kūkai's Principle*, p. 10–11, 18, 23–24; Toganoo, *Mikkyō Bunka* (4), p. 68.

61. Toganoo, *Mikkyō Bunka* (4), pp. 80–81. For an interesting account of how *mandalas* became Japanized within Japanese Buddhism see pp. 78–81.

62. Hakeda, *Kūkai: Major Works*, p. 160.

63. Toganoo, *Mikkyō Bunka* (3), p. 51. In lieu of this quotation we must make an important qualification. *Mantras, mandalas* and *mudras* are all paradigmatic noemata for the purpose of cultivating and sedimenting first order awareness. These are the important noemata upon which the student concentrates. Strictly speaking, however, from the perspective of the enlightened individual, the whole world may be a *mandala*, all sounds are *mantras*, and all postures are *mudras*. That is, once neutral presencing is sedimented the dharma may be seen in all things, sounds, and feelings. To the master, the dharma is not limited to the specific noemata upon which the student focuses his attention. Therefore, from the perspective of the enlightened, "all concrete things or phenomena are identical with truth."

64. Inagaki, *Kūkai's Principle*, p. 29.

65. Toganoo, *Mikkyō Bunka* (4), p. 68.

66. Hakeda, *Kūkai: Major Works*, p. 99.

67. *Ibid.*

68. *Ibid.*, p. 220.

69. *Ibid.*, p. 231.

70. *Ibid.*, p. 220. Note Hakeda's atypical interpretation of *dhyāna* as "body" as opposed to the more traditional "meditation." The somatic aspect of the meditative endeavor is acknowledged.

71. Toganoo, *Mikkyō Bunka* (3), p. 61.

Chapter 4

1. Matsunaga, *Foundation*, vol., I, p. 183 (Interpretative brackets mine].

2. Tamaki, *Philosophical Studies of Japan*, vol., XI, p. 26; *see also* p. 29.

3. Toganoo, *Mikkyō Bunka* (4), p. 84.

4. Hakeda, *Kūkai: Major Works*, p. 210.

5. *Ibid.*

6. *Ibid.*, pp. 230, 234-235; *see also* Tamaki, *Philosophical Studies of Japan*, vol. XI p. 29.

7. Hakeda, *Kūkai: Major Works*, pp. 208-209, 211, 226.

8. *Ibid.*, p. 244. Kūkai's use of *monji* (expressive symbol) includes all sensory objects and is not simply limited to letters or characters; *see* p. 234.

9. Inagaki, *Kūkai's Principle*, pp. 25-26, 35; *see also* Hakeda, *Kūkai: Major Works*, p. 23.

10. Hakeda, *Kūkai: Major Works*, p. 264.

11. *Ibid.*, pp. 250, 256; *see also* p. 253.

12. *Ibid.*, pp. 202–203.

13. *Ibid.*, p. 201.

14. *Ibid.*, p. 201.

15. *Ibid.*, pp. 205, 264, 267.

16. de Bary, *Sources*, p. 155. For further references regarding the use of metaphors depicting a thetically neutral mode of awareness see Ui, *Philosophical Studies of Japan*, vol. I, p. 38; Toganoo, *Mikkyō Bunka* (3); Inagaki, *Kūkai's Principle*, pp. 10, 18, 28, 30; and Hakeda, *Kūkai's Major Works*, pp. 97, 99, 158, 160–162, 219, 221, 226, 231.

17. Hakeda, *Kūkai: Major Works*, pp. 97, 99, 258, 160–162, 219, 221, 226, 231; Inagaki, *Kūkai's Principle*, pp. 10, 18, 28, 30; Ui, *Philosophical Studies of Japan*, p. 38.

18. Hakeda, *Kūkai: Major Works*, pp. 215; 226; Inagaki, *Kūkai's Principle*, p. 10; Toganoo, *Mikkyō Bunka* (3), p. 67.

19. The personification of this keen sensitivity is furthered by statements suggesting that the practitioner becomes aware that the Universe itself is speaking to him. In the context of cultivating various art forms, the Japanese phrases "*Kanyū taido*" and "*Shinryo meisatsu*" reflect this idea. *Kanyū taido* conveys a meaning of a relaxed mind and expansive awareness. *Shinryo meisatsu* conveys a meaning of thorough understanding and deep or heightened awareness. Together these expressions represent a form of sensitivity that enable the practitioner's to acquire an introspective understanding of the Dharmakāya within themselves. This awareness is said to lead them to respect the entire universe wherein the Dharmakāya resides—"*Banyū Aigo*" ("love all creation").

20. Hakeda, *Kūkai: Major Works*, p. 85.

21. *Ibid.*, p. 248.

22. Tamaki, *Philosophical Studies of Japan*, vol. XI, p. 29. *See also* Ui, Philosophical Studies of Japan, vol. I, p. 35.

23. *See* chapter 3, pp. 71–75.

24. Toganoo, *Mikkyō Bunka* (2), p. 54.

25. *See* chapter 1, p. 59.

26. Inagaki, *Kūkai's Principle*, p. 23; Toganoo, *Mikkyō Bunka* (4), p. 84.

27. Ui, *Philosophical Studies of Japan*, p. 35. Quotation by Annen (841–884 A.D.).

28. Hakeda, *Kūkai: Major Works*, p. 213.

29. Tamaki, *Philosophical Studies of Japan*, vol. XI, p. 30.

30. Hakeda, *Kūkai: Major Works*, p. 203.

31. *Ibid.*, p. 176, n. 70 on the "Fourfold Meditation."

32. *Ibid.*, pp. 174–175, 254–255.

33. *Ibid.*, pp. 226–227.

34. *Ibid.*, pp. 231–232. *See also* Inagaki, *Kūkai's Principle*, p. 25.

35. Hakeda, *Kūkai: Major Works*, pp. 232, 254; Inagaki, *Kūkai's Principle*, pp. 26–27, 36.

36. Toganoo, *Mikkyō Bunka* (3), pp. 48–49, 75–76, 78.

37. Hakeda, *Kūkai: Major Works*, pp. 97, 219, 225.

38. *Ibid.*, p. 74.

39. *Ibid.*, p. 78.

40. *Ibid.*, pp. 93, 263.

41. *Ibid.*, p. 78.

42. *Ibid.*, pp. 202, 264, 268. *See also* p. 196, n. 123, and p. 221.

43. *Ibid.*, p. 89.

44. *Ibid.*, pp. 89, 229. *See also* Inagaki, *Kūkai's Principle.*, pp. 10, 23.

45. Ui, *Philosophical Studies of Japan*, vol. I, pp. 38, 57, 63.

46. Hakeda, *Kūkai: Major Works*, p. 220, 221.

47. Toganoo, *Mikkyō Bunka* (3), p. 70.

48. Hakeda, *Kūkai: Major Works*, p. 253.

49. *Ibid.*, p. 91.

50. Inagaki, *Kūkai's Principle*, p. 19.

51. Hakeda, *Kūkai: Major Works*, p. 80.

52. *Ibid.*, p. 79.

53. *Ibid.*, p. 91.

54. *Ibid.*, p. 218.

Chapter 5

1. We will focus our attention upon the fascicles *Genjōkōan, Shinjingakudo, Uji,* and *Kaiinzanmai. Genjōkōan* is considered by many to be the most important fascicle. The principles defined therein are themes which permeate his work. *Shinjingakudō* is a fascicle in which Dōgen specifically addressed issues relevant to our inquiry into the relationship between the mind and body. Dōgen's discussion of temporality is found in the fascicle *Uji.* By interpreting phenomenologically his theory of time, we will be able to understand better the temporal structures of his paradigmatic mode of awareness. Finally in the fascicle *Kaiinzanmai,* Dōgen describes other important features of experience which are valuable for our phenomenological interpretation. Our discussions of these fascicles are not intended to be analyses of the fascicles themselves. On the contrary, these fascicles have been selected simply because some of Dōgen's most explicit statements regarding various characteristics of his paradigmatic mode of experience are described therein.

2. Heinrich Dumoulin, trans. Paul Peachy, *A History of Zen Buddhism* (Boston: Beacon Press, 1969), pp. 152, 306. For a good historical analysis of Dōgen's life see Hee-Jin Kim, *Dōgen Kigen-Mystical Realist* (Tucson, Arizona: 1975), ch. 2.

3. *Ibid.,* p. 153.

4. For this insight I am indebted to Professor Nakamura, who brought this point to my attention in a private conversation on November 5, 1979 (Tokyo, Japan).

5. An incongruence between theory and practice was apparently perceived by Dōgen. We must acknowledge, however, that this problem could have been inflated by Dōgen. That is, we are not in a position to speculate about the social and historical circumstances which may have affected Dōgen's ability to perceive Tendai Buddhism as clearly as his teachers.

6. Norman Waddell and Masao Abe, trans., "Dōgen's Bendowa," *The Eastern Buddhist* NS IV, No. 1 (1971), p. 129.

7. *Ibid.,* p. 138.

8. It should be noted that Dōgen is not the first to hold such a view. The following statements taken from the *Lotus Sutra* captures this notion: "*Sōmoku kokudo shikkai jobutsu,* the grass, trees, earth and natural surroundings all possess Buddhahood." (Unpub. trans by Hajime Nakamura).

9. Kōsen Nishiyama and John Stevens, trans. *Shōbōgenzō: The Eye and Treasury of the True Law,* vol. I (Sendai, Japan, Daihokkaikaku, 1975), pp. 31-35. *See also* pp. 10-11. [This translation of Dōgen's *Shōbōgenzō* has been used sparingly. After checking this translation against the text compiled by Dōshū Okubo, we have discovered that the Nishiyama and Stevens translation is based upon *Gendaigo Yaku Shōbōgenzō* by Soichi Nakamura (Sei shin Shobo). Therefore, we have utilized their translation only after we have consulted the edition compiled by Okubo and determined it to be in accord with the original. There are, however, many fascicles in which (1) the Nishiyama and Stevens text is the only available translation in English, and (2) their translation, although highly readable, significantly strays from the original. In these instances, we have translated the passages ourselves and noted their occurrence. I would like to thank Professor Roger Ames, Professor Alfred Bloom, Professor Thomas Kasulis, Professor Kakuko Shoku and Mr. Shigenori Nagatomo for their assistance in translating these passages].

10. *Ibid.,* pp. 50, 55-56, 74.

11. See Dōshū Okubo, ed., *Dōgen Zenji Zenshū,* vol, I (Tokyo: Chikuma shobo, 1969), p. 37 (my translation).

12. In keeping with our terminology it would be more accurate, but also more cumbersome, to translate *shinjin datsuraku* as "casting off the mind-aspect and body-aspect." In other words rid yourself of such abstractions in order to become aware of the bodymind ground at the base of all experience.

13. Waddell and Abe, "Dōgen's Bendōwa," p. 130.

14. *Ibid.,* p. 133.

15. Matsunaga, *Foundation,* vol. II, p. 239. In this work it is suggested that *shinjin datsuraku* is peculiarly Japanese and would be a most unlikely phrase for Nyojō to utter. It is interesting to note that some scholars hypothesize that Nyojō most likely used "dust" (Jp. *jin,* Ch. ch'en) rather than "body" (Jp. *shin,* Ch. shen). In other words, Nyojō may have said, "cast off the dust of mind" which has been a typical Zen idiom since the days of Enō (Ch. Hui-nêng). Dōgen's possible deliberate misconception, typical of his manner of interpretation, only serves to underscore the importance of bodymind with respect to the enlightenment experience.

16. Reiho Masunaga, trans., *A Primer of Sōtō Zen: A Translation of Dōgen's Shōbōgenzō Zuimonki* (Honolulu: The University Press of Hawaii, 1975), p. 49.

17. *Ibid.,* p. 29.

18. *Ibid.*, p. 25.

19. *Ibid.*, p. 61.

20. *Ibid.*, p. 93.

21. *Ibid.*, pp. 25, 27.

22. Okubo, *Dōgen*, vol. I, p. 778 (my translation).

23. The translation of *shushō* as "cultivation-authentication" was first suggested by Thomas P. Kasulis in his dissertation *Action for Performs Man* (New Haven: Yale University, 1975).

24. Waddell and Abe, "Dōgen's Bendōwa," pp. 133–134.

25. Tamaki, *Philosophical Studies of Japan*, vol. XI, p. 36.

26. The phenomenological nature of Dōgen's project will be specifically discussed at the beginning of Section 3: *The Descriptive Project of Shōbōgenzō*.

27. At this time I refrain from giving the customary etymology as I will discuss this important and rather complex expression in section 3.

28. Norman Waddell and Masao Abe, trans., "Shōbōgenzō Genjōkōan," *The Eastern Buddhist*, NS V, No. 2 (1972), p. 137.

29. "Reflexive transcendence" refers to moving "beyond" discursive modes of thinking through introspective neutralization of thetic positings. By returning to a more primordial level of awareness devoid of noetic/noematic vectors, the experiencer transcends complex thetic modes of awareness in a reflexive direction.

30. See chapter 2, pp. 58–61.

31. Waddell and Abe, "Dōgen's Bendōwa," pp. 135–136.

32. *Ibid.*, pp. 139–140.

33. *Ibid.*, p. 140.

34. Matsunaga, *Foundation*, vol. II, p. 250.

35. Waddell and Abe, "Dōgen's Bendōwa," p. 151. In this passage Abe and Waddell have translated *sokushin zebutsu* as "the mind in itself is Buddha." In an effort to remain consistent with my own previous translation, however, I have taken the liberty to retranslate this phrase as "this very mind is Buddha." In addition I have substituted the word "cultivation" for "practice" (*shu*).

36. Nishiyama and Stevens, *Shōbōgenzō*, pp. 17-20; Waddell and Abe, "Dōgen's Bendōwa," p. 146.

37. Ōkubo, *Dōgen*, vol. I, p. 44 (my translation).

38. *Ibid.*, p. 45 (my translation).

39. Masunaga, *A Primer of Sōtō Zen*, p. 108. For additional information on Dōgen's reference to speech and mind see Nishiyama and Stevens, *Shōbōgenzō*, p. 142 and Waddell and Abe, "Dōgen's Bendōwa," p. 134.

40. Thomas P. Kasulis, "The Zen philosopher: A review article on Dōgen scholarship in English," *Philosophy East and West* 28, No. 3 (Honolulu: The University Press of Hawaii, July 1978), p. 359.

41. *Ibid.*

42. Nishiyama and Stevens, *Shōbōgenzō*, p. 103.

43. *See* Ōkubo, *Dōgen*, vol. I, p. 206.

44. Nishiyama and Stevens, *Shōbōgenzō*, pp. 104–105.

45. For example see Nishiyama and Stevens, *Shōbōgenzō*, pp. 11, 20, 118.

46. For example, Norman Waddell and Masao Abe, "Dōgen's *Fukan-zazengi* and *Shōbōgenzōzazengi*," *The Eastern Buddhist*, NS VI, No. 2 (1973), pp. 122, 124; Waddell and Abe, "Dōgen's Bendōwa," p. 138.

47. This view of *Shōbōgenzō's* purpose is not universally accepted but it is the interpretation which has been adopted. It was first suggested by Thomas P. Kasulis.

48. A complete examination of the etymology of Genjōkōan, including a commentary concerning the philosophical context in which it is employed, is given in Thomas P. Kasulis', *Action Performs Man*, pp. 132–135, 138. I have consulted this work and have adopted the Kasulis translation of "Genjōkōan" as "presencing things-as-they-are."

49. Kasulis, *Action Performs Man*, p. 133.

50. Nishiyama and Stevens, *Shōbōgenzō*, p. 85.

51. Waddell and Abe, "*Shōbōgenzō Genjōkōan*," p. 138. *See also* Matsunaga, *Foundation*, vol. II, p. 248.

52. Matsunaga, *Foundation*, vol. II, p. 248.

53. Ōkubo, *Dōgen*, p. 36 (my translation).

54. *Ibid.*, p. 37 (my translation).

55. Nishiyama and Stevens, *Shōbōgenzō*, p. 11.

56. Ōkubo, *Dōgen*, p. 40 (my translation).

57. Unpub. trans. by Thomas P. Kasulis, "*Shōbōgenzō Uji*", p. 1.

58. *Ibid.*, n. #7, p. 2.

59. Just as body-aspect and mind-aspect have been coined to denote the body or mind abstracted from the experiential correlate bodymind, "temporal-aspect" similarly denotes that the notion of linear time is an abstraction with no direct experiential correlate.

60. Kasulis, "Shōbōgenzō Uji," pp. 2-3.

61. *Ibid.*, p. 4.

62. This term is traditionally associated with Hua-yen meditation.

63. Unpub. trans. by Shigenori Nagatomo, "*Shōbōgenzō Kaiinzanmai*," p. 1. *See also* Ōkubo, *Dōgen*, p. 102.

64. Nagatomo, "*Shōbōgenzō Kaiinzanmai,* " p. 1. *See also* Ōkubo, *Dōgen*, 102.

65. Nagatomo, "*Shōbōgenzō Kaiinzanmai,* " p. 1. *See also* Ōkubo, *Dōgen*, 102.

66. Nagatomo, "*Shōbōgenzō Kaiinzanmai,* " p. 3. *See also* Ōkubo, *Dōgen*, p. 103.

67. Nagatomo, "*Shōbōgenzō Kaiinzanmai,* " p. 2. *See also* Ōkubo, *Dōgen*, pp. 102–103.

68. Nagatomo, "*Shōbōgenzō Kaiinzanmai,* " p. 5. *See also* Ōkubo, *Dōgen*, 104.

69. Nagatomo, "*Shōbōgenzō Kaiinzanmai,* " pp. 6–11. *See also* Ōkubo, *Dōgen*, pp. 104–107.

Chapter 6

1. Norman Waddell and Masao Abe, trans., "Dōgen's *Shōbōgenzō Sammai ŌZammai*" *The Eastern Buddhist*, NS VII, No. 1 (1974), p. 119. *See also* Waddell and Abe, "Dōgen's Bendōwa," p. 148.

2. Waddell and Abe, "Dōgen's *Fukanzazengi*," p. 122. *See also* Waddell and Abe, "Dōgen's Bendōwa," p. 139; Dumoulin, *A History of Zen Buddhism*, p. 167.

3. Waddell and Abe, "Dōgen's *Fukanzazengi*," pp. 122–123. Asterisks denote changes in the translation of specific phrases in order to be consistent with our previous analysis, namely "Without thinking" for Waddell/Abe's "non-thinking," "cultivation-authentication" for practice realization" and "presencing of things-as-they-are" for *genjōkōan* ("manifestation of ultimate reality.") *See* Kasulis, *Actions Performs Man*, p. 113.

4. Waddell and Abe, "Dōgen's *Shōbōgenzō Sammai Ō Zammai*," p. 119.

5. Masunaga, *A Primer of Sōtō Zen*, p. 47.

6. Waddell and Abe, "Dōgen's *Bendōwa*," pp. 146–147; cf., Dumoulin, *A History of Zen Buddhims*, p. 163.

7. Waddell and Abe, "Dōgen's *Shōbōgenzō Sammai Ō Zammai*," p. 121. *See also* Ōkubo, *Dōgen*, p. 540.

8. Waddell and Abe, "Dōgen's *Shōbōgenzō Sammai Ō Zammai*," p. 121. *See also* Ōkubo, *Dōgen*, p. 540.

9. Waddel and Abe, "Dōgen's *Fukanzazengi*," p. 122.

10. Waddell and Abe, "Dōgen's *Bendōwa*," see footnote p. 128.

11. For example in Norman Waddell and Masao Abe, trans., "*Shōbōgenzō* Buddha-nature," Part II, *The Eastern Buddhist*, NS IX, No. 1 (1976), p. 99.

12. This physiological center serves to systematically join the body and mind for a variety of other reasons as well. According to Sōtō tradition, and numerous other forms of *shugyō*, this physiological center is also a spiritual center of the body. Although there are numerous reasons for this phenomenon in the Japanese tradition, we will limit our discussion to the relevancy of focusing one's intention upon this spiritual center during zazen practice. In our phenomenological terminology, the rocking motion which begins practice helps the practitioner to become aware of the dynamism within the horizon of first order bodymind awareness. That is, the distance of the rocking motion decreases by one half each time until one is sitting immovably. However, since the width of the rocking represents a finite distance (line segment) which, when continually halved, never completely becomes diminished to zero, there also remains a feeling of dynamic movement though imperceptible. This "inner dynamism" represents the infinitude of spiritual awareness, i.e., the infinitude of possible experiences of presencing things-as-they-are. It is interesting to suggest that this feeling simultaneously approximates the dynamic structural feature of first order bodymind awareness.

To the practitioner this means that the rocking motion is never calmed to the point of static, motionless sitting. As the practitioner sits in the full lotus position, he or she is aware of the ceaseless dynamic and impermanent character of their given situation. This "inner dynamism" thus simulates the dynamism of zazen awareness and helps the novice to remain steadfast and alert. In fact, drowsy zazen practitioners were frequently and energetically struck by Dōgen's master because this "inner dynamism" was escaping them. Sayings to the effect that "zazen exists in the realm of Buddha and is infinite" (Dumoulin, *A History of Zen Buddhism p. 164*) can thus be understood as representative of the dynamic lived perception of infinity found within each dharma (thing-as-experienced) including one's self. Such statements need not lead us to assume that there is some transcendental other-worldly aspect of zazen awareness.

13. "non-thinking." see Waddell and Abe, "Dōgen's Fukanzazengi," p. 123. "superthinking." see Dumoulin, *A History of Zen Buddhism*, p. 164. "without thinking." see Kasulis, *Action Performs Man*, p. 114. All these translations occur from alternative translations of the introduction to the *zazenshin* fascicle of *Shōbōgenzō*. (*See* Ōkubo, *Dōgen*, p. 90.)

14. Kasulis, *Action Performs Man*, p. 115.

15. Ōkubo, *Dōgen*, p. 36 (my translation).

16. For example, in Waddell and Abe, "*Shōbōgenzō Genjōkōan*," pp. 134–135, "without thinking" is explicitly stated as a precondition for becoming aware of the above-mentioned characteristics of presencing things-as-they-are.

17. Waddell and Abe, "*Shōbōgenzō Genjōkōan*," p. 137.

18. *Ibid.*, p. 139.

19. Ōkubo, *Dōgen*, p. 170 (my translation).

20. Waddell and Abe, "*Shōbōgenzō Genjōkōan*," p. 134.

21. *Ibid.*

22. *Ibid.*, p. 136.

23. Ōkubo, *Dōgen*, p. 27 (my translation).

24. *Ibid.*, p. 563 (my translation).

25. Waddell and Abe, "Dōgen's *Bendōwa*," p. 137; Nishiyama and Stevens, *Shōbōgenzō*, pp. 5, 10, 92, 95, 98, 104–105, 125; Masunaga, *A Primer of Sōtō Zen*, p. 111. For some additional secondary sources see Roshi Philip Kapleau, *The Three Pillars of Zen: Teaching, Practice, and*

Enlightenment (Garden City, N.Y.: Anchor Press/Doubleday, 1980), pp. 56–57; Daisetz Teitaro Suzuki, *The Training of the Buddhist Monk* (Berkeley: Wingbow Press, 1974), p. 116; Tamaki, *Philosophical Studies of Japan*, vol. XI, p. 35.

26. *See* Waddell and Abe, "*Shōbōgenzō Genjokōan*," pp. 138–139, in which Dōgen describes the fish and bird who presence their own situation and adapt themselves accordingly.

27. Masunaga, *A Primer of Sōtō Zen*, p. 39.

28. Nishiyama and Stevens, *Shōbōgenzō*, p. 12.

29. Norman Waddell and Maseo Abe, trans., "Dōgen's *Shōbōgenzō Zenki* 'Total Dynamic Working' and *Shōji* 'Birth and Death,'" *The Eastern Buddhist*, NS V, No. 1 (1972) p. 76.

30. *Ibid.*, p. 79.

31. Waddell and Abe, "*Shōbōgenzō Genjokōan*," p. 135.

32. Waddell and Abe, "Dōgen's *Fukanzazengi*," p. 123.

33. Kapleau, *The Three Pillars*, p. 36.

34. Waddell and Abe, "Dōgen's *Bendōwa*., p. 136 and footnote #51.

35. Nishiyama and Stevens, *Shōbōgenzō*, p. 36.

36. *Ibid.*, pp. 93–94.

37. *Ibid.*, pp. 34–35.

38. Kasulis, "The Zen philosopher," p. 371.

39. *Ibid.*

40. Nishiyama and Stevens, *Shōbōgenzō*, p. 16; Waddell and Abe, "Dōgen's Shōbōgenzō Zenki," p. 74–77.

41. Nishiyama and Stevens, *Shōbōgenzō*," p. 82.

42. Waddell and Abe, "*Shōbōgenzō Genjokōan*," p. 136.

43. Nishiyama and Stevens, *Shōbōgenzō*, p. 28. Unpub. trans. by Shigenori Nagatomo, "Shin-fukatoku": A Translation of the fascicle from Dōgen's *Shōbōgenzō*, p. 1.

44. Since this mode of experience is pre-thetic, it defies all attempts to describe it exactly as it occurs. Therefore, the Zen master's transmission and confirmation (*inka*, 'seal of approval') of this mode of awareness similarly defies linguistic articulation. His role is limited to that of help-

ing his students to break the encrusted habits of second and third order awareness. The master's action must evoke direct mind to mind (*ishin denshin*) communication. (Waddell and Abe, "Dōgen's *Bendōwa*," see footnote #31, p. 132.) The traditional metaphor of the "finger pointing to the moon" (*shigetsu no yubi*) captures the nature of the difficulty of attempting to authentically describe pre-thetic experience. Dōgen recognizes this problem by describing the unobtainable or undefinable mind (*shinfukatoku*). Yet, it is precisely this mode of awareness which enables one to empirically verify the bodymind ground within the primordially given horizon.

45. Waddell and Abe, "Dōgen's *Bendōwa*," p. 134. *See also* Waddell and Abe, "*Shōbōgenzō Genjōkōan*," pp. 136–137 footnote #14; Waddell and Abe, "Dōgen's *Bendōwa*," pp. 136–137.

46. Nishiyama and Stevens, *Shōbōgenzō*, p. 13.

47. *Ibid.*, p. 42. *See also* Nagatomo's translation of "*Shōbōgenzō Kaiinzanmai*," p. 1; Ōkubo, *Dōgen*, p. 102.

48. Nishiyama and Stevens, *Shōbōgenzō*, p. 10. *See also* Ōkubo, *Dōgen*, p. 36 where Dōgen says, "The act of shaving the head and donning the black robes is precisely converting the mind . . ." (my translation).

49. Waddell and Abe, "Dōgen's *Bendōwa*," p. 134; Nishiyama and Stevens, *Shōbōgenzō*, p. 107.

50. Nishiyama and Stevens, *Shōbōgenzō*, p. 108.

51. Masunaga, *A Primer of Sōtō Zen*, pp. 25, 27, 29, 47; Nishiyama and Stevens, *Shōbōgenzō*, p. 119. *See also* de Bary, *Sources*, pp. 254–255.

52. Francis Dojun Cook, trans., *How to Raise an Ox: Zen Practice as Taught in Zen Master Dogen's Shōbōgenzō* (Los Angeles: Center Publication, 1978), pp. 175–176.

53. Waddell and Abe, " Dōgen's *Bendōwa*," pp. 146–147.

54. Yūhō Yokoi, trans., *Zen Master Dōgen: An Introduction with Selected Writings* (New York-Tokyo: Weatherhill Inc., 1976), pp. 57,63.

55. Waddell and Abe, "Dōgen's *Fukanzazengi*," p. 122. *See also* Dumoulin, A History of Zen Buddhism, p. 167.

56. Nishiyama and Stevens, *Shōbōgenzō*, p. 130.

Chapter 7

1. *See* Husserl, *Ideas I*, ch. 10, section 111, for an examination of the role of free fancy as an imaginative technique.

2. The suggestion that one's posited theories (noemata) provide a "transcendent clue" to help understand the manner in which meaning is bestowed (noesis) is underscored in Husserl's *Cartesian Meditations*, sections 21 and 43. Edmund Husserl, *Cartesian Meditations*, trans. by Dorion Cairns, The Hague: Martinus Nijhoff, 1973, pp. 50–53. *See also* the works of Husserl's student, Roman Ingarden. Ingarden's *The Literary Work of Art*, trans. George G. Grabowicz (Evanston: Northwestern University Press, 1973) and *The Cognition of the Literary Work of Art*, trans. Ruth Ann Crowley and Kenneth R. Olson (Evanston: Northwestern University Press, 1973) both attempt to explain those aspects of a text which are given some independent ontic value, through the efforts of the author working within the limitations of his/her transcendental apparatus, and those indeterminate aspects of a text that will be "concretized" by the reader; hence, the development of reader-oriented theories of interpretation.

3. Kim, *Dōgen Kigen-Mystical Realist*, p. 128.

4. *Ibid.*, *see also* footnote 172 on p. 339.

5. *Ibid.*, pp. 129–130.

6. Husserl, *Phenomenology and the Crisis of Philosophy*, pp. 149–192.

7. *Ibid.*, p. 192.

8. As a case in point see Husserl, *Phenomenology and the Crisis of Philosophy*, p. 171.

9. *Ibid..*, p. 181.

Glossary

Amaterasu Ōmikami	天照大神
banyu aigo	万有愛護
basho	場所
Bendōwa	弁道話
Benkenmitsu nikyō ron	弁顕密二教論
busshin ichinyo	物心一如
ch'en (Ch)	塵
Daibirushana Jōbutsu Jimben Kaji-kyō	大毘盧遮那成仏神変加持経
Dainichi-kyō	大日経
Dainichi Nyorai	大日如来
Daigo	大悟
datsuraku	脱落
Dōgen Kigen	道元希玄
Enō	慧能
Fukanzazengi	普勧坐禅儀
fushiryo	不思量
ga	我
ga soku butsu	我即仏
Genjōkōan	現成公案
go-dai	五大
goshin-pō	護身法

229

gyōbutsu	行 仏
gyōshū	行 修
heijōshin	平 常 心
himitsu sammaji	秘 密 三 味
himitsu zen	秘 密 禅
hishiryō	非 思 量
hō	法
hōben	方 便
hongaku	本 覚
honnu hongaku	本 有 本 覚
honnu sammaji	本 有 三 摩 地
honnu sanmitsu	本 有 三 密
hosshin	法 身
hosshin seppō	法 身 説 法
hotsubodaishin	発 菩 提 心
Hui-kuo (Ch)	恵 果
Hui-nêng (Ch)	慧 能
ichiji	一 時
ichijo	一 処
Ikkamyōju	一 顆 明 珠
inka	印 可
ishin denshin	以 心 伝 心
Izana-gi	イ ザ ナ ギ
Izana-mi	イ ザ ナ ミ
ji ri funi	地 理 不 似
jigen onyō	慈 眼 温 容
jijuyū	自 受 用
jin	塵
Jinen chishū	自 然 智 宗
Jippo	十 法
jisetsu	時 節

jōbutsu	成 仏
Ju-ching (Ch)	如 浄
Juki	授 記
kabuki	歌 舞 技
Kaiinzanmai	海 印 三 味
kaji	加 持
kami	神
Kannon	観 音
kanyū taido	寛 裕 大 度
karada	身 体
Kegon-shu	華 厳 宗
keiko	稽 古
keireki	経 歴
kenkyō	顕 教
kōan	公 案
Kōbō Daishi	弘 法 大 師
Kobutsushin	古 仏 心
kōge	高 下
kōjō	向 上
kokoro	心
Kokū	虚 空
Kōmyō	光 明
koya-hijiri	高 野 聖
kū	空
Kūge	空 華
Kūkai	空 海
kyōryaku	経 歴
Lao Tzu (Ch)	老 子
mi ni sokushite butsu to naru	身 に 即 して 仏 と 成 る
mikkyō	密 教
mitsu	密

mon	文
mondō	問 答
monji	文 字
mu	無
muga	無 我
musō	無 相
Nakamura, Hajime	中 村　元
nikon	而 今
nikon no ima	而 今 の 今
niōmon	仁 王 門
niō zen	仁 王 禅
Nishida, Kitarō	西 田　幾 多 郎
no-en	能 縁
Noh	能
Nyojō	如 浄
Nyūga ganyū	入 我 我 入
Ōkubo, Dōshū	大 久 保　道 舟
otomo	お 伴
sanmitsu	三 密
sanmitsumon	三 密 門
sangai isshin	三 界 一 心
satori	悟
sennigedō	先 尼 外 道
setsu	説
Shamon Dōgen	沙 門 道 元
shi-igi	四 威
shigetsu no yubi	指 月 の 指
shikantaza	祇 管 打 坐
shin	身
shin	心
shin-dai	心 大

shin shin	身　心
shin shin toitsu aikido	身心統一合気道
Shinfukatoku	心不可得
Shingon-shū	真言宗
shinjin	身　心
shinjin datsuraku	身心脱落
Shinjingakudō	身心学道
shinjin ichinyo	身心一如
shinjitsunintai	真実人体
shinryo meisatsu	深慮明察
Shintō	神　道
shiryō	思　慮
shō	証
sho-en	所　縁
Shōbōgenzō	正法眼蔵
Shōbōgenzō Zuimonki	正法眼蔵随門記
Shōji	生　死
Shotoku Taishi	聖徳太子
shu	修
shugyō	修　行
shūgyōshite jibun no karada ni osameru	修行して自分の身に修める
Shugendō	修験道
shushō ichinyo	修証一如
soku	即
soku-ji-shin	即地地真
sokushin jōbutsu	即心成仏
Sokushin Jōbutsu-gi	即心成仏儀
Sokushin Zebutsu	即心是仏
sōmoku kokudo shikkai jōbutsu	草木国土悉皆成仏
Sōtō-shū	曹洞宗
sumiyakani mi butsu to naru	速やかに身仏と成る

sunawachi mi nareru	即 身 成 れ る
taigi	体 技
taizen fudō	泰 然 不 動
Tamaki, Kōshirō	玉 城 康 四 郎
Tao (Ch)	道
Tendai-shū	天 台 宗
Tsuki	都 儀
uchi deshi	内 弟 子
Uji	有 時
usō	有 相
Watsuji, Tetsurō	和 辻 哲 郎
wu (Ch)	無
wu-wei (Ch)	無 為
Yuasa, Yasuo	湯 浅 泰 雄
zazen	坐 禅
Zazenshin	坐 禅 箴
Zen	禅

Bibliography

Brownowski, Jacob. *A Sense of the Future.* Cambridge, Massachusetts: Massachusetts Institute of Technology Press, 1977.

Carnap, Rudolf. *Philosophical Foundations of Physics.* New York: Basic Books, Inc., 1966.

Cook, Francis Dojun. *How to Raise an Ox: Zen Practice as Taught in Zen Master Dōgen's Shōbōgenzō.* Los Angeles: Center Publications, 1978.

de Bary, William T., et al. *Sources of Japanese Tradition.* New York and London: Columbia University Press, 1971.

Dumoulin, Heinrich, S. J. *A History of Zen Buddhimm.* Trans. Paul Peachey. Boston: Beacon Press, 1969.

Hakeda, Yoshito S. *Kūkai: Major Works.* New York: Columbia University Press, 1972.

Hall, David L. *Eros and Irony: A Prelude to Philosophical Anarchism.* Albany: State University of New York Press, 1982.

Heidegger, Martin. *Being and Time.* Trans. John Macquarrie and Edward Robinson. New York: Harper and Row, 1962.

Hegel, George Wilhelm Friedrich. *Reason in History.* Trans. Robert S. Hartman. New York: Bobbs-Merrill Co., 1953.

Husserl, Edmund. *Ideas I: General Introduction to Pure Phenomenology.* Trans. W. R. Boyce Gibson. London: Collier-Macmillan Ltd., 1962.

– – –, *Cartesian Meditations.* Trans. Dorian Cairns. The Hague: Martinus Nijhoff, 1973.

— — —. *Phenomenology and the Crisis of Philosophy*. Trans. Quentin Lauer. New York: Harper and Row, 1965.

— — —. *The Crisis of European Sciences and Transcendental Phenomenology*. Trans. David Carr. Evanston: Northwestern University Press, 1970.

Hutchinson, John A. *Paths of Faith. New York: McGraw-Hill Co., 1969.*

Inagaki, Hisao, trans. *Kūkai's Principle of Attaining Buddhahood with the Present Body*. Ryukoku Translation Pamphlet Series 4. Kyoto: Ryukoku Translation Center Ryukoku University, 1975.

Kapleau, Roshi Philip. *The Three Pillars of Zen: Teaching, Practice and Enlightenment*. Garden City, N.Y.: Anchor Press/Doubleday, 1980.

Kasulis, Thomas P. *Zen Action/Zen Person*. Honolulu: The University Press of Hawaii, 1981.

— — —. *Actions Perform Man*. Ph.D. Dissertation. New Haven: Yale University, 1975.

— — —. "The Zen philosopher: A review article on Dogan scholarhips in English." *Philosophy East and West* 28, No. 3 Honolulu: The University Press of Hawaii, July 1978.

— — —. (From an unpublished manuscript of a lecture delivered at the Blasdell Concert Hall, Honolulu, April 1978.)

— — —. Unpub. trans. "Shōbōgenzō Uji," Honolulu, 1978.

Kim, Hee-Jin. *Dōgen Kigen-Mystical Realist*. Tucśon: The University of Arizona Press, 1975.

Kiyota, Minoru. *Shingon Buddhism Theory and Practice*. Los Angeles-Tokyo: Buddhis Books International, 1978.

Kūkai, "Sokushin Jōbutsugi". in *Chosaku Zenshū*, vol. 1. Tokyl: Sankibō-Busshōrin, 1968-70.

Lao Tzu. *Tao te Ching*. Trans. D. C. Lau. Baltimore: Penguin Books, 1963.

Masunaga, Reiho, trans. *A Primer of Sōtō Zen: A Translation of Dōgen's Shōbōgenzō Zuimonki*. Honolulu: The University of Hawaii Press, 1975.

Matsunaga, Alicia and Matsunaga, Daigan. *Foundation of Japanese Buddhism*, vol. I (The Aristocratic Age). Los Angeles-Tokyo: Buddhist Books International, 1976.

– – –. *Foundation of Japanese Buddhism*, vol, II (The Mass Movement: Kamakura & Muromachi Periods). Los Angeles-Tokyo: Buddhist Books International, 1976.

Nagatomo, Shigenori. Unpub. trans. "Shōbōgenzō Kaiinzammai," A translation of a fascicle included in Dōgen's *Shōbōgenzō*, Honolulu, 1978.

– – –. Unpub trans. "Shin-fukatoku": A translation offascicle included in Dōgen's *Shōbōgenzō*.

Nakamura, Hajime. *A History of the Development of Japanese Thought: from A.D. 592–1868*, vol. I. Tokyo: Japan Cultural Society, 1969.

– – –. *A History of the Development of Japanese Thought*, vol. II. Tokyo: Japan Cultural Society, 1969.

– – –. *Ways of Thinking of Eastern Peoples*, Honolulu: The University of Hawaii Press, 1974.

Nitta, Yoshihiro and Tatematsu, Horotaka, ed. *Analecta Husserlina: The Yearbook of Phenomenological Research Bol VIII Japanese Phenomenology.* Dordrecht, Hollan/Boston/London: D. Reidel Publishing Co., 1979.

Ōkubo, Dōshū, ed. *Dōgen Zenji Zenshū*, vol. I. Tokyo: Chikuma Shobo, 1969.

Plato. *Plato: The Collected Dialogues.* Ed. Edith Hamilton and Huntington. Cairns. Princeton, N.J.: Princeton University Press, 1961.

Suzuki, Daisetz Teitaro. *The Training of the Buddhist Monk.* Berkeley: Wingbow Press, 1974.

Takakusu, Junjiro. *The Essentials of Buddhist Philosophy.* Westport, Conn.: Greenwood Press, Publishers, 1976.

Tamaki, Koshiro. "On the Fundamental Idea Underlying Japanese Buddhism." *Philosophical Studies of Japan*, vol. XI. Tokyo: Japan Society for the Promotion of Science, 1975.

Toganoo, Shozui Makoto. "The Symbol-System of Shingon Buddhism (1)." *Mikkyō Bunka.* Koyasan: The Esoteric Buddhist Society, September 1971.

– – –. "The Symbol-System of Shingon Buddhism (2)." *Mikkyō Bunka*, Koyasan: The Esoteric Buddhist Society, December 1971.

– – –. "The Symbol-System of Shingon Buddhism (3)." *Mikkyō Bunka.* Koyasan: The Esoteric Buddhist Society, June 1972.

— — —. "The Symbol-System of Shingon Buddhism (4)." *Mikkyō Bunka*. Koyasan: The Esoteric Buddhist Society, March 1973.

Ui, Hakuju. "A Study of Japanese Tendai Buddhism." *Philosophical Studies of Japan*, vol. I. Tokyo: Japan Society for the Promotion of Science, 1959.

Waddell, Norman and Abe, Masao, trans. "Dōgen's Bendōwa." *The Eastern Buddhist*, NS IV, No. 2 (1971).

— — —. trans. "Dōgen's Fukanzazengi and Shōbōgenzō Zazengi." *The Eastern Buddhist*, NS VI No. 2 (1973).

— — —. trans. "Shōbōgenzō Genjōkōan." *The Eastern Buddhist*, NS V, No. 2 (1972).

— — —. trans. "Shōbōgenzō Buddha-nature Part II." *The Eastern Buddhist*, NS IX, NO. 1 (1976).

— — —. trans. "Dōgen's Shōbōgenzō Sammai Ō Zammai." *The Eastern Buddhist*, NS VII, No. 1 (1974).

— — —. trans. "Dōgen's Shōbōgenzō Zenki 'Total Dynamic Working' and Shōji 'Birth and Death.'" *The Eastern Buddhist*, NS V, No. 1 (1972).

Yokoi, Yuho, trans. *Zen Master Dōgen: An Introduction with Selected Writings*. New York-Tokyo: Weatherhill Inc., 1976.

Yuasa Yasuo. "Religious tradition in Japan." (From a manuscript of a lecture on National Culture and World Peace," at Seoul, Korea, 1976).

Index